Learning About Language

General Editors: Geoffrey Leech and Mick Short,
Lancaster University

Already published:

Patterns of Spoken English

An Introduction to English Phonetics

Gerald Knowles

Longman
London and New York

Longman Group Limited
Longman House, Burnt Mill, Harlow
Essex CM20 2JE, England
and Associated Companies throughout the world

Published in the United States of America
by Longman Inc., New York

First published 1987
Second impression 1987
Sixth impression 1995

British Library Cataloguing in Publication Data
Knowles, Gerald
  Patterns of spoken English: an introduction to
  English phonetics. — (Learning about language)
  1. English language — Phonetics
  I. Title   II. Series
  421.5   PE1135

ISBN 0-582-29132-1

Library of Congress Cataloging in Publication Data
Knowles, Gerald, 1945–
  Patterns of spoken English.

  (Learning about language)
  Bibliography: p.
  Includes index.
  1. English language — Phonetics.   I. Title.
II. Series.
PE1135.K66   1986   421'.5   85-23819
ISBN 0-582-29132-1

Set in Linotron 202 11/11pt Bembo

Transferred to digital print on demand, 2002
Printed and bound by Antony Rowe Ltd, Eastbourne

Contents

Preface

Most introductory textbooks in phonetics are designed to turn the people who use them into phoneticians. People who take phonetics courses, on the other hand, do not in general wish to become specialists, but rather need to know what the study of phonetics has to offer in some other field. This book is intended for those involved in any way with the study of the English language: for students of linguistics or literature, teachers of English, and those involved with the study of literacy, or the analysis of discourse or conversation.

The conventional approach to English phonetics concentrates on vowels and consonants – which in Britain generally means the vowels and consonants of Received Pronunciation – and scant attention is paid to rhythm and intonation. The beginner is taken through the anatomy and physiology of speech, and examines the ways in which speech sounds contrast with each other. Fascinating and essential as these things may be for the specialist, it requires some experience of working with phonetic data before the point of studying them becomes apparent. Secondly, it is not reasonable to assume that the beginner is familiar with RP: the fact that students from Northern England or outside Britain passively understand RP does not mean that they can use it actively as a model. Nor, for most people, can an active knowledge of the sounds of RP be regarded as essential.

Vowels and consonants and RP are certainly dealt with in this book, but they are placed in context. The vowel and consonant systems are a part, and an important part, of the structure of the spoken language; RP is one variety, and an important variety, of spoken English. A large proportion of this book is concerned with the much wider range of sound patterns referred to generally as 'rhythm and intonation', and where appropriate, varieties other than RP are described. The relationship between spoken and written English is dealt with at the appropriate points and in some detail. And for the benefit of that large proportion of students of English phonetics who are also students of English literature, the final section of each chapter is devoted to some phonetically relevant aspect of the literary language.

No previous knowledge or experience of phonetics or linguistics is assumed. Technical terms are commented on as they are introduced, and those which are absolutely essential are given in capital letters the first time they are mentioned. Other terms which are sufficiently common, and which the reader is likely to come across in the literature, are referred to in single quotation marks.

Phonetics is not a new subject, and I make no claim to originality for a large proportion of the material used. Much of it would have been familiar to Henry Sweet a century ago, and indeed some of the best ideas can be traced through European scholarship back to Greece and Rome, and even ancient India. What I do claim is that I have attempted a new organization of the material to present a coherent picture of the spoken language. The description of vowels and consonants is consistent with the description of the syllable, which is in turn consistent with the description of accentuation.

In the case of rhythm and intonation, a consistent and coherent picture is conspicuously lacking in the literature. There are many detailed studies of odd corners of the system, but no study of the system as a whole. My view is that we need an overall study of English rhythm and intonation before exploring details of the system. I have attempted to provide an overview of this kind at an elementary level.

This book has developed from courses in English phonetics which I have given over the last few years at the University of Lancaster. Faced with groups of students from a variety of backgrounds, both native speakers and foreign, and with different interests and different needs, I have found it essential to develop techniques of presenting English phonetics in a more general way. Without these students, and their successes and failures, I would not have

been in a position to write this book at all. I must also thank
my editors and colleagues, Professor Geoffrey Leech and
Mr Mick Short, for their careful and painstaking work on
early drafts of the text. The responsibility for any blunders
and obscurities that remain is entirely my own.
27.2.85

Acknowledgement

We are grateful to Faber and Faber Ltd & Random House
Inc for permission to use the poem 'Night Mail' by W H
Auden Copyright 1938 by W H Auden from *W H Auden:
Collected Poems* edited by Edward Mendelson.

CHAPTER 1

Spoken and Written English

If you have never studied phonetics before, it is likely that your view of the spoken language is partly conditioned by your experience of the written language. Written language has the advantage that it is permanent, so that it can be studied conveniently and at leisure. Spoken language, however familiar it might be, is more elusive. Until the invention of the record player – or perhaps more importantly the tape recorder – speech was uttered and gone for ever. So, although you will have developed an understanding of the workings of the written language in the course of your education, you are less likely to have a corresponding awareness of speech. For this reason I shall take as little as possible for granted about the nature of speech, and where appropriate relate spoken language to the more familiar written form.

The kind of English most often studied at school is also special in two other respects: it is literary, and it is standard English. We shall be paying particular attention to literary language, but I shall also be relating it to non-literary language. The relationship between standard and non-standard English is another important question, and I shall deal with this immediately.

1.1 Standard English and dialects

The development of a standard language is of enormous advantage to English speakers. The standard form of the language has considerable prestige, and non-standard varieties are downgraded accordingly. It is quite understandable that people have jumped from 'prestige' to 'correctness', and have assumed that the standard form is correct, and all others incorrect.

A large number of books have appeared over the last two hundred and fifty years or so, attempting to lay down what is 'correct' in English, and what is not. The best of these contain some excellent common sense, e.g. Sir Ernest Gowers's *The Complete Plain Words*. Others merely retail misconceptions and unfounded assertions picked up from other books e.g. that there is something wrong with the sentence *It is me*, or that a sentence should not end with a preposition. The allegedly 'correct' forms confuse the structure of English with the structure of Latin. Where an Anglo-Saxon would have said *Hit eom ic* 'it am I' we now say *it is me*: the form *it is I* has never been commonly used except by people attempting what they imagine to be correct English. Although a Latin sentence could not end in a preposition, this does happen in English, e.g. in the question *What are you looking at?*: far from being 'correct', *At what are you looking* is just not something speakers of English would naturally say at all. Despite the absurdity of some of these 'rules of correctness', they have achieved wide currency, probably because few people know where they come from, and are not in a position to challenge them.

Linguists in the present century have reacted sharply against this PRESCRIPTIVE approach to language, and insisted that the job of the linguist is purely DESCRIPTIVE, to describe the language as it is, and not as some people might think it ought to be. In some cases the pendulum swung too far, and the impression was given that 'anything goes in language', that there was no such thing as incorrect language, and that anyone's language was every bit as good as anyone else's. But the student of literature might rightly find it hard to believe that every backstreet urchin or rural swain is an unrecognized Shakespeare.

The point is that we must make a clear distinction between the scientific study of the forms of language, and our personal feeling about varieties of English. You may find a Devon accent delightfully quaint and rustic, you may warm to the mid-Atlantic accent of a radio disc jockey or you may regard a Glaswegian accent as the ugliest accent in the world. We all have such personal feelings about language, and you are quite entitled to yours. But we must not confuse these subjective reactions with objective descriptions of language. If we take this more reasonable approach, non-standard forms can be seen as simply *non*-standard: there is no reason to infer that they are also *sub*standard.

What we now regard as standard English can be traced back to about the time of Chaucer. Before that, the prestige of the different dialects of English changed with the political fortunes of the region in which they were spoken. The dialect of Wessex is the variety of Old English generally studied as 'Anglo-Saxon', but after the transfer of the political capital of England to London, the dialects of the South East grew in prestige and were to form the basis of the standard language. Meanwhile, as the political import-ance of the West Country declined, the prestige of West Country dialects declined with it.

Standard English was for a long time essentially a written form of the language, but it did influence the use of grammar and vocabulary in speech, and even pronunci-ation. In all parts of the country, local forms and usages have been subject to displacement; as fashions have changed, new forms have been accepted in the standard language and have gradually spread to local dialects. The popular assumption that local dialects somehow 'corrupt' the pure standard language could not be further from the truth: in reality they tend to preserve older forms of the language. Dialects have of course also been open to non-standard developments; but for the mass of English speakers non-standard usages are much more likely to be preserved archaisms.

The standardization of pronunciation really began in the late eighteenth century. Faced with various pronuncia-tions of the same word, elocutionists and orthoepists ('those concerned with correct pronunciation') recommended their own pronunciation as the correct one, and condemned others as incorrect. This continues today: there are still people who argue about whether the first syllable of *either* and *neither* ought to rhyme with *by* or *be*, on the false assumption that there is one correct answer. Agreement in matters of pronunciation seems to have developed in the nineteenth century, especially in the public schools of the south of England. This has led to a widespread acceptance in England of one variety of pronunciation as a standard, and this is the type that was adopted in the 1920s for broadcasting by the BBC. It is known as RECEIVED PRONUNCIATION, or more commonly as RP. (The word *received* is here used in the older sense 'generally accepted'.) An RP speaker is somebody whose speech belongs to England, but cannot be pinned down to any region of England. RP has had a powerful influence on all regional varieties, but relatively few people actually speak it.

The vast majority of English speakers today have a standardized variety of English. In England their pronunciation is likely to be influenced by RP, but retains some local flavour. If we wish to generalize about the speech of England, we have mainly to describe the speech of a few conurbations, including London, Birmingham, Greater Manchester, Merseyside, Leeds-Bradford and Newcastle-upon-Tyne. Note the difference between the two terms 'standard English' and 'RP': 'standard English' refers to the form of the language as a whole, and includes grammar and vocabulary, whereas 'RP' refers specifically to pronunciation. Australians, Scots and Americans generally have standard English, but RP is spoken as a prestige accent only in England.

The kind of English spoken outside England is in many cases more conservative than the speech of England itself. When a language is taken to a new area, dialect differences among the immigrants tend to be levelled out in the speech of the new population, so that a more homogeneous variety is formed; and the new variety then tends to preserve features of the language of the time of its introduction. American English thus preserves many features of seventeenth-century English, and although there are dialects of American English, they are not as diverse as those of England. It is much easier to generalize about American pronunciation, and the standard model is actually called GENERAL AMERICAN or *GenAm*. We shall be referring to RP and GenAm collectively as the *'standardized varieties'* of English.

The English of the 'Celtic' areas of the British Isles varies according to the time of the introduction or reintroduction of English. The dialects of the Scottish lowlands derive from the northern dialect of Old English, so that English is as indigenous there as in England itself. Further north, in the Highlands, English was introduced as a foreign language, particularly in the eighteenth century after the union of England and Scotland. The lack of a traditional non-standard local dialect is presumably the source of the claim that the 'purest' English is spoken at Inverness. (It is not of course possible to prove or refute such a claim, as it is a purely personal and subjective feeling.)

English has been introduced to Ireland on several occasions since the Norman period. Ulster was colonized from England and Scotland in the seventeenth century, and this is reflected in Ulster English: the speech of County Antrim and adjoining areas is markedly Scottish, while further south in the Lagan valley and the areas round Belfast, local accents are influenced by the dialects of England.

1.2 Speech and writing

If you have occasion to write a conversation down, you are very likely to find it disjointed, stumbling and inarticulate. If you do react like this, that is because what you expect to find in speech follows your expectations of written language, particularly prose. It is difficult not to regard speech as an imperfect version of the written language.

Exercise

As a preliminary exercise, find or make a recording of a natural conversation. Write down exactly what you hear, complete with *ums* and *ahs*, mistakes and repetitions. Avoid the temptation to edit the original: even though you can work out what the speaker really meant to say, write down what you actually hear. This is much more difficult than it sounds!

Which comes first: speech or writing?

The view conventionally taken by linguists and phoneticians is that speech is logically prior to writing. As individuals, we all learn to speak before we learn to read and write; and all societies have had speech before writing. There are still languages which have never been written down. When writing systems are devised, they are designed to represent aspects of the spoken language. Some systems attempt to represent words as a whole, others individual syllables, and alphabets have (in principle at least) a single character for a single speech sound. From this point of view, writing looks like an imperfect version of the spoken language.

But if writing simply mirrored speech, learning to read would essentially involve visually recognizing familiar words. In fact, except in the very early stages, we learn new words and concepts through reading, and from reading these pass into speech. Literate adults find it natural to work from writing to speech. You can probably recall meeting new written words as a child, and mispronouncing them; as an adult you will probably be quite accurate at guessing the correct pronunciation. For instance, you are unlikely to have heard the word *sesquipedalian* in speech, but you probably know immediately how to pronounce it. The habit of working from spellings to sounds has had the effect of changing the pronunciation of some words to fit the spelling. For instance, most people now pronounce the word *humble* with a /h/, although the word was formerly pronounced without it; the pronunciation of several proper names including *Darwen, Bristol, Cirencester, Boleyn* has been changed to fit the spelling. These are examples of 'spelling pronunciations'.

Actually, for over four centuries, standard written English has been influencing the spoken language, not only in determining the pronunciation of words but also in providing the words themselves. At the time of the Renaissance, scholars and writers attempted to enlarge the English vocabulary, in order to do in English what had formerly been done in Latin. A large number of words were borrowed from Greek and Latin into written English as learned words, or as opponents at the time dubbed them, 'inkhorn terms'. It was in response to these new words that the first English dictionaries were produced, including Robert Cawdrey's *Table Alphabeticall of Hard Words* in 1604. Many of these words, including *horrid, admire* and *prevent* have since passed from the written language into everyday speech.

If we were talking of newly-literate Saxons carving runes on pieces of bone, or even of a scribe taking a heroic poem like *Beowulf* from the oral tradition and preserving it in writing, then perhaps writing would be simply a representation of speech. But that is far removed from the normal modern use of writing. Most of the things we write – whether a literary masterpiece or a humble shopping list, a poster or our name in a book or other property – are not the sort of thing we would normally speak aloud anyway. It is better to regard speech and writing as parallel but different forms of the same language: it is actually rather naïve to regard one simply as a reflection of the other.

Letters and sounds

The basic principle of an alphabetic writing system is that each character in the written language stands for a single sound of the spoken language. This simple relationship is upset in practice by a number of complications. First, writing of its very nature preserves texts, and this in turn preserves older writing conventions. The sounds of the language change in the course of time, but people keep on writing in the traditional way. For instance, the vowel spelt **i** in the word *five* was formerly pronounced like the **ee** of *green*, and this has changed considerably since the spelling began to settle down five hundred years or more ago. Speakers of other languages may find our use of the letter **i** rather eccentric, but for us it remains a perfectly good way of writing the vowel known as the **long-i**. In other cases, when sounds drop out of pronunciation, e.g. the **k** or the **gh** of *knight*, they remain fossilized in the spelling. Of course, from the point of view of meaning, especially for highly literate users of the language, it is rather useful to distinguish *knight* from *night*, or *might* from *mite*, but this does not alter the fact that the spellings no longer fit the sounds. The confusion is increased in some words when the change in one sound makes it identical to some other sound of the language. For instance, the spellings **ee** and **ea** at one time represented quite different vowel sounds, but these are now identical in most dialects, so that *meet* sounds exactly like *meat*. In this way, as a direct result of the normal changes that take place in pronunciation, a regular spelling system eventually gets out of step.

The problem is compounded when spelling conventions are borrowed from one language to another. English has always had an irregular spelling system, because it was first written down with an alphabet and spelling conventions designed for Latin. We have also adopted conventions from French and other languages.

Latin had five vowel sounds, **a, e, i, o** and **u**, long and short. This is why we have only five main vowel letters. Most varieties of English have a much bigger vowel system, with over twenty vowels, and this has been true throughout the history of the language. The Latin alphabet is glaringly inadequate for the representation of English vowels, and in order to spell some of them, especially the long ones, it has been necessary to place two characters together, e.g. **ea, oa**, as in *beat* and *boat*. Most of these combinations are – or have become – arbitrary, in that the sound of the whole vowel is not made up of the sounds represented by the separate characters. Such double letter symbols are known as DIGRAPHS. We also use digraphs for consonants which did not exist in Classical Latin, e.g. **ch, sh, th** as in *chin, shin* and *thin*.

Old English used the Latin alphabet supplemented by a few extra characters and digraphs. These included two equivalent characters, ð called 'eth' – pronounced to rhyme with *Beth* – and þ known as 'thorn'. Both of these were used for the **th** sound, so that the word *than* could be written ðan, or alternatively þan. The letter eth has long been obsolete in English, but thorn survived in handwriting into the nineteenth century. It is now used only for self-consciously old-fashioned inn signs and shop signs, where it is generally confused with the letter **y**, e.g. *Ye olde village shoppe*. The word *the* has never been pronounced *ye*, of course, except by modern people reading old-fashioned writing.

Some of our more illogical spelling conventions were

brought over by French scribes after the Norman conquest. The use of **qu** for the sound sequence /kw/ as in *question* was inherited by French from Latin – where it was already an oddity borrowed from Etruscan – and from French it came to English. This was no improvement on the Old English spelling **cw** as in *cwene* 'queen'. The sounds represented by **c** and **g** in Latin had changed in French before the vowels **e** and **i**, and this too was transmitted as an irregularity to English. The word *house* was spelt *hus* in Old English, but the corresponding vowel was spelt **ou** in French, and the spelling **ou** was imposed on the English word, despite the fact that it was less well motivated than the old one. The letter **h** was added to other consonant letters to form digraphs including **ch, sh**, and **th**, and the spelling **hw** was reversed to **wh**, e.g. *hwy* became *why*. This was no improvement, as the older pronunciation of **wh** is actually like a *h* sound followed by *w*, and the spelling **wh** is quite illogical. In this and other ways, practice in the spelling of English had already in the medieval period moved away from the basic alphabetic principle of one character for one sound.

Following the introduction of printing in the late fifteenth century, English spelling began to fossilize. Pronunciation, of course, continued to develop as before. Within a hundred years, would-be spelling reformers were already complaining about English spelling. In 1568 Sir Thomas Smith published his *De recta & emendata linguae Anglicae scriptione Dialogus* 'Dialogue concerning the correct and emended writing of the English language' in which he attempted to introduce special phonetic characters to spell certain English sounds. This was followed by *An Orthographie* written in 1569 by John Hart, who is sometimes regarded as the first serious English phonetician.

Although many of our spelling conventions were fossilized by the sixteenth century, there were still different possible ways of spelling individual words, e.g. *yoke* could equally well be spelt *yoak*, and *music* could also be spelt *musick*. Fixed spellings for words date only from the eighteenth century. Dr Johnson's dictionary of 1755 was important here: Johnson was quite clear that in choosing spellings he had often had to make an arbitrary choice; but other people took his dictionary to be an authority on the subject. As a result, there has been little change in spelling for the last two hundred years.

The result of fixing archaic spellings is that modern English spelling does not really represent modern English pronunciation at all, but rather that of the centuries before it became fixed. Even when we have to spell a new word, such as *telephone*, we use a final silent **e**, which is half a millenium out of date as far as the pronunciation is concerned – not to mention the digraph **ph** for /f/, which reflects a sound change in ancient Greek!

1.3   Phonetic notation

The strained connection between sound and spelling on the one hand, combined with dialect differences on the other, makes it difficult to use spellings to refer to pronunciation. We need to start again and reestablish the basic alphabetic principle of one character per sound, and make clear what variety of English we are referring to. We shall also find that the term 'sound' is not accurate enough: we shall instead use the term PHONEME.

Very roughly, phonemes are the sounds which you would regard as distinctively different in your speech. You probably regard the vowels of *bit* and *beat* as different phonemes, and the vowels of *beat* and *bead* as the same phoneme. You may be able to detect a slight difference in the vowels of *beat* and *bead*, but this does not alter your classification of them as the 'same'. In other words, the difference is not 'distinctive'. In order to represent the phonemes of speech accurately, we need a set of phonemic characters.

It matters little where we get our characters from. We could simply number the phonemes, and call the first phoneme in *dog* no. 4, the second no. 15, and the last no. 7. In some applications, e.g. in a computer program, this is actually a good way of identifying phonemes, but it would be inconvenient for human beings. We could invent a special set of characters, as many nineteenth-century phoneticians did (including Henry Sweet, the supposed original of Professor Higgins in *Pygmalion*); but these are as difficult to deal with as numbers until you are used to them. Foreign alphabets, e.g. the Arabic alphabet or an Indian alphabet, could be used by those who are familiar with them. In practice, the most commonly used set of characters is taken from the Latin alphabet supplemented as necessary by characters specially invented or borrowed from other alphabets. Wherever the characters come from, the important requirement is that they provide one character for each phoneme of the language, so that each phoneme can be written down unambiguously.

I emphasize the arbitrary nature of phoneme characters, because the point is frequently misunderstood. People who learn to use one particular set of phonemic characters may form the impression that that set is the only 'correct' one and that others must somehow be inferior or wrong. Since the choice of characters is arbitrary, it does not make sense to talk of right and wrong. Let us imagine that an extremely eccentric phonetician devised a set of characters so that the first phoneme of *dog* was written **c**, the second **a** and the third **t**: the word *dog* would then be written **cat**. This system would be difficult to use and would be unlikely to attract many followers, but it would still not make sense to describe it as 'wrong'. Some systems are more appropriate for a given purpose than others.

Phoneme characters for English and other languages are by convention taken from the alphabet or set of symbols provided by the International Phonetic Association (IPA). These are usually referred to as 'IPA characters' or simply as 'phonetic symbols'. Actually, IPA characters have as their primary role the representation of precise sound qualities irrespective of the language in which a sound occurs. If we use these same characters as labels for the phonemes of a particular language, we are using them for a rather different purpose.

The IPA has never made official phonemic analyses of any language, nor does it recognize any particular set of symbols for transcribing any language phonemically. There is no such thing therefore as an IPA phonemic transcription of English. Different scholars have made their own selection of characters from the IPA alphabet to use as labels for English phonemes.

Most introductions to English phonetics describe just

one variety of English: RP as a matter of course in Britain and usually the author's own variety of English in America. For one variety, it is possible to select special symbols which indicate minute shades of sound in the pronunciation of the phonemes. This is fine for people who speak the variety in question: but for anyone else the attempt to indicate phonetic detail is merely confusing. More seriously, it may obscure entirely the whole point of phonetic notation. Instead of being a simple matter of identifying phonemes and writing them down, it becomes a mysterious art in which words are encoded in perversely eccentric characters to no obvious purpose.

The set of phoneme characters adopted in this book is the first one suggested by Daniel Jones in the *Principles of the IPA* (1949). Jones used several different sets of symbols for different purposes, and this is the one most suitable for generalizing about English as a whole; it is for that reason the most suitable for this book. These symbols are listed in Appendix 1. Once you have learnt the basic principles of phonemic notation, it is a simple and trivial matter to switch to another set of symbols. (This is like learning to drive: driving any car at all is the difficult part, but if you have learnt to drive a Ford, it is not very difficult to drive an Austin.) If you read other phonetics books you will find minor differences in the symbols used.

A further point which follows from the arbitrary nature of symbols is that different symbols may be appropriate for different purposes. In mathematics, for instance, the product of two numbers **a** and **b** can be written **ab**, **a.b** or **a × b**, and none of these is 'correct' to the exclusion of the others. In phonetics there is a convention whereby a colon is equivalent to doubling a symbol, thus [a:] is exactly equivalent to [aa]. As in mathematics, it will sometimes help to clarify the argument if advantage is taken of alternatives of this kind.

1.4   English phonemes

English vowel phonemes are most commonly represented in spelling by the letters **a,e,i,o,u**. The 'semi-consonant' letters **w** and **y** sometimes represent part of a vowel sound, as in the case of *now* or *they*, and sometimes a consonant as in *wet* or *yacht*. The remaining letters represent consonant sounds.

Phonemes are conventionally referred to in phonetic terminology, e.g. /b/ is a 'voiced bilabial stop', which is very difficult to follow until you have learnt enough phonetics to understand the individual terms. It may be helpful in the early stages to refer to phonemes by name. If there is a good correspondence between the phoneme and a particular written letter, no harm is done in using the conventional letter name, e.g. the phoneme /b/ can be called 'bee'. Some phonemes which do not have corresponding letters have also been given conventional names, and these will be indicated below.

Consonants

The majority of consonant letters are used fairly consistently, so that we can use them in a phonetic notation with their usual values. Those that have only one main value include **b d f h k l m n p r s t v w z**.

In cases where a consonant character has several phonetic values, we shall have to choose one value, and use it consistently. Where a digraph is used to represent a single consonant phoneme, we shall have to invent a special single character for the phoneme.

C: the letter **c** is popularly said to have a 'hard' and a 'soft' value. The **hard c** is pronounced like **k** in words such as *cat* or *clock*, and the **soft c**, which occurs before **e, i** or **y**, is pronounced like **s** as in *cell* or *fence*. We can thus always write **c** phonetically as /k/ or /s/, e.g. /kat, klok, sel, fens/. The letter **c** itself is redundant, and we never need to use it.

X: the sound which this letter represents is made up phonetically of /k/ followed by /s/, e.g. *box* /boks/. Occasionally it stands for /gz/ as in *exam* /igzam/. In every case we can write it out as a sequence of phonemes, and so the letter **x** is redundant.

Q: the letter **q** is also redundant, as it represents /k/, e.g. *quest* /kwest/. It is nearly always followed by **u** pronounced /w/; the word *Iraq* /ira:k/ is an exception.

SH: the digraph **sh** represents a single consonant phoneme, as in *ship* or *fish*. Since there is no way of writing this with our alphabet, we shall adopt the symbol ʃ, thus /ʃip, fiʃ/. The symbol ʃ is called 'esh' /eʃ/ to parallel 'es' **s** and 'ef' **f**.

CH: the two letters of the spelling here represent two sounds in pronunciation, but obviously not /k/ followed by /h/. The **ch** sound is in fact like /ʃ/ preceded by a /t/ sound: compare *ship* /ʃip/ and *chip* /tʃip/ or *hash* /haʃ/ and *hatch* /hatʃ/. As this last example shows **ch** is sometimes preceded by a redundant **t** in the spelling. Although /tʃ/ is made up of two sounds, there are many reasons for regarding it as a single phoneme in English.

J: the sound usually spelt **j** is closely related to /tʃ/. It has a /d/ followed by a z-like sound which we shall write with the '**long-z**' symbol ʒ, thus *jam* /dʒam/. Note how the /d/ corresponds to the /t/ of /tʃ/ and /ʒ/ to the /ʃ/. This /ʒ/ element occurs on its own as a separate phoneme, but it is rare and has a variety of spellings. It is spelt **s** in *pleasure* and *leisure*, and **ge** in *rouge*. It sometimes alternates with /dʒ/, as in the case of the word *garage*.

G: the letter **g** has 'hard' and 'soft' pronunciations corresponding to those of **c**. Before **e, i** and **y**, it is pronounced 'soft' as /dʒ/, e.g. *gem* /dʒem/, *gin* /dʒin/ and *gym* /dʒim/. This /dʒ/ can be preceded by **d** in the spelling e.g. *edge* /edʒ/. We shall reserve the symbol /g/ for the 'hard' value, as in *got* /got/ or *grin* /grin/.

TH: the digraph **th** represents two different phonemes, the first as in *thin* and the second as in *then*. These are spelt the same because originally they were a single phoneme. The latter phoneme is conventionally written with the Old English letter ð, e.g. *then* /ðen/. In older phonetics books, the letter thorn þ is used or the first consonant of *thin*, but this has been superseded by the Greek letter 'theta' θ, thus *thin* /θin/. There is no theoretical significance in the change: it is merely a change of fashion, but the new symbol now has general currency. The traditional name of /ð/ is /eθ/, which rather confusingly contains the other **th**-sound; it is for that reason more commonly known now as /eð/.

NG: in some varieties of English, the letters **ng** represent a variety of /n/ sound followed by /g/. However, it is more commonly the case that these two sounds have fused to form a single new phoneme, which we shall write ŋ. Thus *sing* /siŋ/ has three phonemes like *sin* /sin/, and *hang* /haŋ/ has three phonemes like *ham* /ham/. We can call this phoneme '*eng*' to parallel '*em*' **m** and '*en*' **n**.

Y: although we are using our symbols just for English, phonetic characters are in principle intended to be useful for any language. Some letters including **j** and **y** have very different values from one language to another. We have already used /dʒ/ for the English value of the letter **j**. In some continental languages, including German, the letter **j** is given the value which in English we give to **y**. It is this continental value that is conventionally given to **j** in works on phonetics. Thus we can write *yam* /jam/ and *yacht* /jot/. The /j/ phoneme has a traditional name '*yod*', which is taken from its name in Hebrew.

Exercise

Identify the words which are here written down in IPA characters:

kat   kwik   woz   ʃal   θeft   briŋ   ðis   dʒak   jak   fiks

Write down the sequence of phonemes which corresponds to the following words. In cases where digraphs represent a single phoneme, make sure you use just one symbol. For the vowels use the conventional letters **a, e, i, o,** and **u**. The first one has been done for you:

thick /θik/

wig   bang   gnat   yell   six   quick   chop   push   this jack

---

The representation of words by phonemic symbols is known loosely as 'phonetic transcription' (although since phonemes are being transcribed, it might better be called 'phonemic transcription'). When transcribing, you should use only the symbols which we have decided to use above. Since capital letters are not included in our set of symbols, you should disregard them when they occur in the spelling, and use only lower-case characters. When transcriptions are introduced into a text alongside ordinary spellings, they should be preceded and followed by slashes ("/"). (Go through the above section again and notice how we have used slants for transcriptions. Note too that words quoted in their normal written form have been put in italics: the corresponding convention in handwritten or typed documents is to underline them.)

Vowels

To refer to the vowel phonemes we can make use of everyday names, as long as we are consistent and always use the same name for the same vowel phoneme. Since the vowel phonemes are spelt in several different ways, and the same spelling can represent several different phonemes, we shall have to choose the name that best represents the connection between sound and spelling. For instance, if we define the **short-a** as the vowel of *hat*, we must find some other name for the vowel of *was*. If we refer to the vowel of *hot, shock,* and *block* as the **short-o**, we shall also have to refer to the vowel of *was* as the **short-o** despite its spelling. **Short a, e, i, o** correspond to their spellings, as in the words *pat, pet, pit,* and *pot,* and we shall write these phonemically with the symbols /a, e, i, o/ respectively, thus /pat, pet, pit, pot/. In the case of **short-u** we have to make a choice between the vowel of *put* and the vowel of *putt*. We shall reserve the term **short-u** for the vowel of *put,* and write it with the symbol /u/, thus /put/. For the vowel of *putt* we shall have to invent a new symbol, /ʌ/, thus /pʌt/; this vowel has no agreed name. (If you come from the North of England, you may find that for you *put* and *putt* sound exactly alike, and that our references to the /ʌ/ vowel make little or no sense. In that case, disregard the /ʌ/ symbol, and write /u/ in each case, thus *put* /put/ and *putt* /put/. This will be explained further in Chapter 3.)

Exercise

Transcribe the following words, paying particular attention to the vowels. If you are not sure what symbol to use, consult the list of phonemes in Appendix 1, and find the key word containing the vowel you are looking for.

> lamb   pin   pet   top   pull   cough   tough   rhythm   swap
> flood

There is another short vowel, which as a rather different status, and which is by far the commonest vowel sound in English. It is known as SHWA, and its symbol is /ə/. It has no regular spelling, and although it is often spelt **a** as in the first and last syllables of *banana, America* and *madonna*, all the vowel letters are sometimes used for it, as in *surplice, hopeless, potato, pursue.* Shwa frequently replaces other vowels in certain circumstances. Some whole words, e.g. *the, a, for, of, than* have different vowels when pronounced in isolation, but in the context of a sentence they almost always have the shwa vowel. For instance, you would pronounce *of* /ɒv/ in isolation, but /əv/ in the phrase *a cup of tea* /ə kʌp əv tiː/.

Exercise

Identify the vowels in these words, paying particular attention to those which become shwa. Note how the shwa vowel is spelt.

milkman	cottage	Scotland	women	woman	goodness
kingdom	witness	pigeon	burial	medicine	

Some of the long vowels can be referred to by their familiar names, and we shall take **long a, e, i, o, u** to be respectively the vowels of *mate, meet, nice, note* and *cute.* The long vowels are often spelt with a single vowel which is followed by a single consonant letter; if this consonant would otherwise come at the end of the word, a final unpronounced **e** is added, as in the case of four of the five key words we have just given. Using the symbol C to stand for the single consonant letter, we can refer to these spellings as **aCe, iCe** etc. In other cases, as in *meet,* digraphs are used to represent the long vowel; taking typical spellings we can refer to the **oo** vowel or the **aw** vowel. For several reasons, including the merger of formerly distinct phonemes, many of the long vowels have alternative spellings, with a single letter or with a digraph.

The pronunciation of a long vowel is in some cases like an extended short one. But much more commonly in English, a long vowel is like two short vowels run together. Say the word *wide* slowly to yourself, and notice how the **long-i** divides into two different vowel elements. As a first step, we can try to identify these elements with the short vowels and shwa. The first element of **long-i** is obviously not /i/ or /u/: for most speakers of English it is more like /a/ than any of the other short vowels, although not exactly like it. The second element is similar to /i/, but again not exactly the same. In this way we can make up the phonemic symbol /ai/ for **long-i**, and this will be sufficient for most practical purposes. Some people will disagree, and people from the home counties may feel that the first element of **long-i** is more like the /o/ of *hot* than the /a/ of *hat*. We shall be dealing with dialect variation in some detail in Chapter 3, but for the present we shall analyse the long vowels in the way that applies to the greatest number of native varieties of English.

Vowel phonemes which consist of two identifiable elements are called DIPHTHONGS. (Do not confuse diphthongs with digraphs: a diphthong is a sound, and a digraph is a written symbol.) Now it would be very convenient if the digraph spellings divided spoken diphthongs into their constituent elements, but unfortunately this is rarely the case. There was a better match at the time of Caxton, but this has been obliterated by changes in pronunciation. The analysis of long vowels and diphthongs thus presents us with our first major problem.

> LONG-A: this is spelt a**Ce** or **ai**, as in *bake, made, maid, rain*. We shall write this vowel /ei/, taking the first element to be something like short /e/ and the second element like /i/, thus /beik, meid, meid, rein/.

> LONG-E: the e**Ce** spelling as in *cede* is now not as common as **ee** as in *green*. Other spellings include **ie** as in *relief*, or **ei** following the letter **c**, as in *receive*. Although the two elements of **long-e** are different in most varieties of English, they are both in the general region of /i/. We can accordingly write **long-e** /ii/, or by using the colon to represent a double character /i:/. In this way we can write our key words /gri:n, rili:f, risi:v/.

> LONG-I: this is almost always spelt i**Ce**, as in *bike, mile, size*, and it is pronounced /ai/, thus /baik, mail, saiz/. Another but much less common spelling is **igh** as in *high* /hai/ and *nigh* /nai/, and this in many of its occurrences comes before **t**, as in *fight, right* /fait, rait/.

> LONG-O: spelt o**Ce** or **oa** as in *coke* and *cloak*. The second element of this vowel is close to /u/ in most varieties of English, but the first is more variable. For the moment we shall treat the phoneme as /ou/, thus /kouk, klouk/. This will

suit large numbers of English speakers, but not those of the standardized varieties. In RP the first element is closer to shwa, thus [əu]. For the use of square brackets in phonetic transcription see Chapter 3 Section 2.

LONG-U: spelt **u**C**e** or with several digraphs, including **ui, eu** and **ew**, as in *cute*, the first vowel of *nuisance, eulogy* and *pew*. In nearly all varieties of English this is not a diphthong, but a TRIPHTHONG, i.e. a vowel phoneme with three elements. The first is [j], and this is followed by two elements both in the region of /u/, giving /juu/ or /ju:/, thus /kju:t, nju:səns, ju:lədʒi, pju:/.

OO: the **oo** vowel. As a rough generalization we can say that this is like the **long-u** but without the initial [j], thus *food* /fu:d/, *balloon* /bəlu:n/. In some words where we might expect **long-u** from the spelling we actually have /u:/ in pronunciation, e.g. *rude* /ru:d/, *bruise* /bru:z/. In other cases the **oo** vowel has been replaced by the shorter /u/ e.g. *hood* /hud/, or even by /ʌ/, e.g. *flood* /flʌd/.

OW: the digraph **ow** actually represents two different phonemes. In the case of *sow* meaning 'cast seeds' or *bow* 'contraption that fires arrows' it represents the **long-o**, thus /sou, bou/; but in *sow* 'female pig' or *bow* 'lower the head' it represents what we are here calling the **ow** vowel. The pronunciation of **ow** typically starts somewhere close to /ʌ/ and moves up to /u/, thus /sau, bau/, and also *bough, fowl* /bau, faul/.

AW: this is the vowel of *law* and *laud*, and it is also spelt **ough** in *thought* and *bought*. In many varieties of English this is like a lengthened version of /o/, and we shall write it /o:/, thus /lo:, lo:d, θo:t, bo:t/.

AH: this bears the same relationship to /a/ as **aw** does to /o/ and will be written /a:/. It is the vowel of *shah* /ʃa:/ and also usually occurs in *father* /fa:ðə/ and *palm* /pa:m/. This vowel alternates in some words with **long-a**, e.g. *tomato* and *vase* have **ah** in a typical British pronunciation, /təma:tou, va:z/, and **long-a** in an American one, thus /təmeitou, veiz/. The third vowel of *Copenhagen* alternates between **ah** and **long-a** thus /koupənha:gn, koupənheign/.

OY: spelt **oy** in *toy* and **oi** in *void*. When spelt **oi** this is the only long vowel for which the spelling matches the pronunciation: /toi, void/.

The long vowels we have dealt with so far have conventional names or spellings which are associated with them. Most varieties of English have a further set of vowel phonemes which are spelt with an **r**. More precisely, English has developed these further phonemes only before /r/. These have no recognized names, and we shall refer to them as **long-a + r, oo + r** etc. After these vowels, the **r** in the spelling is not pronounced in some varieties of English, and so we shall put the corresponding /r/ in parentheses in our transcriptions.

> ER: this vowel is spelt **er** and sometimes **ir** or **ur**. Phonetically it is like an extended shwa, which we shall write /əː/, e.g. *Bert, girl, urn* /bəː(r)t, gəː(r)l, əː(r)n/.
>
> LONG-A + R: this vowel, which occurs in *hare* and *scarce*, is subject to considerable dialect variation, but commonly starts in the region of /e/ and moves in the direction of shwa. It will be written /eə/, e.g. /heə(r), skeə(r)s/.
>
> LONG-E + R: before **r, long-e** begins in the usual way near /i/ and then moves towards shwa, e.g. *beer* /biə(r)/, *here* /hiə(r)/.
>
> LONG-I + R: in this case shwa is added to the **long-i** to form the triphthong /aiə/, e.g. *fire* /faiə(r)/, *lyre* /laiə(r)/.
>
> LONG-U + R: this starts off like **long-u** but moves off quickly towards shwa, to form the triphthong /juə/, e.g. *pure* /pjuə/, *cure* /kjuə/.
>
> OO + R: the **oo** starts near /u/, and then moves off towards shwa, e.g. *poor* /puə(r)/, *tour* /tuə(r)/.
>
> OW + R: shwa is added to the **ow** vowel, e.g. *tower* /tauə(r)/, *flour* /flauə(r)/.

1.5 The sound of written texts

A speech or a piece of conversation can be written down in a reasonably satisfactory way. Some aspects of the original cannot be represented in our conventional writing system, and people may disagree on details of punctuation, or on whether a particular chunk of text should be written as one sentence or divided into two. But in general, it is possible to produce something which counts by common consent as a written version of the original.

It may appear that the reverse is also true: that corresponding to a written text there is a generally agreed spoken version. Thus we talk of rhymes in verse, and of lines of verse or purple patches of prose which have a powerful rhythm. We may even generalize about the roughness of the

verse of Elyot and contrast it with the smooth mellifluous-
ness of Spenser. These take for granted a general agreement
on the sound of the text.

However, a written text consists of marks on paper:
any sound it may be said to possess is supplied by the
reader. This is a self-evident but important point, and one
to which we shall return. It has a number of consequences,
some of which may not be immediately obvious, particularly for the study of literary texts in which the sound plays
an important role.

In the first place, the 'sound' depends on the
performer's or the silent reader's own variety of English.
Our view of the sound of Shakespeare is determined by the
performances of twentieth-century actors speaking RP or
GenAm: in either case this is far removed from what Shakespeare heard in London or Stratford. If you come from
London or Glasgow, the sounds you imagine to yourself
when you read *Under Milk Wood* are unlikely to be the same
as Thomas imagined when he wrote it.

It would not be realistic to argue that the only valid
version of the text is the writer's own, because in many
cases we do not know how the writer spoke. The sound
of *The Wreck of the Deutschland* is an important aspect of the
poem, but who knows how Hopkins recited it? And what
about dumb poets, those with speech defects, and those
who are just not very good at reading their own work
aloud?

In practice we have to accept that there is not just one,
but an indefinitely large number of spoken versions of a
written text. This presents an interesting problem for
aspects of the sound of literary texts which need to be fixed,
and agreed on by literary critics. For instance, if rhyme is
part of the structure of a poem, it must be recognized as
a rhyme by the reader. But rhymes can change in the course
of time, and you may have been puzzled by some nursery
rhymes:

Goosey Goosey *Gander*	Whither shall I *wander*?
I love little pussy	Her coat is so *warm*
And if I don't hurt her	She'll do me no *harm*.

In former times, *wander* rhymed with *gander*, and *warm* with
harm. Another problem arises in dialect verse: the words

verse and *scarce* may rhyme perfectly for a Liverpool poet, but the effect is lost if they are read with different vowels.

The 'sound' of a text also depends on what happens when we read it aloud, and 'bring it to life'. We do not just mouth the words, nor is there a resident sound pattern lying dormant in the text waiting to get out. We have to analyse the text, decide what the writer intended it to mean, and then search the resources of the spoken language for an appropriate way of speaking it. Compare these two sentences, for instance:

> He took the lead off the dog's neck.
> He took the lead off the roof.

In order to decide how to pronounce the letters **l-e-a-d** you first scan the rest of the sentence for the most likely interpretation. Of course, the dog could have had a /led/ weight round its neck, or someone could have thrown a dog's /li:d/ on to the roof: but we do not normally consider such unlikely possibilities unless there are compelling reasons for doing so. The pronunciation of a word like *convict* varies according to whether it is interpreted as a noun or a verb:

> The convict was sewing mailbags.
> I expect they'll convict him on all charges.

Again, the word *convict* does not have an inherent sound 'there in the text'; the pronunciation is imposed upon it in response to the grammar.

In the case of a single word, once the reader has decided on the interpretation, there is little further choice to be made. You cannot say '*convict* is a verb, so I'll pronounce it /mju:zli/': the English language obliges you to say /kənvikt/. However, there is considerable choice in the way we pronounce groups of words together. Consider this ambiguous sentence:

> Don't do it for my sake.

You can read this out to convey quite different meanings: 'for my sake, don't do it' and 'do it, but not for my sake'. The 'sound' depends on the meaning you choose.

The dependence of 'sound' on meaning is important, as 'sound' is often confused with meaning. In our everyday speech, we respond to language as an undifferentiated whole: we do not consciously sort out sound from grammar and meaning. But if we are studying a text in detail, it is essential to get clear exactly what we are talking about, and this includes separating out sound from meaning. A point which will come up several times in the following chapters is that some patterns which are often thought of as sound patterns are in fact responses to meaning.

If you have occasion to comment on the sound of a written text, then obviously you cannot lay down exactly what it should sound like. You need to be able to distinguish a possible reading from an impossible one, and a likely one from a less likely one. In short, you need a sufficient grasp of the sound patterns of English to know something of the range of sensible readings. Several of the exercises in this book deal with written texts: when you do these, it would be useful to start by writing down in transcription what you would expect to find in the spoken version. Record someone else reading it out to you, and compare what you actually get with what you expected. Unless your text is only two or three words long, they are not likely to be identical.

CHAPTER 2

The Formation of Sounds

In this chapter we shall be describing the formation of speech sounds in some detail. Since everyday language cannot cope with phonetic descriptions, we shall have to introduce a number of technical terms. If you find the vocabulary rather complicated at first, remember that the important things to get to grips with are the fundamental concepts themselves. Phonetic terms are of no value except insofar as they refer to concepts which are properly understood. There is no virtue whatever, for instance, in knowing that /f/ is a voiceless labio-dental fricative, unless you have a clear idea what these terms mean: otherwise you would be much better off simply calling it an /ef/.

The basic concepts of phonetics are fortunately very simple, and once you know what to look for, you can make some of the necessary observations directly for yourself. You can usually see something of how a sound is produced by making it in front of a mirror; and for most consonants at least, you can also feel what is going on inside your mouth. It takes a bit of practice to do this precisely and accurately, but many observations require no training at all. Anybody can observe that a /p/ sound is made with the lips, or that the tongue is involved in forming a /s/. If you concentrate on the basic concepts, and on observation, the job of finding the correct technical term quickly becomes a simple matter.

2.1 Channels and cavities

Some speech sounds, including /s, t, dʒ/, appear to be made up of a hissing or rushing noise which may begin or end abruptly. These 'noisy' sounds contrast with vowel sounds and a number of consonants, such as /m, n, l, r/, which are rather more musical or 'resonant' in nature. This distinction is an important one for the study of sound production, and also of interest for the study of the aesthetic properties of speech sounds.

The production of RESONANCE can be illustrated by comparison with a musical instrument such as a Spanish guitar. If you pluck one of the strings of a guitar, it vibrates in a complex way, with a fundamental frequency which you hear as the pitch, and a number of harmonics or 'overtones'. The vibrations of the string cause the air inside the body of the instrument to vibrate also, and depending on the size and shape of the cavity, some harmonics are strengthened, and others weakened. It is this resonance that gives the characteristic 'guitar' quality to the note that you hear. You can play the same note with the same pitch on another instrument, but it will not sound quite identical, as the size and shape of the cavity inside the instrument will be different.

In speech, the mouth acts like not one instrument, but a whole range of instruments. If you make an /i:/ vowel as in *pea* /pi:/, and then move to /a:/ as in *pa* /pa:/, you can keep the pitch constant, but you change that aspect of the sound that we perceive as the quality of the vowel phoneme. To get from /i:/ to /a:/, you move your tongue and your jaw, and this alters the size and shape of the cavities of the mouth and throat, and consequently its resonance properties. The mouth corresponds to the body of the guitar. Corresponding to the string are the VOCAL FOLDS which vibrate and set the air in the vocal cavity in motion. (The vocal folds are also known as the 'vocal cords', which is a less accurate term, and exaggerates the similarity to the guitar string. The musical image is taken even further in the alternative spelling 'vocal chords'.)

The other important sound-producing mechanism is the one that generates noise. When air is forced through a narrow channel, it becomes TURBULENT, and produces a kind of hissing noise. You can very easily demonstrate this for yourself. Put your hands together in the 'praying' position, and then move them about 5 mm apart. If you blow through the gap you will generate audible turbulence. A number of speech sounds are made in a very similar way, as the breath from the lungs is forced through a narrow gap made somewhere in the mouth, e.g. /f, θ, s/ as in *fin, thin, sin.* In phonetics this turbulence is generally referred to as 'friction', and sounds produced in this way are known as FRICATIVES. (The term derives from the Latin verb *fricare*, meaning 'rub', but 'rubbing sound' gives quite the wrong impression. If there is any friction in a fricative, it is made between the air and the gap left in the mouth, not by any of the organs of the mouth rubbing together!)

Put your hands back in the praying position, this time bringing your palms and fingers tightly together, and leaving no gap at all. It is obvious that in this position you cannot blow through the gap, as your breath is stopped. Try it. While you are blowing against the blockage, pull your hands suddenly apart: the air escapes noisily with a slight explosive sound immediately the blockage is released. This is the kind of mechanism used for /p, t, k/. Practise making these sounds, and feel for the closing of the gap, the holding back of the breath, and finally the noisy release. Sounds of this type are known simply as STOPS.

Open the gap again, this time to about 20 mm. If you blow hard, you can still produce the turbulence, but as you reduce the flow, the noise gradually subsides. The wider gap is clearly less efficient for generating noise. This is why sounds made with a wide channel in the mouth are not of the noisy type, but of the 'resonant' type, being made with vocal fold vibrations and with the vocal tract acting as a resonator.

Exercises

For each of the following sounds decide whether it belongs to the 'noise' category or the 'resonance' category:

     f   u: p   θ   l   o   ə   k

Transcribe the following words, placing each phoneme in the 'noise' or 'resonance' category:

     calm   picture   murmuring   elephant

Obstruent types

The term OBSTRUENT is used to refer collectively to all the types of sound in the 'noise' category.

As we have seen, a stop is produced by bringing the relevant organs together and stopping the air stream for a short while, and then releasing the stricture. Different types of stop can be made by varying the speed with which the phases of the articulation are carried out.

The release is in most cases made quickly, as for /p, t, k, b, d, g/, and stops of this kind are also known as 'plosives'. In other cases the release is slow, and consequently the organs linger for a time in the fricative position: the result is that the stop appears to be followed by the corresponding fricative, e.g. /tʃ, dʒ/. Stops of this type are 'affricates'. You can compare the rapid release of /t/ with the slow release of /tʃ/ by saying the words *tip* and *chip*; and similarly compare the rapid release of /d/ in *din* with the slow release of /dʒ/ in *gin*. The manner of the release of /tʃ, dʒ/ is reflected in the use of the digraphs [t] + [ʃ], [d] + [ʒ]. You may note, incidentally, that the stop phase of /tʃ, dʒ/ is actually made a little further back than the plosives /t, d/.

All fricatives are made by narrowing the channel so that turbulence is generated as air passes through the mouth. The set of fricatives consists of /f, v, θ, ð, s, z, ʃ, ʒ, h/.

Some of these, namely /s, z; ʃ, ʒ/, are made on the ridge just behind the teeth, at a position from where the air stream is directed towards the teeth. This has the effect of generating a greater degree of turbulence. The fricatives /s, z; ʃ, ʒ/ are generally noisier than /f, v; θ, ð/ and are known as 'sibilants'. The direction of the air is made more efficient by forming a groove down the central line of the tongue, and since this grooving is as a rule greater for /s, z/ than for /ʃ, ʒ/, /s, z/ are also known as 'grooved fricatives'.

2.2 Voicing

Your vocal folds are in your LARYNX or 'voice box', which you can locate in your neck (see the diagram in Appendix 3). If you put your hand on your throat and swallow, you should be able to feel the larynx – or at least that part of it known as the 'Adam's apple' – rising and then returning to its normal position. The Adam's apple tends to protrude in men, and so men usually have less difficulty than women in finding it.

The primary job of the larynx is to control the entrance to the windpipe and the lungs. When you breathe, the larynx is open, allowing air in and out of the lungs; when you swallow, it closes up to prevent food going down 'the wrong way', and directs it down the food passage to the stomach. The vocal folds are a part of this opening/closing mechanism which has been developed for speech. They are stretched across the windpipe, and when they are pulled apart they leave a V-shaped aperture called the GLOTTIS through which air can pass. When they are pulled together, they stop the flow of air. (Note that the organs themselves are the 'vocal folds'; the 'glottis' is the space between them.)

The vocal folds are able to adopt a number of different positions. If they are widely separated, leaving an open glottis, the air from the lungs passes through the larynx relatively unimpeded; sounds produced in this position are called VOICELESS sounds. The stops and fricatives that we considered above were all voiceless. To make the vibrations for VOICED sounds, the vocal folds are held in a loosely closed position. As air is pushed up from the lungs, it forces the folds apart, upon which they quickly snap together again as a result of their own elasticity. Then the air from the lungs forces them apart again, and so the cycle continues. You can get some idea of the action of the vocal folds if you can hold your lips in a loosely closed position and make them vibrate. (The sound conventionally written *brrr*, which people make when they are cold, is produced by a simultaneous vibration of the vocal folds and the lips.) The frequency with which the cycle is repeated is what gives the impression of PITCH. In women's and children's voices, the folds may vibrate several hundred times per second, but in a low-pitched man's voice the rate may be down below about 75 cycles per second.

We have so far treated the generation of noise and the production of resonance as quite separate, some sounds being in one category, and some in the other. In fact, voicing is quite independent of the size of the channel left in the mouth, and the two mechanisms can be combined.

Make a /s/ sound followed by /z/: these are made in exactly the same way except that /s/ is voiceless, and /z/ is voiced. If you put your fingers on your throat while making a long /z/ sound you should be able to feel the vibration made by the voicing: this vibration is of course absent when you make a /s/ sound. Or if you cup your hands over your ears you can hear the voicing of /z/ as a buzzing noise that reaches your ears through the bones of your skull: again the buzzing is absent from /s/. Another property of voiced sounds is that they have a musical pitch: you can sing /z/ and change the note, but if you try to sing /s/ all you get is the hissing fricative noise. When you have got the feel of voicing and voicelessness, instead of saying /s/ and /z/ separately, try switching directly from one to the other and back again in an unbroken [szszszsz]. If you can do this, you can probably feel yourself switching the voicing on and off. Do the same with /f/ and /v/; with the /θ/ of *thin* /θin/ and its voiced counterpart /ð/ as in *then* /ðen/; and also with /ʃ/ as in *fresher* /freʃə/ and its voiced counterpart /ʒ/ as in *measure* /meʒə/.

The opening and closing of the glottis controls the flow of air in much the same way as a tap controls the flow of water. When the glottis is wide open for a voiceless sound, it lets a lot of air through, which in turn generates a high level of turbulence; conversely, when it is loosely closed for voicing, it cuts down the flow of air and the turbulence. On account of their greater breath flow and noisiness, voiceless sounds are also described as 'fortis' ('strong') as opposed to 'lenis' ('weak') voiced consonants. For instance, /f, θ, s, ʃ/ are noisier than their voiced counterparts /v, ð, z, ʒ/. In fact, the channel for /v, ð/ may be so wide that when the flow of air is reduced by the voicing, virtually no turbulence is produced at all. You will notice that /v/ is the consonant which is elided in words which have special poetic forms, e.g. *o'er, e'er, e'en* for *over, ever,* and *even(ing)*. A fricative which has lost its friction is phonetically very close to a vowel sound.

Stops can also be voiced, but in this case the voiced/voiceless distinction is more difficult to perceive. In order to get the vibrations going, air has to pass through the larynx; but if the air stream is blocked somewhere in the mouth, it follows that not much air will get through the larynx. The main difference between voiced and voice-less stops is not in the sound produced while the stop is being held, but in the influence of the stop on neighbouring sounds.

Exercise

Each of the following sounds is voiceless. What is the corresponding voiced sound?

    k ʃ p θ f s t

Transcribe the following words, and identify each phoneme as voice as voiceless:

    pan   crack   bend   toffee   shorts

Say the words carefully to yourself: identify the points at which the voicing is switched on and off.

Approximant types

In order to describe the more open types of articulation, we need to combine two ideas which we have already discussed. First, the wider the air channel, the less efficient it is at generating noise: the more open types of articulation consequently tend to be voiced. Secondly, the effect of voicing is to reduce the flow of air, and this in turn reduces further the amount of noise produced. For instance, if we make a /r/ sound, it is voiced, and there is too little air flow to produce any turbulence. Now if we were for some reason to make the /r/ voiceless, that would increase the breath flow: if the organs remain at the same distance apart, the increased flow might now be sufficient to generate turbulence. In fact, English /r/ is sometimes voiceless and turbulent; this happens when it follows /p, t, k/ at the beginning of a syllable, as in *priest, crow, train*. If you say these words slowly to yourself – or better still, get someone who knows nothing about phonetics to say them for you – you may be able to detect this voiceless /r/. It will prob-ably be easiest to hear in *train*. On the other hand, no matter how much you increase the breath flow when you make an

/a/ sound, you are very unlikely to produce any turbulence in the mouth: indeed, you will almost certainly produce a bronchial wheeze first!

We can use these properties to subdivide the category of sounds made with resonance. We shall use the term APPROXIMANT for sounds where the articulators are close enough to generate turbulence when there is a high breath flow, and reserve the term RESONANT for sounds which are never noisy. There is no absolute cut-off point where 'approximant' gives way to 'resonant'; rather there is a scale with the organs fairly close together at one end, and the mouth wide open at the other. We shall simply call this the scale from 'close' to 'open'.

When we described the formation of a stop, we made the assumption that any side exits or other escape routes which the air stream might take are sealed off. As a result, when the stop is formed, the air flow stops completely. Some types of approximant, e.g. /m, n, ŋ, l/, are made by opening up an alternative escape route. Practice making these sounds, and see if you can detect the route by which the air escapes.

The remaining approximants include /j/ and /w/: /j/ is made by bringing the body of the tongue up and forwards, and /w/ is made by raising the back of the tongue and simultaneously rounding the lips. In either case the organs remain far enough apart to avoid turbulence. These two sounds are often described as 'semi-vowels' or 'semi-consonants'. These are not strictly phonetic terms at all, for they do not refer to the way the sounds are made, but to the position they occupy in the syllable. They are very similar to the vowels /i, u/ respectively, but they are like consonants in that they occupy the syllable margin rather than the syllabic position itself. We shall come back to this point when we discuss syllables.

2.3 The organs of speech

In order to say exactly where a sound is made, we have to be able to identify the ORGANS OF SPEECH. Most of these are familiar, such as the lips, the teeth and the tongue; but some of the names for the parts of the roof of the mouth are not used in everyday language, and so a few comments are necessary. A diagram of the organs of speech is given in Appendix 3.

Place your tongue tip behind your upper front teeth. If you slide your tongue back a little, you can feel, immediately behind the teeth, a hard bony ridge known as the ALVEOLAR RIDGE. From here backward the roof of the mouth arches upwards into the dome of the PALATE, remaining hard and bony. Outside phonetics, the term 'palate' normally refers to the whole of the roof of the mouth, but we shall use it to refer specifically to this hard area behind the alveolar ridge. The more explicit term 'hard palate' is also frequently used. You can probably feel with your tongue tip that at the top of the dome the hardness gives way and the palate becomes soft and fleshy; this is the 'velum' of the palate, known simply as the VELUM, or as the 'soft palate'. If you examine your velum in a mirror you will see that it ends in a soft, fleshy protuberance that hangs down at the entrance to the throat; this is the 'uvula'.

When you close your mouth, your tongue will remain close to or touching the roof. The BACK of the tongue is that part of it that lies behind the junction of the hard palate and the velum; the FRONT of the tongue is forward of this point. However, the tongue is so important in speech production that we have to divide up the front more narrowly: the TIP is self-explanatory, and the BLADE is the area just behind the tip which lies opposite the alveolar ridge. In fact the term 'front' is often used to exclude the tip and blade, and to refer specifically to that part of the front of the tongue opposite the hard palate.

The velum controls the rear entrance to the nose. When you breathe through your nose, the velum is lowered to allow air in and out; when you eat and swallow, it is raised against the back wall of the throat to prevent food going up. The velum is normally in this raised position during speech. The stops /b, d, g/ have a raised velum; the NASALS /m, n, ŋ/ respectively are produced in exactly the same way except that the velum is lowered, allowing air to escape via the nose. Practice making these sounds to yourself, and see if you can feel the connection between them. If you exaggerate /b, d, g/ you may be able to feel the pressure of the air building up behind the blockage, whereas in the nasals you can feel the air escaping through your nose. The word *wooden* is normally pronounced /wudn/, without any vowel sound between /d/ and /n/, and to get from /d/ to /n/ all you do is move the velum. Practice and exaggerate the syllable /dn/ a few times, and you may be able to feel this movement of the velum at the back of your mouth.

The stop /d/ also has a LATERAL counterpart /l/, in which the air escapes through a side exit. For all alveolar consonants other than /l/, the sides of the tongue make an air-tight seal against the side teeth and gums; but for /l/ the sides of the tongue are pulled away and the seal is broken. In the normal pronunciation of *medal* /medl/. the /d/ is immediately followed by /l/, and the transition between them is simply effected by breaking the seal at the sides. If you practice the syllable /dl/ on its own you may be able to bring this mechanism under conscious control.

To make the English /r/ the tip of the tongue is usually raised and held close to the back part of the alveolar ridge, but not close enough to generate turbulence, and a bit further back than for /z/ or /d/. Thus /r/ is a (post-)alveolar approximant. Some people may in some words like *very* touch the alveolar ridge briefly in the formation of /r/, making it into a 'tap'. If the tap is repeated a few times, the result is a 'roll'. The Scots are popularly supposed to roll their /r/s, and stage Scots frequently do; but in real life the tap is more common. In English as a whole, the approximant type of /r/ is the most common.

Articulation

The organs involved in making a sound are the ARTICU-LATORS. The normal meaning of the verb 'articulate' is to 'joint' or to 'divide into sections'; when we articulate the stream of speech we divide it up into sections of different sizes, such as words, syllables, and ultimately phonemes. In phonetics the word has shifted from referring to the sectioning process, to the actual production of the small sections, and thus has the special sense of to 'produce a speech sound'.

The organs attached to the lower jaw are able to move, and when used to make a sound are called the ACTIVE articulators, whereas those connected to the upper jaw are in general fixed, and so known as the PASSIVE articulators. This neat distinction breaks down somewhat in the case of the lips, because they move together, so that neither is properly 'passive'. The velum is attached to the upper jaw, and so normally a 'passive' articulator, but it does move during the formation of nasal consonants, and to that extent it could perhaps be claimed as an 'active' articulator for nasals.

Place of articulation

For the most part we can assume that the air channel is narrowed between a given part of the roof of the mouth and the organ which normally lies opposite it, e.g. that the back of the tongue rises towards the velum. In other words, if we know the passive articulator, we can usually predict the active one. We can thus describe most places of articulation by giving just the passive articulator. For this we need a set of adjectives corresponding to the nouns for the parts of the roof of the mouth:

NOUN	ADJECTIVE
lip	labial
teeth	dental
alveolar ridge	alveolar
palate	palatal
velum	velar

From the adjectives we can form nouns to refer to sounds, e.g. labial consonants are referred to as 'labials', and dental consonants as 'dentals' etc. This simple classification breaks down slightly in the case of labial and dental sounds, because the active articulator cannot always be predicted from the passive one. If you make the sounds /p, b/, the lower lip moves up to the upper lip, as expected. But in the case /f, v/, it is the lower lip that moves up towards the upper front teeth. To clarify matters we can call /f, v/ LABIO-DENTAL, leaving the term DENTAL for the true dentals /θ, ð/, for which the tongue tip – the expected active articulator – moves up to the teeth.

We are now in a position to classify English consonants according to their place of articulation:

LABIAL: /p, b, m/, produced by stopping the air at the lips.

LABIO-DENTAL: /f, v/, the air being forced through a narrow gap between lower lip and upper teeth.

DENTAL: /θ, ð/, the air being forced through a narrow gap between tongue tip and teeth.

ALVEOLAR: /t, d; s, z; n; l, r/. Of these, /t, d/ are stops, and /s, z/ are fricatives made by forcing the air between the tip and blade of the tongue and the alveolar ridge. The rest are approximants, /n/ being a nasal, and /l/ lateral.

PALATAL: /j; ʃ, ʒ; tʃ, dʒ/. The only true palatal here is /j/; /ʃ, ʒ/ are made further back than /s, z/ in an area intermediate between those normally regarded as alveolar and palatal, and are more precisely described as 'palato-alveolar'.

VELAR: /k, g, ŋ/, of which /k, g/ are stops, and /ŋ/ is a nasal.

There remain two consonants, /w/ and /h/. The former is obviously some kind of labial consonant: what is less obvious is that it also involves raising the back of the tongue towards the velum. It therefore has a 'double articulation', being labial and velar at the same time. (You may see /w/ described as 'labio-velar'. However, the first part of a hyphenated term such as 'labio-dental' is normally taken to refer to the active articulator, and so 'labio-velar' would – absurdly – imply that the lower lip is raised towards the velum.) We shall describe /w/ as a 'labial and velar approximant'.

All consonants except /h/ are produced at some specifiable point in the mouth. By contrast, /h/ cannot be localized in this way. Foreign learners of English sometimes have difficulty with /h/, and substitute sounds with a narrowing somewhere at the back of the mouth; but any turbulence thus produced is very salient to the native speaker's ear, and such sounds are not accepted as versions of English /h/. It is consequently difficult to pin down a place of articulation for /h/, but since the greatest degree of narrowing between the lungs and the outside air is found at the glottis – the vocal folds are brought together, but not in the manner that produces voice – /h/ is usually defined by default as a 'glottal fricative'.

You will occasionally find consonants classified according to the active articulator. Adjectives in this case derive not from the English name for the articulator, but from the Latin name. Sounds produced with the tongue tip (apex) are 'apical'; those made with the blade (lamen) are 'laminal', and those made with the back of the tongue (dorsum) are 'dorsal'. An older equivalent for 'dorsal' is 'guttural', deriving from Latin *guttur* meaning 'throat': this is a perfectly good phonetic term which happens to have gone out of fashion. However, just because it is a word not now used by phoneticians, you should be on your guard when you come across it.

2.4 Vowel sounds

Identifying where consonants are made is relatively easy, because there is considerable contact between the articulators, and you can actually feel where the narrowing is being made, and how close together the organs involved are. The place of articulation of vowels is much more difficult to pin down, as the channel is much wider, and the organs consequently further apart. You may find that you have no 'feel' at all for the place of vowels in the mouth.

If you make a /j/ sound followed by /iː/, you may recognize the two as having very similar gestures. We classed /j/ above as a palatal sound, and so /iː/ must also be palatal. In fact, for many people /iː/ is like a short /i/ followed by a /j/ sound, thus phonetically [ij]. In much the same way, /uː/ is similar to /w/, so that /uː/ must also be a labial and velar sound. There is thus no absolute phonetic distinction between vowels and consonants: vowels are sounds which are like /j, w/ but have a more open channel. And like /j, w/, all vowel sounds are normally voiced.

Consider now the short /i, a, u/ vowels of *pit, pat, put.* For /i/ the tongue is raised towards the palate, and for /u/ it is raised towards the velum, but for /a/ the jaw is lowered and the tongue is pulled away from the roof of the mouth, leaving the maximum size of channel. Let us call /i, u/ CLOSE vowels; /a/ is an OPEN vowel. Short /e/ as in *pet* is intermediate between /i/ and /a/, while short /o/ as in *pot* is intermediate between /a/ and /u/:

CLOSE   /i/   /u/

                    /e/   /o/

OPEN   /a/

Although it might be reasonable to describe /i/ as 'palatal', the wider channel for /e/ and /a/ makes the pinpointing of a 'place' of articulation more nebulous. For this reason it is actually rather rare to describe vowels as 'palatal', and they are commonly described more vaguely as FRONT vowels. For the same reason 'velar' vowels are described as BACK vowels. Front vowels are made with the mass of the tongue pushed forward in the mouth, while back vowels are made with the mass of the tongue retracted, or pulled back.

When vowel systems are listed, it is conventional to go from close front to open to close back. Thus whereas the vowel letters are usually listed **a, e, i, o, u,** the phonemes in the short vowel system are listed /i, e, a, o, u/.

We have plotted the vowels /i, e, a, o, u/ in the form of a triangle, with all the vowels on its outer edges. There are also CENTRAL vowels, including /ə/ and /ʌ/. Note that shwa – the 'neutral' vowel – is intermediate between front and back, and close and open. It could thus be plotted in the middle of the triangle. If you have the /ʌ/ vowel in a word like *cut*, so that it does not rhyme with *foot*, then your /ʌ/ is probably a central vowel, more or less similar in quality to /ə/, but unlike /ə/ it occurs in accented syllables.

The long vowels written with the colon can also be plotted in a triangle:

              FRONT   BACK

CLOSE   /i:/   /u:/

                        /ə:/   /o:/

OPEN   /a:/

In many varieties of English there is a gap in the long vowel triangle corresponding to short /e/, while /ə:/ occupies the position corresponding to /ə/. It must be emphasized that we are making here an extremely crude classification of vowels: it does not follow that corresponding long and short vowels sound exactly alike, and have exactly the same 'vowel quality'. For example, whereas /a/ is the most open of the short vowels, /aː/ is the most open of the long vowels; but in most varieties of English they are kept apart by a difference of quality as well as duration.

2.5   The aesthetic properties of sounds

Phoneticians study the vowels and consonants of a language purely as sounds, and the meaning of the words in which those sounds occur is in most cases irrelevant. This is the reverse of our everyday experience of language, for the sound is normally a vehicle for the transmission of meaning, and receives little attention for its own sake.

However, for the student who wishes to apply phonetics to the study of literary texts, the connection between sound and meaning is of considerable potential interest. In poetry, for instance, an attempt is sometimes made to bring the 'sound' of the text out of the background, and to create some kind of recognizable pattern that is pleasing or appropriate to the sense. The aesthetic properties of sound patterns depend on several factors, including rhythm and parallelism, and also on the auditory effect of individual phonemes.

It must be emphasized that this connection between sound and meaning is found only in exceptional cases. It is not the normal state of affairs in literary language, nor is it usual even in poetry. The normal case is that the sound has a conventional and an entirely arbitrary relationship to the meaning. For instance, there is no necessary connection between the sequence of phonemes /ʌgli/ and the meaning 'ugly' beyond the fact that the English language uses the one to refer to the other. Someone who did not know English would be unlikely to guess the meaning of the word from the sound alone. We can only claim a non-arbitrary relationship between sound and meaning when we have very, very cogent reasons for doing so.

In the case of ONOMATOPOEIA, the normal

connections between sound and meaning are apparently bypassed, and superficially it may seem that sound and meaning are related directly. The simplest case of onomatopoeia involves words which seem to have very suitable pronunciations. This applies as much in everyday language as in literary texts. Most people would probably agree, for example, that at least to some small extent it is possible to assess the suitability of words which might be used to refer to noises, such as *peep* and *bang*.

Suppose you had the job of advertising a new electric drill and you found that you needed a word to describe the sound of the drill boring into masonry. The drill motor itself has a 'whine', but there is no obvious ready-made word for the noise made by the bit in the masonry. There are several unused but potential English words available, such as /biʃ/, /kaŋ/ or /si:v/, but none of these sounds quite right. Perhaps the /i:, i/ vowels suggest something high-pitched, and so the first and third possibilities are not very good; /k/ suggests a sound with a sharp onset, so /kaŋ/ is not much better. How about /ra:m/, with a slow onset, a 'loud' /a:/ vowel, and gradual decay? There is a subjective element here: you may or may not feel that /ra:m/ is a reasonable suggestion. In this section we shall try to find a phonetic explanation for the suitable naming of sounds.

In the first place, we can relate speech sounds to natural sounds which are made in a similar way: stops and fricatives are to turbulent noises as approximants and resonants are to sounds made by cavity resonance. For instance, escaping steam may be said to 'hiss': where the /s/ represents the noise of the steam in an obvious and direct way.

In the production of stops, the stopping of the air stream and the release are sudden events: the air channel is open, and a fraction of a second later it is shut, and it reopens equally sharply. Stops are thus suitable for sounds which start or end abruptly: *pop, tick, bang*. Fricatives are more appropriate for noises with a gradual onset or decay, e.g. *hiss, zoom*. It is perhaps not too fanciful to think of a *crash* as a noise which starts abruptly (with a stop) and ends more gradually (with a fricative).

Approximants are more suitable for sounds which lack the noisy element: *ring, roll, murmur*. Consonants in this category are also called 'liquids'; this is not really a descriptive term – describing how the sounds are made – but rather an aesthetic term. (Its use is not consistent; it includes /l, r/, and possibly other approximants. When you come across the term 'liquid', you should always check to see exactly what kinds of consonants it includes.)

If consonants have aesthetic properties, this is very much more true of vowels. With vowels, however, it is as well to observe that not all English vowels take part in the aesthetic system. There are over twenty vowel phonemes in English, but we can deal with their aesthetic properties by reference to a subsystem of three basic vowel types: [i, a, u]. The close front category is represented by [i], [a] represents the open category, and [u] close back vowels. These vowels vary on the scale of loudness, and the scale of apparent pitch. Loudness is the easier to explain. Open vowels like [a] are made with the mouth open, and so [a] has, as it were, full volume. Noise words containing /a/ tend to represent loud noises: *clang, smash, bang, crash, smack*. The mouth being more closed for [i, u], these vowels tend to represent softer sounds, e.g. *boom, tick, ping*.

The apparent pitch of vowels is more complex. If you put your hand on your throat and sing up the musical scale, you will probably find that your larynx rises as the pitch gets higher. (If you are a trained singer, you may have learned not to do this for certain styles of singing. But for the normal speaking voice, we can assume a connection between the pitch and the height of the larynx.) When you make the vowel [i], you push your tongue upwards and forwards, and since the tongue is linked mechanically to the larynx, this movement of the tongue tends to pull the larynx up with it into the position for higher pitch. Close front vowels are as a rule slightly higher in pitch than other vowels in similar conditions.

Another, and probably more important, contributor to the apparent high pitch of [i] has to do with what is called its 'formant structure'. You can get some idea of the relevant formant by whispering vowels. Now whispered sounds, being voiceless, do not have a true pitch; but they do have a pitch-like quality by means of which they can be plotted on a scale relative to each other. Whispered [i] is clearly higher on this scale than [a], which in turn is higher than whispered [u]. (It is obvious that you have to whisper:

you can sing [i] on a low note and [u] on a high note if you wish to!)

There are several examples of words containing the vowels /i:, i/ which refer to high pitched noises, e.g. *ping, clink, squeak, scream, screech*. Examples of /u:, u/ for low pitched sounds can be found, e.g. *boom, vroom* /bu:m, vrum/, but they are rarer. This is partly because the phonemes of a language are subject to historical change, and this process take no account whatever of the aesthetic associations of sounds. The short English /u/ has in most dialects become more open /ʌ/. In Northern English, words like *bump, thud, rumble* – which all represent low-pitched sounds – retain the close back /u/ vowel; elsewhere the pronunciations /bʌmp, θʌd, rʌmbl/ have lost their echoic effect.

The associations between vowels and pitch and vowels and loudness have a direct phonetic explanation. Vowels may also be linked to a variety of sensations which are indirectly associated with loudness or pitch. For instance, soft high-pitched sounds are associated with objects small in size, and loud low-pitched sounds with large objects. This follows from the kind of sound we expect to hear when an object is struck: a small bell or pipe gives a softer and higher note than a large one. In this way higher pitched [i] may be linked indirectly with small objects, and lower pitched [a] with large ones. The word *ping* refers in the first place to a high-pitched sound, but you probably expect it to be used for the sound of a small object like a kitchen timer rather than, say, a train. Conversely, you probably associate *clank* with a large object.

Another possible case of this transference between senses or 'synaesthesia' concerns back vowels. You may feel that low-pitched sounds are 'dull' and indistinct to the ear, whereas high-pitched sounds are 'bright'. If we could talk of focus with respect to hearing, high-pitched sounds would be more in focus than low-pitched ones. The [u] vowel – or its replacement /ʌ/ – is used for sounds which are indistinct or ill-focussed, e.g. *mutter, thunder, rumble*; by extension it is used to refer to sensations involving visual indistinctness, e.g. *gloom, obscure*. Indistinctness is associated with distance, and perhaps noise words with [u] refer to distant sounds. Thus one talks of the *boom* of thunder: cannon *roar* when they are close at hand, but at a distance they *boom*.

The study of the aesthetic properties of sounds can be very interesting, but you also have to be careful. Just because you can occasionally find a link between sound and meaning, it does not follow that you can always do so. You may feel that the vowels /i̩/ and /ɑː/ of *little* and *large* respectively are ideal for the representation of their meanings: but *big* has the vowel suggesting smallness. In the next chapter, we shall argue that the apparently direct link between sound and sense in the case of onomatopoeia is actually an illusion.

Secondly, it is important that any claimed link is based on firm phonetic criteria: you cannot just make up an explanation as you go along. A Frenchman once pointed out to me that the Latin word *nox* 'night' had become *nuit* in French, with the 'dull' [o] vowel replaced by the 'bright' [i], and that conversely *dies* 'day' had been replaced by *jour*, the 'bright' [i] giving way to 'dull' [u]. This, he explained, was because the Romans were busy during the day and went to bed early, whereas the French are lethargic during the day and come to life in the evening. This is a delightful piece of pseudo-scientific nonsense, but it has nothing whatever to do with phonetics.

Exercise

Describe the kind of sensation conjured up by the following words:

> gloom, screech, plop, thwack, clunk-click, whoosh, glimmer

To what extent can you give a phonetic explanation for the effect of these words? Find some more examples of your own, and explain them.

Comment on the meanings of the words in italics in these phrases and sentences:

(1)   *loud* music; a *loud* shirt
(2)   a *chink* of light; the *clink* of coins.
(3)   Have a *peep* in at the dog before you leave. It was so quiet I never heard a *peep* out of it.

CHAPTER 3
The English Sound System

In the last chapter we discussed the ways in which individual sounds are made. The points made so far apply in principle to any language. We shall now consider English phonemes as a system, so that when discussing any one phoneme we take into account its relationship to other phonemes. Much of the information in this chapter applies specifically to English.

3.1 The consonant system

When we consider the consonant system as a whole, it is usual to present it in the form of a table, with the consonants arranged in relation to other consonants. Thus /b/ is paired with its voiceless counterpart /p/, and grouped both with the other voiced stops /d, g/, and with the other labial consonants /p, f, v, m/. You will see English consonants presented in this way in Appendix 4.

When referring to consonants, it is conventional to specify

(i) the state of the glottis, i.e. whether the sound is voiced or voiceless.
(ii) the place of articulation, and
(iii) the manner of articulation.

Thus /p/ is a 'voiceless bilabial stop', and /z/ is a 'voiced palato-alveolar fricative'.

If information is predictable, it is not necessary to specify it. For example, only obstruents (stops and fricatives) enter into the contrast of voicing, and the more open sounds are voiced as a matter of course. While it is necessary to specify /p/ as voiceless, on the grounds that it contrasts with /b/, the voicing of the nasals /m, n/ can be taken for granted. 'Bilabial nasal' or 'alveolar nasal' are unambiguous. In the case of place of articulation, it is enough in most cases to specify the passive articulator, since the active one is predictable. In the case of manner of articulation, all affricates are in fact affricated stops, and all nasals and laterals are approximants; the more general terms 'stop' or 'approximant' are consequently unnecessary in these cases. Similarly, although /ŋ/ is actually a voiced dorso-velar nasal approximant, the definition 'velar nasal' is sufficient to distinguish it from all other English phonemes. Remember that we are talking specifically about English here: the relationships among phonemes may be very different in other languages.

Exercise

Identify the consonants that answer to the following definitions, and write down the appropriate symbol:

> alveolar lateral
> voiceless dental fricative
> voiced bilabial stop
> velar nasal
> voiced alveolar stop
> voiceless glottal fricative
> voiced palato-alveolar fricative
> palatal approximant
> voiceless alveolar fricative
> voiceless palato-alveolar affricate

Now classify the following phonemes:

> /g dʒ r m s θ v w k b /

Start off by giving a 3-term classification, and then check to see if voicing is predictable: if so, delete the word 'voiced'. When you have done that, study the following series of consonants. Exactly what do you have to do to get from one consonant to the next in the series? Apart from minor adjustments, there is only one significant change in each case, which may be in voicing, in place of articulation, or in manner of articulation.

k t s ʃ tʃ dʒ ʒ ð θ f v b m ŋ g d l
r j w ɡ k

3.2 Cardinal vowels

In the last chapter we introduced a rough method of indicating vowel quality, plotting the vowels of English relative to each other on scales from close to open and from front to back. This was the kind of accuracy generally achieved by linguists until the early years of the present century. An improved – but still rough – method was devised by Daniel Jones, and uses a set of vowel qualities known as the CARDINAL VOWELS.

The use of the word *cardinal* is related to its use in the phrase 'cardinal points of the compass'. Two fixed points are established, and three front and three back intermediate cardinal points are set up between them. The quality of speech vowels is identified by reference to the nearest cardinal vowel. It is rare for speech vowels to be identical to cardinal vowels – just as directions on the ground are rarely due north or due east – and a mere coincidence when they are.

The cardinal vowels are auditory qualities, and the only way you can learn them is to hear them produced by someone who knows them. Unless you have a teacher who can demonstrate them for you, the best thing you can do is to listen to Jones's recording of the vowels, which is listed in Appendix 6. It is impossible to learn them from a book, and foolish even to try. The description here is intended only to tell you about the system, and how it is used.

The first fixed point is cardinal [i]. This is made by pushing the front of the tongue as close as possible to the palate without producing turbulence. You will come close to /i/ if you prolong the /j/ of *yeast*. The other fixed point is [ɑ], which is made by pulling the tongue back and down into the throat as far as it will go, again without producing turbulence. If a doctor wishes to examine the back of your throat, he may ask you to say **ah**, and this is a reasonable approximation to cardinal [ɑ]. Note that [i] is the closest and frontest possible vowel, while [ɑ] is the openest and backest. These are therefore the extreme vowels, and the vowel phonemes of any language must fall somewhere in between.

You can move your tongue from the [i] position to the [ɑ] position taking several different routes, and in this way make an infinite number of different intermediate vowel sounds. If you move from [i] to [ɑ] keeping the tongue as front as possible, you produce a continuum of front vowel sounds. Three cardinal points on this continuum are picked out, and are the cardinal vowels [e, ɛ, a]. Three cardinal vowels, namely [ɔ, o, u] are picked out on the continuum of back vowels made by moving from [ɑ] back to [i] keeping the tongue as far back as possible. Cardinal [u] is similar to a drawn-out version of the [w] sound of *woo*. The cardinal vowels are plotted on the outside edges of a quadrilateral:

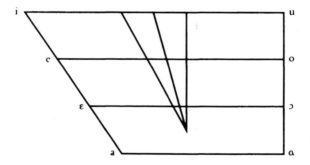

Very, very roughly, the position of the cardinal vowels on the quadrilateral corresponds to the position of the highest point of the tongue when the sound is made. As you move from [i] to [a] the movement of the tongue is essentially downwards until you get to [a], and then backwards to [ɑ]. At the back, the movement is essentially upwards from [ɑ] to [u], and then forwards to [i]. The quadrilateral is actually a highly stylized representation of these points, with convenient parallel lines joining [i, u], [e, o], [ɛ, ɔ] and [a, ɑ]. Although the cardinals are all peripheral, the vowels of speech are usually to be plotted inside the quadrilateral.

The point of this stylization is that it enables us to describe vowels more efficiently in terms of front/back and close/open.

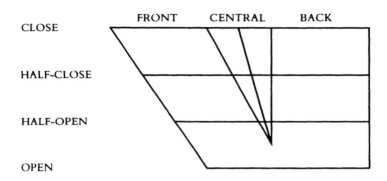

Any vowel which is reasonably near the line joining [i] and [u] can be described as 'close', and any vowel between the front line, and the parallel sloping line inside the quadrilateral can be described as 'front'.

For ease of reference the cardinal vowels are numbered:

1.	i	**8.**	u
2.	e	**7.**	o
3.	ɛ	**6.**	ɔ
4.	a	**5.**	ɑ

'A vowel in the region of cardinal 2' is exactly equivalent to 'a vowel in the region of [e]': both refer to a 'half-close front vowel'.

The cardinals we have discussed so far are actually the 'primary' cardinal vowels. The first five are produced with spread lips; this spreading is very vigorous for [i] but gets progressively weaker with the openness of the vowel, so that [ɑ] is virtually lip neutral. The last three are lip rounded, and progressively so as the vowel gets closer. Although these lip shapes commonly pattern with the tongue positions in the languages of the world, this is not always the case. Lip position is in principle independent of tongue position. To handle this third dimension of vowel quality, a set of 'secondary' cardinal vowels are established with lip positions reversed, the first five being rounded and the last three spread:

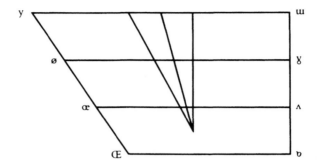

These are numbered 9–16. You do not need to know exactly what they sound like: the reason that they are mentioned here is that the symbols of two of them – [ʌ] [ɒ] – are frequently used to represent English phonemes. If you know French, the vowel of *rue* /ry/ 'street' is in the region of cardinal 9, that of *oeux* /ø/ 'eggs' in the region of cardinal 10, and that of *oeuf* /œf/ 'egg' in the region of cardinal 11.

One important application of the cardinal vowel system is to provide a set of phonetically motivated symbols for the vowel phonemes of any language. Although the realization of phonemes will not coincide with the cardinal positions, the symbol of the nearest cardinal vowel can be used. For a vowel which falls in the middle between two cardinal vowels, a choice has to be made, and preference is given to a familiar Roman character over a more exotic one. For example, English /e/ is usually between cardinals 2 and 3, and the Roman letter **e** is chosen in preference to the Greek letter ɛ. If two vowel phonemes are close together near the same cardinal vowel, some other means has to be found to distinguish them, perhaps by adding a special mark (or 'diacritic'), or by adopting a special character for one of them.

This method works quite well if we are choosing phoneme symbols for a single variety of the language at a single point in its history. It becomes very cumbersome and confusing if we have to compare different varieties, or discuss historical developments. For instance, if we were to say that in the history of English '/iː/ becomes /ai/ and /eː/ becomes /iː/' we would be using /iː/ as the label for two different phonemes. We have already been using slants for phonemes, and square brackets for their phonetic realizations. This distinction will now become more important, and a bit more complicated.

To illustrate the point, consider the case of a school which has a group of seven-year-olds in class 1, and eight-year-olds in class 2. In the course of time, the seven-year-olds become eight-year-olds, and at an agreed moment they cease to be referred to as 'class 1' and instead become 'class 2'. We take it for granted that the label 'class 1' refers to different actual bodies in different years, and that the same bodies are referred to at different times by different labels.

Suppose now that we have two phonemes, A and B, and that A is in the region of cardinal 1, and accordingly written /iː/. If at some future date A has moved away from cardinal 1, while B has moved into that area, we might stop using the symbol /iː/ for A, and use it instead for B. In such cases it would be clearer to use labels for the phonemes rather than the usual IPA characters. For the study of English vowels, we shall temporarily return to the everyday names that we used in Chapter 1.

3.3 English vowels

We have already dealt in an incidental fashion with some of the ways in which the phoneme system differs among varieties of English. Some variables can be traced back before the Norman conquest, especially in the case of the rural dialects of the Scottish lowlands and the extreme north of England. But as far as the mainstream standardized dialects of England are concerned, and overseas varieties of English which derive from them, the major sources of variation have arisen since the introduction of printing in the fifteenth century. These are mostly to be found in the vowel system, the earlier state of which is fossilized in the spellings of words. We shall refer loosely to the medieval form as the 'original' pronunciation, although we could of course trace the pronunciation back further, if we so wished. Secondly, since it has always been the case that some dialects are more conservative than others, it would be impossible and meaningless to put a date on this 'original' form, and say when it was used. Conservative dialects may retain old forms five hundred years and more after a change has been completed in more advanced varieties.

Short vowels

In our table of phonemes, we listed six short vowels for RP / i e a o ʌ u/, Northern English preserves the earlier system of five short vowels /i e a o u/, which is represented in the spelling. Outside the North, the /u/ phoneme has split, remaining in some words – especially following a labial consonant – and changing elsewhere to /ʌ/. The minimal pair *put~putt* /put, pʌt/ shows that this is a new phonemic distinction, and not just the development of a new minor variant. Thus RP has *push* /puʃ/, *butcher* /butʃə/, *full* /ful/ and *mud* /mʌd/, *buff* /bʌf/, *pun* /pʌn/: Northern English has /u/ in all these words, thus /puʃ, butʃə, ful, mud, buf, pun/.

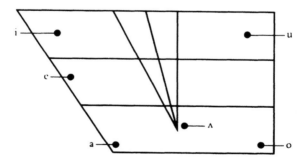

The short vowels /i, u/ written without the colon are in this way distinguished from the corresponding long vowels /i:, u:/, and this notation is perfectly clear and unambiguous. Short /a/ is somewhere in the region of cardinal 4 in many varieties of English, and the cardinal 4 character is a good symbol for it. In (old-fashioned) RP, and more generally in American English, a closer variant is found, intermediate between cardinals 3 and 4. However, the Old English alphabet had a special character – æ known as 'ash' – for a vowel of this type, and since the phoneticians of the last century were also philologists, the practice grew of using ash to represent short /a/. While this may be reasonable for RP, its use for the short /a/ of Northern or Scottish English is misleading and confused; for all varieties of English the Roman letter **a** is more familiar and its use is more consistent in principle.

You will recognize the symbol ʌ used for the vowel of *but* /bʌt/ as the back spread secondary cardinal 14. This represents its pronunciation in Ulster English, and possibly in the RP of the last century: it is extremely archaic for contemporary RP. The vowel of *pot* you will see plotted on the vowel chart above between half-open and open. It is also slightly rounded in most British varieties of English. If we select our symbol strictly according to convention, we have the choice of primary cardinal 6 [ɔ] or secondary cardinal 13 [ɒ], and both of these are in widespread use. Since the character **o** is used for cardinal 7, which is not very close to the vowel of *pot*, its use as the phoneme symbol has become a matter of controversy. However, for the vast majority of people who need to represent the vowel phonemes of English, but who do not have long experience of using the cardinal vowel system, this controversy is nitpicking and pointless.

Exercise

Transcribe the following words as you would pronounce them in your own variety of English. Paying particular attention to the vowels spelt **u**:

> mud pudding but bush such brush gum push
> put butter bull tummy shun gun hum cut

Long vowels

The long vowels have changed more dramatically than the short vowels over the last 500 years or so by a series of changes known together as 'the great vowel shift'. Although there is a wide range in the pronunciation of the long vowels, the variation is not haphazard, but follows a number of identifiable patterns which make up the mainstream development in English as a whole. Some dialects are more conservative than others, and have progressed less far, but at least they are on the same road. This is very convenient, as it means we can account for a wide range of dialect forms with a single explanation. Of course we cannot predict the exact shade of sound for every dialect, but we can give an approximation which should enable you to get to grips with your own variety of English if it is different from RP.

A characteristic of English long vowels is that they tend to change in quality towards the end. A 'pure' vowel that remains the same in quality from the beginning to the end is called a MONOPHTHONG. A vowel that changes from one quality to another is a DIPHTHONG. If we have a long monophthong [e:], the end of which becomes closer and more like [i], we can say that the monophthong has diphthongized to [ei]. Conversely, if a diphthong /au/ ceases to change in quality, and the initial quality is maintained throughout, we can say it has monophthongized to [a:]. Changes of this kind are important in the history of English.

General principles of change

Although the details of the changes which have taken place are different for each vowel, the same sort of changes have taken place several times. There are three main rules at work:

1. Long monophthongs become closer.
2. When monophthongs have become about half-close, they tend to become closing diphthongs, i.e. the second element is closer than the first. The first element of a closing diphthong becomes more open.
3. A wide diphthong – i.e. one in which the first element is open and the second close – weakens and loses its second element, and thus becomes a monophthong.

Note that rule 3 produces an open long vowel which can then feed rule 1 and become closer. In this way, the three rules operate in a continuous cycle.

To illustrate the operation of rules 1 and 2, consider

long-a and **long-o**, which have developed roughly in parallel. As the name and spelling suggest, **long-a** was originally a longer version of short /a/, phonetically [a:]. This became a closer and fronter vowel by rule 1, moving towards cardinal 3 and then to 2. The Northern English 'broad a' is fairly monophthongal and intermediate in quality between Cardinals 2 and 3; Scottish English tends to have a closer vowel [e:]. Elsewhere, the vowel has generally diphthongized by rule 2 to [ei], which is also the quality in RP and GenAm. In the South of England, the diphthong has kept on developing, and becoming more open and centralized to [ʌi], thus *bake* [bʌik], *today* [tədʌi] This form is spreading up through the Midlands.

Long-o is by origin a lengthened /o/ which has become closer and then diphthongized. The Northern English 'broad o' is fairly monophthongal and between Cardinals 6 and 7. The Scottish [o] is closer to Cardinal 7. Elsewhere, it generally diphtongizes to [ou]. This type is common in American English, Ulster English, Northern English, and was formerly the RP vowel. In RP the first element of the diphthong has become more central, thus [əu], and in the south of England this is more open, and more like [ʌu], e.g. *soap* [sʌup], *road* [rʌud].

In the north of England, roughly north of a line from the Lune to the Humber, these vowels have developed historically in a markedly different direction: they are diphthongized, but instead of moving to a closer vowel quality, they move to [ə], thus *bake* [beək], *place* [pleəs], *soap* [soəp], *road* [roəd]. In this type, the first element of the vowel continues to get closer, and forms like [biək, pliəs, suəp, ruəd] are heard. These are CENTERING diphthongs.

As these vowels have developed, other less common vowels have merged with them in most varieties of English. For instance, the vowel spelt **eigh**, as in *weight* and *eight* has generally merged with **long-a**. Some dialects in the North of England preserve the distinction between *weight* [weit] and *wait* [we:t]. Similarly, one of the vowel phonemes formerly written **ow**, as in *know*, has generally merged with **long-o**, so that *know* and *no* are identical. Some dialects preserve the distinction, e.g. *no* [no:] vs *know* [nou]. (Where the contrasts survive, we need distinct phoneme symbols to distinguish /weit/ from /we:t/ or /nou/ from /no:/.)

The development of **long-e** and **oo** has followed the same route as **long-a** and **long-o**, but it is less dramatic. The usual spelling of **long-e**, with the doubling of the letter **e** as in *green* /gri:n/, suggests a vowel similar to short /e/ but longer. The original [e:] has in the course of time become closer [i:] and is now becoming a diphthong. Since this starts in the position of short /i/ and moves to a closer quality, we can make up a symbol [ij] using [j] to represent a vowel closer than /i/. In final position the diphthong has widened to [əi] in some urban dialects of England, thus *free* [frəi]. The spelling **oo** similarly represents the fact that this was formerly a more open vowel, and more like a longer equivalent of short /o/. Having become [u:] by rule 1, it is now becoming a diphthong, and can be transcribed [uw], e.g. *boot* [bu:t, buwt] or *tool* [tu:l, tuwl]. (In Scotland and Northern Ireland, **oo** has not diphthongized, but has instead moved forward to a central position. This vowel is represented by a bar through the symbol **u** thus [bʉt, tʉl].)

The vowel spelt **ea** as in *bead* /bi:d/ was formerly a phoneme separate from **long-e**, but has merged with it in most varieties of English. The original value of **ea** was a long vowel intermediate in quality between /e/ and /a/, hence the spelling. This is about half open on the cardinal vowel chart, in the region of cardinal 3 [ɛ:]. This became [e:], and in most dialects eventually [i:] where it caught up with and merged with /i:/. There are just a few words, including *great* and *steak* in which the older form survives in standard pronunciation and has merged with **long-a** as in *grate* and *stake*. In parts of Scotland and Ireland the older more open sound has survived as an independent phoneme, or else it has merged more generally with **long-a**.

The development of **long-i** and **ow** illustrates rules 2 and 3. The former vowel was originally a long version of /i/, i.e. something like [i:]. This became a diphthong [ij], the first element of which became increasingly open, first [əi], and later [ai]. Some conservative dialects, including those of Scotland and Ireland, preserve [əi], but the standard realization in RP and GenAm is [ai]. Although /ai/ has got no further than [ai] in the standard varieties, it is still developing in local dialects. In many parts of the English-speaking world, from Texas to New Zealand to North Yorkshire, the second element of /ai/ is being weakened and dropped.

In this way *tide* becomes [taːd], *time* [taːm], and *five* [faːv]. The [i] may survive before voiceless consonants, e.g. *kite* [kait], *pipe* [paip].

The vowel **ow** was formerly a long close back [uː] which diphthongized to [uw], and the first element has now become more open via [əu] to [au]. RP and GenAm have [au]; conservative varieties may retain [əu]. In some non-standard varieties, the second element of [au] is weakened to [ə], e.g. Cockney *house* [aəs], or becomes an extension of the first element, e.g. [aːs].

Both **long-i** ([ai]) and **ow** ([au]) ultimately lose their second elements, but they do not merge. In order to see why, we need to investigate in more detail the quality of the first element when it becomes open. In most kinds of English it has a central quality intermediate between front and back, and is not significantly different for /ai/ and /au/. RP has a back starting point for /au/ in the region of Cardinal 5, [ɑu], and a front starting point for /ai/ near Cardinal 4, [ai]. Non-RP Southern English as a whole,

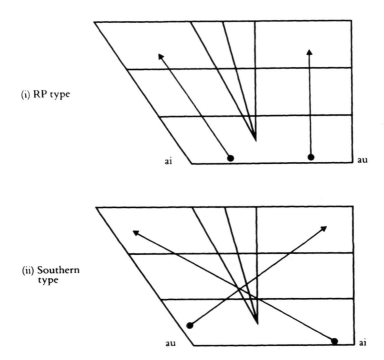

(i) RP type

ai   au

(ii) Southern type

au   ai

however, has the reverse, a front starting point for /aʊ/, and a back starting point for /ɑɪ/.

Long-i has in the course of its development merged with the vowel written **igh** in *night, light, right*, etc. These originally had short /i/ followed by the velar fricative represented by **gh**. This pronunciation is preserved in the stage Scots phrase *a braw bricht moonlight nicht*, where the fricative is spelt **ch**. As the fricative disappeared, the vowel was lengthened to [i:] and thus became identical to **long-i**. In some dialects, **gh** survived until after **long-i** had become a diphthong; in this case the lengthened vowel remained [i:]. In Lancashire [ni:t, ri:t] survive as traditional pronunciations of *night* and *right*.

There remain three long vowels and diphthongs, **ah, aw** and **oi**. In conservative varieties, **aw** as in *lawn, daughter* is fairly open, between cardinals 5 and 6, but in other varieties, it becomes closer according to rule 1. In transcriptions of RP it is given the symbol for cardinal 6 [ɔ], indicating a half open vowel, while in more advanced varieties it is nearer to Cardinal 7 [o], and even becomes a diphthong. The conservative form of **ah** as in *calm, father* is a fairly front vowel, rather like a lengthened short /a/. This [a:] is characteristic of Australian accents, some Welsh accents, and older Northern English. As **aw** has moved closer, **ah** has moved back to take its place. A conservative **aw** is thus similar to an advanced **ah**, and e.g. an American or Yorkshire pronunciation of *caught* is similar to an RP pronunciation of *cart*.

The **oi** phoneme does not vary much, except that the quality of its first element varies in more or less the same way as **aw**, i.e. it varies from fairly open to about half close.

3.4   Phonemes and allophones

We have thus far treated phonemes as though they had only one pronunciation in any variety of English. In fact there may be a wide range of phonetically different forms which the native speaker will accept as pronunciations or REALIZATIONS of the same phoneme. To put it another way, we have to explain the paradox that sounds can simultaneously be the 'same' but 'different'.

This paradox is familiar in other areas of human experience. Take for example the letters of the alphabet. Consider first the kind of variation you would expect to find in cursive handwritten forms of a single letter. If you write *cell* and *well*, you will probably find that you approach the **e** from the bottom line in *cell* and from higher up in *well*, so that you draw different shapes for the 'same' letter **e**. You can easily explain this as the result of smooth and efficient joining of successive characters. A rather different explanation is needed for the characters **d** and **D** which are quite different physical shapes, and yet also classed as variants of the same 'letter'. You cannot prove that they are the same letter by examining them or by logical argument; it is something you have to find out when you learn the writing system. To find an explanation you have to delve into the history of the alphabet. However obvious these things may be for anyone who knows the system, they are by no means obvious in advance. It is not at all self-evident, for instance, that if a handwritten **F** is written backwards it counts as the 'same' letter, whereas a reversed **d** is the completely different letter **b**. If you learn the Arabic or Japanese writing systems you may be surprised at the different shapes which are regarded as equivalent, and by the major modifications of characters that are allowed and by the minor ones that are not.

There are many ways in which the realization of phonemes is modified by the environment. Compare for example the /f/ of *feel* and *fool*. Part of the specification for /iː/ in *feel* is a slight spreading of the lips, and this is anticipated during the production of the preceding /f/; similarly, the /f/ of *fool* has slight lip-rounding in anticipation of the /uː/. As far as the English language is concerned, this minor difference between the /f/s is of no significance, and most English speakers are probably unaware of it until it is brought to their attention. Nevertheless, from a phonetic point of view, the /f/ phoneme has two different variants in these words. Such phoneme variants are known as ALLOPHONES.

Most allophones are probably due to the influence of neighbouring sounds. In other cases we have to accept an arbitrary fact that a particular sound is an allophone of a given phoneme. For instance, /t/ between vowels may be realized as a glottal stop in many local varieties of British English. To form the glottal stop, the vocal folds move together to block the air stream, and then suddenly release it. The symbol for it is [ʔ], e.g. *water* /wo:tə/ is pronounced [wo:ʔə]. Although English speakers may feel that [t] and [ʔ] in some way sound similar, speakers of other languages – such as Arabic – may feel that they sound utterly different, and regard them as quite different phonemes.

If we argue that the allophones of phonemes that actually occur in words are affected by their environment, this presupposes that phonemes have some kind of 'ideal' or 'standard' versions. If you produce a phoneme out of context, e.g. /ai/ or /z/, you give it the allophone that occurs by default, when there is no reason to do anything else. We shall call this the 'default allophone'. For consonants the default allophone is typically the one that occurs at the beginning of a word and followed by shwa, so that e.g. the default form of /t/ is [t] rather than [ʔ].

Not all variation in phonemes is due to the environment. In some cases different variants are found in the same environment. An English /r/, for instance, is most commonly a post-alveolar approximant as described above, and it is accompanied by a greater or lesser degree of lip-rounding. Some people give it vigorous lip-rounding, and have a weak tongue gesture if any at all: this makes /r/ a labial approximant sounding rather like [w]. (The letter w is sometimes used to represent it, thus *wun, wabbit wun.*) Yet another version of /r/ is a uvular approximant, with the tongue pulled up and back towards the uvula. This kind of variation, being free of the phonetic environment, is known as 'free variation'. It is not strictly free, but subject to social forces, prestige and fashion. A variant may be associated with a particular social group, and consequently have high or low prestige, or it may be on a scale from trendy to old-fashioned. A labial /r/, for instance, is rather fashionable in England, and is used by a number of senior politicians.

Levels of transcription

It is clear from the use of slashes and square brackets that there are different kinds of activity loosely described as 'phonetic transcription'. Whenever we use a symbol to identify a phoneme or string of phonemes, we use slashes, e.g. /t/, /e/, /wo:tə/; this is properly 'phonemic transcription'. If on the other hand we are referring to variants of phonemes, whether allophones or free variants, we use square brackets, e.g. [tʰ], [ẹ], [wɔ:ʔə]; this is properly 'phonetic transcription'. The distinction was originally made by Henry Sweet who called them 'broad' and 'narrow' transcriptions. In Sweet's time, the concept of the phoneme had not yet been explicitly formulated, although the basic idea behind it was familiar enough.

Before making a phonemic transcription, we have to choose a set of symbols to represent the phonemes, and we have to keep strictly to these symbols, and no others. In this book, RP phonemes are represented by the symbols listed in Appendix 1. For a detailed phonetic transcription, we can draw on the whole resources of the International Phonetic Alphabet to give as much detail as required. Although you can be expected to read detailed phonetic transcriptions, none of the exercises in this book will expect you to do them yourself.

The relationship between symbol and sound is different in the two types of transcription. Symbols in square brackets represent conventional IPA values, and can be interpreted without a knowledge of the language or dialect in question, so that e.g. [i:] always represents a vowel in the region of cardinal 1. Phoneme symbols cannot be directly interpreted, e.g. /i:/ is equivalent to **long-e**, and you need an indication of what a **long-e** sounds like in order to interpret /i:/. Using slashes and square brackets we might say that the phoneme /i:/ is pronounced [i:].

Choice of phonemic symbols

Although the choice of a phonemic symbol is in principle arbitrary, linguistics prefer in practice to choose an IPA symbol which represents the realizations of the phoneme. Since a phoneme may have several realizations, a choice has to be made, and the obvious choice is the symbol representing the default allophone. The phoneme with the initial allophone [t] and the intervocalic allophone [ʔ] is as a matter of course written /t/ and not /ʔ/. But notice that even if someone were to choose the symbol /ʔ/, it would be representing exactly the same phoneme, and the same phonetic realizations.

This is a point to bear in mind when you see transcriptions of different varieties of English. If you see transcriptions of American English, for example, most of the consonant symbols will be the same as those in this book, but some of the vowels will be different. In some cases, such as the vowels of words like *cot, caught, cart, court* different symbols reflect different phonemes and different phonetic realizations. In other cases the use of the same symbol may disguise phonetic and phonemic differences.

3.5 Manipulating sound

In the last section of this chapter, we shall examine the English sound system from a rather different point of view. Instead of treating phonemes and their realizations just as sounds, we shall consider ways in which patterns of phonemes can be used for literary effect. When you read a literary work, you may sometimes form the impression that the writer has in some way deliberately manipulated the sound system of the language. Consider these well-known lines for example:

(1)   And murmuring of innumerable bees (Alfred Lord Tennyson, *The Princess.*)
(2)   The curfew tolls the knell of parting day. (Thomas Gray, *Elegy in a Country Churchyard.*)
(3)   I galloped, Dirck galloped, we galloped all three. (Robert Browning, *How they brought the Good News from Ghent to Aix.*)
(4)   This is the night mail crossing the border.
       Bringing the cheque and the postal order. (W. H. Auden, *Night Mail.*)

Now unless you are totally insensitive, or devoid of imagination, you can probably 'hear' the humming of bees in (1), the bell in (2), the galloping in (3), and the train in (4). This is a kind of onomatopoeia, but not of the simple kind that we discussed in Chapter 2, for its effect extends over several words or phrases. Let us start with the hypothesis that there is something in the sound of the text that evokes or 'triggers' the meaning.

If this is so, then two consequences follow. First, the sound should still suggest the meaning when phonetic details not directly involved in the onomatopoeia are removed or changed. In (1), for example, the humming is associated with the /m/ sounds rather than the word *bees* itself, and so we should still hear the humming if *bees* is changed to, say *peas*. But the resulting nonsensical line would also lose its onomatopoeia. Secondly, the same sound pattern should trigger similar sensations in different environments. Consider the line which in Tennyson's poem immediately precedes (1):

(5)   The moan of doves in immemorial elms.

Like (1) this line contains several /m/ sounds; but it does not suggest the humming of bees at all. The essential difference between (1) and (5) is that (1) actually refers to the humming of bees, while (5) does not. In the same way, (2)–(4) refer explicitly to the sensations apparently suggested by the sound. It is evident that the sensations have to do with the meanings of the words, and to claim that it is the sound that triggers them is to confuse the roles of sound and meaning.

A similar sceptical point can be made about noise words which are held to be intrinsically onomatopoeic, words like *crack* or *shush*. If these words trigger a sensation because of the sounds they contain, then words of similar phonetic make-up should arouse similar sensations. In this way, *fish* should have an effect similar to *shush*, and *track* a similar effect to *crack*: they clearly do not. The more one examines the trigger hypothesis, the more one is driven to the conclusion that words and lines of verse are only ono-matopoeic when the meaning allows them to be.

A weaker but more promising hypothesis is that in cases of onomatopoeia the reader is able to recognize an appropriate match of sound and sense, or – to borrow Pope's phrase – 'an echo to the sense'. In the lines above it is not difficult to find something in the form of the language which matches the sense in a pleasing way. When the meaning is changed – e.g. by substituting *peas* for *bees* – then sound and sense can no longer be matched, and so the onomatopoeia breaks down. In words like *shush* or *crack*, it is possible to find a phonetic link between the sound of the word itself, and the sound it refers to. There is no sound involved in a phrase like *railway track*, and so nothing for the sound of the words to match or echo, and the concept of onomatopoeia is inapplicable. When you recognize patterns of sound in a poem, it is tempting to look for some appropriate match with the meaning and it is very satisfying when such a link can be found. The vast majority of sound patterns have no such link with meaning.

Let us suppose we have established such a link between sound and meaning. Our next job is to find what it is in the sound of the text that makes the match or echo. In some rare cases, such as (1), it will be the actual phonetic quality of the phonemes used, but there are other possibilities. A pattern of long, heavy monosyllables – *strives, rock's, vast, weight*, etc – is used to effect in:

> When Ajax strives some rock's vast weight to throw.
> The line too labours and the words more slow. (A. Pope, *Essay on Criticism*, 370–71.)

In examples (2) to (4) it is the rhythm of long and short syllables, and strong and weak syllables, that seems to match the bell, the gallop, or the noise of the train.

The source of the onomatopoeia may not strictly be phonetic at all. Consider this extract from *Paradise Lost* concerning the expulsion of Satan from heaven:

> Him the Almighty Power
> Hurld headlong flaming from th' Ethereal Skie
> With hideous ruine and combustion down
> To bottomless perdition, there to dwell
> In Adamantine Chains and penal Fire,
> Who durst defie th'Omnipotent to Arms. (I, 44–49)

You may find an interesting match here between the meaning and the arrangement of bigger chunks of the text. When you read a sentence you have certain expectations about the order of its different parts. You do not expect the object to come before the subject, but here *him* not only comes before the subject *the Almighty Power*, but it is not fully completed before the last line *Who durst defie th'Omnipotent to Arms*. The topsy-turvey syntax matches Satan's headlong fall out of control.

Although we can be reasonably precise and objective about the phonetic facts on which we might base a case of onomatopoeia, the claimed link between sound and meaning is ultimately a subjective matter, and depends on whether a given person can perceive it or not. Compare the following two examples from Shakespeare's sonnets:

> When I do count the clock that tells the time, (XII).

You may feel that the regular metre matches the regular tick of the clock; this is reinforced by the sequence of stops /k . . k . . t . . t/ which matches the sudden onset of the tick.

> Lo, as a careful housewife runs to catch
> One of her feather'd creatures broke away,
> Sets down her babe, and makes all quick dispatch
> In pursuit of the thing she would have stay; (CXLIII)

If you are easily persuaded, I might be able to convince you that the metre here imitates the movement of the housewife running about and knocking into things. If you are more sceptical, you might object that I have simply let my imagination run riot. Were this example to be taken seriously, then perhaps we could claim that the /ks/ of *Cox's Orange Pippin* represents the crunching sound of someone biting into an apple, or that the sequence of labial stops /b . . p . . p . . b/ in the phrase *Blackpool pleasure beach* represents the oompah, oompah of a municipal band playing on the promenade. If onomatopoeia is to be taken seriously, there clearly has to be a limit on the kind of claims made. Flights of fantasy must be excluded.

Onomatopoeia is one important way in which the sound of a text can be manipulated, but not the only one. The poet can also make use of devices like rhyme and alliteration which – except when they are purely ornamental – link sound and syntax. We shall be referring to these devices as cases of PHONETIC PARALLELISM. We shall be dealing with these in Chapter 4.

Exercise

Here is the full text of Auden's *Night Mail*, which was written as a commentary for a film made for the Post Office. Read through it carefully, looking for examples of onomatopoeia. If possible you should do this exercise in discussion with a group of people, rather than on your own.

I

This the Night Mail crossing the border,
Bringing the cheque and the postal order,

Letters for the rich, letters for the poor,
The shop at the corner, and the girl next door.

Pulling up Beattock, a steady climb:
The gradient's against her, but she's on time.

Past cotton-grass, and moorland boulder,
Shovelling white steam over her shoulder,

Snorting noisily, she passes
Silent miles of wind-bent grasses.

Birds turn their heads as she approaches,
Stare from the bushes at her blank-faced coaches.

Sheep-dogs cannot turn her course;
They slumber on with paws across.

In the farm she passes no one wakes,
But a jug in a bedroom gently shakes.

II

Dawn freshens. Her climb is done.
Down towards Glasgow she descends,
Towards the steam tugs yelping down a glade of cranes,
Towards the fields of apparatus, the furnaces
Set on the dark plain like gigantic chessmen.
All Scotland waits for her:
In dark glens, beside pale-green lochs,
Men long for news.

III

Letters of thanks, letters from banks,
Letters of joy from girl and boy,
Receipted bills and invitations
To inspect new stock or to visit relations,
And applications for situations,
And timid lovers' declarations,
And gossip, gossip from all the nations,
News circumstantial, news financial,
Letters with holiday snaps to enlarge in,
Letters with faces scrawled on the margin,
Letters from uncles, cousins and aunts,
Letters to Scotland from the South of France,

Letters of condolence from Highlands and Lowlands,
Written on paper of every hue,
The pink, the violet, the white and the blue,
The chatty, the catty, the boring, the adoring,
The cold and official and the heart's outpouring,
Clever, stupid, short and long,
The typed and the printed, and the spelt all wrong.

IV

Thousands are still asleep,
Dreaming of terrifying monsters
Or a friendly tea beside the band in Cranston's or Craw-
    ford's:
Asleep in working Glasgow, asleep in well-set Edinburgh,
Asleep in granite Aberdeen,
They continue their dreams,
But shall wake soon and hope for letters,
And none will hear the postman's knock
Without a quickening of the heart.
For who can bear to feel himself forgotten?

There are examples of onomatopoeia here which should
convince all but the most sceptical critic. Make a note of
sounds referred to the poem: in how many cases is the
sound suggested phonetically?

If you release your imagination, you can 'hear' all sorts
of sounds that would be familiar on a steam rail journey.
You may 'hear' the train slowing down, speeding up,
crossing the points, and even stopping towards the end of
the poem. To what extent is this phonetically motivated,
and how much is pure fantasy?

CHAPTER 4

The Syllable

In previous chapters we have examined sounds one at a time. We shall now turn to the groups and combinations into which sounds enter in connected speech. The smallest such group is the SYLLABLE. Since the concept of the syllable is a familiar and everyday one, it might be expected that linguists had long since agreed what the syllable is, and how and why sounds group themselves into syllables. In fact this is not so. The Swiss linguist de Saussure in his *Course in General Linguistics*, which was first published in French in 1916, suggested that the syllable was based on the opening and closing of the vocal tract as the speaker moved from one sound to the next. This idea has an elegant simplicity which must be substantially correct. But as de Saussure himself pointed out, this basic idea does not account for all the patterns we might regard as syllables. We shall therefore start with the basic syllable and deal with the complications later.

4.1 The principle of the syllable

The chief criterion which governs the division of a string of phonemes into syllables is the size of the oral cavity required for the different sounds. The SYLLABIC is the most open sound, generally a vowel. You can as a rule count the number of syllables in a word or phrase by counting the number of vowel phonemes. The segment at the syllable boundary is the closest sound. Any sounds between the boundary segment and the syllabic are arranged in order of increasing cavity size, and if any sounds follow the syllabic they are in decreasing order of cavity size.

There are no generally agreed symbols for marking the parts of a syllable, and what conventions there are arbitrary, untidy and unsystematic. A vertical dash is used in British works to mark the syllabic when it happens to be a consonant, e.g. *button* /bʌtn̩/. But since in the opening sequence each segment has an aperture LESS THAN the next, we could use the symbol '<' between each pair of segments, and similarly in the closing sequence, where each segment is GREATER THAN the next, we could use the symbol '>'. These symbols enable us to indicate the opening and closing of the syllable, e.g. *drunk* /d<r<ʌ>ŋ>k/. This word begins with the stop /d/, which is closer than the approximant /r/, which is in turn closer than the vowel /ʌ/. The vowel is the most open sound, and this is indicated by the symbols < and > on either side. The nasal /ŋ/ is closer, since the air passage is blocked at the velum and the air is diverted through the nose, and /k/ is maximally close, all air exits being closed off.

Exercise

Transcribe the following words, putting one of the symbols < or > between each pair of phoneme symbols. Count the number of syllables in each word, and identify the syllabic of each syllable, and the segment at the boundary between each sequence of syllables.

> linen   language   drinking   beautiful   Christmas
> pelargonium   television   hatchet   rhododendron

Not all theoretically possible opening and closing sequences are tolerated in practice. For instance, /p<ʃ<j<a>l>s>b/ constitutes a single syllable according to the explanation we have just given, but it does not look like an English syllable. Our task is not just to define the syllable in general, but to say what kinds of syllable are 'legal' in English. (The term LEGAL is here and elsewhere used to mean 'well-formed according to the normal rules of the language'.)

Languages differ considerably in the number and type of phonemes that are allowed to combine in the syllable.

In some languages, such as Japanese, only the structure (C)V is generally legal, with a single consonant C – which is in parentheses to show that it is optional – followed by a single vowel V. English, by contrast, tolerates clusters as complex as CCCVCCC, so that we consider the word *strengths* to consist of just one syllable.

A language which has very complex syllable structures has some extra principle at work. For example, we cannot explain *strengths* or *sixths* in terms of a single opening and closing sequence, because they manifestly contain more than one. We have somehow to reconcile our basic notion of the syllable with what the English language treats as a syllable. We shall have to say that the basic syllable is AUGMENTED by the addition of extra segments. If we were to attempt to deal with all types of syllable at once, the picture would become extremely complicated. We shall therefore deal with the simple type of syllable first, and postpone discussion and explanation of augmented syllables until the next chapter.

4.2   The basic English syllable

Every syllable must by definition have a syllabic, but other segments are optional. In English, the syllabic can be preceded or followed by a consonant, with the restrictions that /h/ cannot end a syllable and /ŋ/ cannot begin one. If the syllable begins with an obstruent, then it can be followed by an approximant before the syllabic, and similarly in the closing sequence, an approximant can come between the syllabic and an obstruent.

Opening sequences

An opening sequence of stop plus fricative is a theoretical possibility, but it is not in fact legal in English. When faced with **ps** in Greek words like *psychology*, we regard /ps/ as an impossible cluster and simplify it to /s/, thus /saikolədʒi/. There is nothing intrinsically difficult about /ps/ and it presents no problems in *topside* /topsaid/ or *maps* /maps/. The problem is not that initial /ps/ is difficult but simply that it is illegal in our language. (The affricates /tʃ, dʒ/ might seem to be an exception to the ban on opening sequences of stop plus fricative. Although these are written with two symbols, they are best considered a single phoneme each rather than as a sequence of phonemes.)

If the syllable begins with a stop or a fricative it may be followed by one of the approximants /r, l, w/ in the following combinations:

Before /r/			Before /l/			Before /w/		
p	b	f	p	b	f			
t	d	θ				t	d	θ
		ʃ		s				s
k	g		k	g		k	g	

There are several clusters which used to be legal in English, but which have ceased to be. In some cases they are still reflected in the spelling, such as /wr/ in *write* and *wrong* which has been simplified to /r/ as in /rait, roŋ/. More recently, the cluster /hw/ has been simplified to /w/ in most of the dialects of England, although the contrast survives in some dialects in Scotland, Ireland and the USA.

Exercise

Does /hw/ survive in your variety of English? Transcribe the following words:

    wet   whet   weather   whether   wine   whine   were   where

If you have any difficulty in deciding how to transcribe **wh** and **w**, it probably means that for you /hw/ has merged with /w/.

The loss of /wr/ and /hw/ are relatively recent, but some gaps in the system of legal clusters are of considerable antiquity, and are older than the English language itself. Voiced fricatives as a set distinct from the voiceless fricatives developed after the Old English period, and you will notice that only the voiceless series occurs in clusters, so that we can start a syllable with /θr/ – e.g. *throw* – but never with

/ðr/. The series /t, d, θ/ do not occur before /l/, and /p,b,f/ do not occur before /w/: these changes took place in Germanic, the historical ancestor of English. Again, there is nothing difficult about these clusters, but at some time in the past they have ceased to be legal. Actually, phonetic [tl, dl] do occur in some kinds of English, but as realizations of /kl, gl/: if you say [tliːn dlʌvz] this is likely to be perceived as 'clean gloves' by a native speaker of English.

Closing sequences

The approximants which can occur between the syllabic and an obstruent include /l, r/ and a nasal which is /m/ before labials, /ŋ/ before velars and otherwise /n/. However, historical changes in closing sequences have removed many possibilities, and left a ragged and untidy pattern. In particular, in most dialects of English, /r/ no longer occurs in final clusters, and this loss is currently being followed in the South East of England by the loss of /l/. So whereas most American English will have *farm, bird* /farm, bərd/, most British English has /faːm, bəːd/; and much Southern English has *film, bell* [fium, beu] instead of [film, bel].

AFTER /r,l/   AFTER /m,n,ŋ/

p	b	f					p			
		θ								θ
t	d	s	z	n			t	d	s	z
tʃ	dʒ						tʃ	dʒ		
k							k			

Where post-vocalic /r/ survives it mostly occurs in the same combinations as /l/, though with one or two additional possibilities, such as /rv, rg/, e.g. *carve, morgue* /karv, morg/. Final /mb/ although still written in *lamb, comb* etc, has been simplified to /m/, and most dialects of English have simplified /ŋg/ to /ŋ/. Older /ŋg/ survives in the North West of England roughly in the area bounded by Liverpool, Preston, Manchester, Sheffield and Birmingham, thus *bring, song* [briŋg, soŋg] corresponding to the standard forms [briŋ, soŋ].

Exercise

Transcribe the following words paying particular attention to the sounds spelt *ng*:

> sing singer long longer finger banging banger
> Bangor anything anger

After /l,n/, /tʃ/ can also be pronounced /ʃ/. It is of course easy enough to make a clear distinction between /ltʃ/ and /lʃ/ or between /ntʃ/ and /nʃ/, but in practice many English speakers do not do so. The spelling of *Welsh* suggests /welʃ/, but /weltʃ/ is also common, and indeed this is suggested by the spelling in the title *The Royal Welch Fusiliers*; and similarly while the spelling of *lunch* suggests /lʌntʃ/, it can equally well be pronounced /lʌnʃ/. This problem does not arise after post-vocalic /r/, and dialects which pronounce the /r/ still distinguish /rʃ/ and /rtʃ/ as in *harsh* /harʃ/ and *parch* /partʃ/ respectively. These are of course pronounced /ha:ʃ, pa:tʃ/ in RP and some other dialects.

In some dialects, /nts/ is not kept apart from /ns/. In the North of England they are generally distinguished, so that *mince* is quite different from *mints*; but in the South these words are likely to sound the same.

Glides

We have already noted the phonetic similarity of [j] and [i] on the one hand, and of [w] and [u] on the other. In fact [j] is simply a non-syllabic [i], and [w] is a non-syllabic [u]. In the word *yet* /jet/, for instance, /e/ is the syllabic, and the preceding close front vowel is in the opening sequence, and accordingly transcribed /j/. Similarly, in *was*, the syllabic is /o/, and the close back vowel is in the opening sequence. Given our convention for marking relative aperture size we could also transcribe these words /i<e>t/ and /u<o>z/, and similarly *music* /m<i<u:>z<i>k/ and *well* /u<e>l/.

Non-syllabic /j, w/ have an interesting property which distinguishes them from syllabic /i, u/. When you pronounce any syllabic in isolation, you give it a steady state, which means that you can maintain the posture for a short time without moving the articulators. You cannot do this with /j, w/, for these are essentially moving sounds, and for this reason they are often termed 'glides'. The degree of closeness achieved for /j, w/ depends on the following syllabic. Before an open vowel, the glide may not be very close at all, e.g. *yam* /jam/ or *want* /wont/. Compare *ye* /ji:/ and *woo* /wu:/: /i:/ and /u:/ are the closest syllabics in English, and if /j/ and /w/ are in the opening sequence they have to be closer still. If you practice saying *ye* and exaggerate the movement slightly, you will feel your tongue pushing hard against your palate, but without closing the gap enough to produce turbulence; and if you practice saying *woo* you will feel the tightening of your lips, but again avoiding turbulence.

Whereas most IPA symbols identify a particular sound quality, [j, w] indicate vowel glides which are closer to [i, u] respectively than neighbouring vowel sounds. In this way they express a relationship between sounds. Closing diphthongs such as /ai, au, oi, ou/ could equally well be written /aj, aw, oj, ow/: the use of **i** or **u** indicates the quality towards which the diphthong is moving, while **j** and **w** indicate the fact that they end closer. We have already used the symbol [ij] for a diphthongized /i:/. The different symbols pick out different aspects of the same phonetic reality.

Diphthongs which have the syllabic in first position, and a glide in second position, are known as FALLING diphthongs. Most English diphthongs are of this type. One exception is the phoneme /ju:/, which occurs in e.g. *beauty* /bju:ti/, and *muse* /mju:z/. This vowel has a number of peculiarities. In other diphthongs, one element is clearly more open than the other, but [j] and [u] are roughly equal in aperture size. It so happens that most varieties of English treat [u] as the syllabic, and [j] as an initial glide; syllabic [u] patterns more like long /u:/ than short /u/, and hence the symbol /ju:/. With an initial glide, and the syllabic in second position, this is described as a RISING diphthong. A characteristic of Welsh English is that it treats this vowel like other diphthongs of the falling type, and this produces the vowel [iw], e.g. [biwti, miwz].

When /ju:/ follows a consonant at the beginning of a syllable, it produces complex opening sequences, e.g. /bj/

in *beauty* and /mj/ in *muse*. Some of these sequences are subject to simplification, while others have ceased to be legal in some varieties of English:

(i) After /t/ or /d/ in some varieties of English, [j] coalesces with the stop to make the affricates /tʃ/ and /dʒ/ respectively, thus *tune* /tʃu:n/ and *duke* /dʒu:k/, and *due* is often identical to *jew* /dʒu:/.

(ii) In most dialects [j] is dropped after /r, l, tʃ, dʒ/, e.g. *rude* /ru:d/ and *lewd* /lu:d/, while *chews* is identical to *choose* /tʃu: z/, and *June* (dʒu:n/)originally with [dʒ + j] may be exactly like *dune* (originally [d + j]). Dialects which do not coalesce [j] after /t, d/ may drop it, thus *tune* /tu:n/ and *duke* /du:k/; these dialects are also likely to drop [j] after /n/, thus *news* /nu:z/.

(iii) The development of [j] after /s/ is very variable, and inconsistent across the vocabulary. The cluster [sj] has coalesced in the word *sugar* to form /ʃ/, thus /ʃugə/; most people probably do not think of this as [sj] at all, and consider **s** an irregular spelling for /ʃ/. In *super* and *sue* (including *Sue* and *Susan*), [j] is dropped, thus /su:pə, su:, su:zn/. The [j] remains for some speakers in *suit* /sju:t/, but this is giving way to /su:t/. In *assume*, [j] can remain /əsju:m/, coalesce /əʃu:m/ or drop altogether /əsu:m/. Similar variation is found when /s/ is voiced to /z/, thus *resume* /rizju:m/, /rizu:m/ and possibly even /riʒu:m/; note also *please* /pli:z/ but *pleasure* /pleʒə/.

The dropping of [j] is sometimes regarded as an Americanism, even though it occurs in many parts of England, including London. For some reason, the coalescence of [tj, dj] is regarded by some people with considerable hostility.

Exercise

Transcribe these words for your own variety of English. Decide whether [j]-dropping or [j]-coalescence are normal in your speech.

bruise	presume	view	beauty	sewer	Luke	superb
music	nuisance	suet	Tuesday	jewel	duel	tube
zeugma	nuclear	rule	lute	lure		

As non-syllabic vowels, [j, w] are intermediate between typical vowels and typical consonants, and this status is reflected in the terms 'semi-vowel' and 'semi-consonant' by which they are often known. In the course of time, a palatal consonant can become a vowel, passing through the stage [j], and in the reverse direction, a front vowel can become a consonant; similarly in the velar region, vowels can pass through the stage [w] to become consonants, or vice versa.

Changes of this kind explain the relationships among the letters **i, j, y** on the one hand, and **u, v, w** on the other. In the Latin alphabet, **i** and **j**, and **u** and **v**, were originally variants of the same letter, and were used interchangeably in both syllabic and non-syllabic position. In pronunciation, as Latin developed into French, non-syllabic **i** became closer and closer, until eventually it was made with actual contact on the palate: this sound developed into [dʒ]. Under French influence, we borrowed this use of the letters **i** and **j** into English, but we now use **i** for the syllabic, and **j** for the [dʒ] sound. We have also adopted the letter **y** mainly in non-syllabic positions. In the case of **u**, the non-syllabic [w]-sound eventually became [v] in Latin, so that both /u/ and /v/ were written with the same letter. This convention was borrowed into English, and survived into the eighteenth century. Eventually the rounded shape **u** was restricted to the syllabic /u/, and the angled shape **v** to the fricative /v/. Meanwhile, from medieval times a doubled letter **u** was used to represent the English non-syllabic sound: the **w** is indeed a double **u**, but unlike the single **u** it can still be written with either the rounded or the angled shape.

4.3 Allophones

The position which a phoneme occupies in the syllable is an important factor controlling the occurrence of its allophones. For instance, the syllable governs the distribution of time among its phonemes. Segments in the 'leading' position before the peak tend to be rushed over, while those in the 'trailing' position after the peak are given more time, and any surplus time is distributed between them. The amount of time allotted to a segment in turn determines other details of its pronunciation.

The speed with which an opening sequence is executed means that while producing one sound, the speaker has to be getting the next one ready. This leads to considerable anticipation or overlapping in articulation between segments, and a feature which in principle belongs to one segment may spread over neighbouring segments. We have already discussed the overlap of /f/ and the following vowel in words like *feel* and *fool*. In a similar way, we produce minor variants of most consonants depending on the quality of the following vowel.

Voicing is also affected by syllable position, and sounds normally classed as 'voiced' may in fact be devoiced by neighbouring voiceless sounds. For instance, all the approximants are normally voiced, but they are devoiced when they follow a voiceless obstruent at the beginning of a syllable. In this way, /l/ is voiced in *laid, glade, blade* but partly voiceless in *play* and *clay*. Say these last two words slowly: as you release the stop, the air which has built up behind the closure suddenly escapes; since you will have put your tongue into position for /l/ before releasing the stop, the /l/ is voiceless for a short time before you switch on the voicing.

Devoicing may combine with other kinds of overlapping of articulation. If you say the word *twin* slowly, you may notice that the first thing you do is to round your lips for the /w/, and that when you get to /w/ it is voiceless. In isolation, /w/ is voiced and rounded, and /t/ is voiceless and neutral as to the rounded/spread distinction. When these two sounds come together at the beginning of the syllable, the rounding of /w/ spreads to the /t/, while the voicelessness of /t/ is extended to /w/. The same is true of /kw/ in e.g. *queen* /kwiːn/.

The combinations /tr/ and /dr/ are rather special. This is because /r/ is made in the same general region as the alveolar consonants. To get from the alveolar stop position to the approximant position, the tongue necessarily passes through the close narrowing which produces turbulence. The articulation of /tr, dr/ is consequently very similar to that of affricates. Since /r/ is devoiced after /t/, /tr/ and /dr/ pattern as a voiceless and voiced pair. They are sometimes classed as affricates in phonetics books, but as far as the English language is concerned they are just as much combinations of stop and approximant as /kl, tw, br/ etc.

Velar fronting

The velar stops /k, g/ are also subject to a different kind of modification. Compare *key* /ki:/ and *car* /ka:(r)/. To make the /i:/ the body of the tongue is brought up and forward towards the hard palate. The default position for /k/ is further back, on the velum, and the movement from /k/ to /i:/ is made more efficient if the /k/ is brought forward, nearer to the hard palate. We shall indicate the fronting by means of the plus sign, thus *key* [k+i:]. Before the open back vowel of *car*, the position for /k/ is correspondingly brought back, and we shall write this [k-], thus [k-a:]. The assimilation of the stop to the position for the vowel is so natural that you may at first have difficulty in recognizing it. If you get the allophones the wrong way round, it is immediately obvious. In some kinds of Irish English the fronted allophone actually occurs before back /a:/, e.g. *car, garden* [k+a:r, g+a:rdn], and this is represented in non-standard spellings such as *cyar, gyarden*, etc.

The fronting of velar stops before close front vowels is a common change, and by no means confined to contemporary English. It also took place in Southern dialects of Old English, but in this case the stops became fully palatal. Palatal stops sound very like the affricates [tʃ, dʒ], and English /tʃ, dʒ/ do indeed derive in many cases from fronted /k, g/. Scots and Northern *kirk* corresponds to Southern *church*, in which /k/ has become /tʃ/. Roman camps in the North tend to have a name ending in *-caster*, e.g. *Lancaster, Doncaster*, whereas those further South have *-chester*, e.g. *Chester, Rochester*, with /k/ fronted to /tʃ/.

Velar fronting in Latin explains the origin of 'soft' **c** and **g**. These were originally pronounced /k, g/ respectively, but eventually became [s, dʒ] before /i/ or /e/. The **c, g** spellings have been retained in words of Latin origin which have been borrowed into English, either directly or through French. This is why we have *collar* with /k/ and *cellar* with /s/, or *gentle* with /dʒ/ and *govern* with /g/. Note that the fronting of **g** and the development of non-syllabic **i** both result in the sound [dʒ]: in modern English spelling 'soft' **g** has the same pronunciation as **j**.

Clear and dark /l/

In the isolated case of /l/ there is another kind of allophonic variation which is associated with syllable position. Although this is usually ascribed to 'English' it is in fact a feature of RP and dialects related to RP, and in Britain it does not really apply outside the southern half of England. If you do not come from the South of England, the distinction we are about to make between 'clear' and 'dark' /l/ may not make much sense to you. If so, it probably does not apply to your variety of English: if possible get someone from the South of England to illustrate the examples for you.

The consonant articulations described in Chapters 2 and 3 dealt only with the main or PRIMARY ARTICULATION, and the positions of organs not essentially involved were left unspecified. To describe /f/, for example, we refer to the upper teeth and lower lip, but say nothing about the position of the tongue. A CLEAR consonant is made with the body of the tongue moved into the position for [j], in so far as this is compatible with the primary articulation; [j] is described as a SECONDARY ARTICULATION. For a DARK consonant, the tongue moves in the position for [w] in so far as this is compatible with the primary articulation, and this may be accompanied by the lip rounding characteristic of [w]. In this case, [w] is the secondary articulation. In IPA notation consonants are assumed to be clear or neutral unless marked otherwise; dark consonants are marked with a tilde (˜) drawn through the character, e.g. [z̃, ɫ].

When you make the [l] sound, the tip of your tongue has to make contact with the alveolar ridge, and a gap is left at the sides of the tongue for the air to escape laterally. As long as these basic requirements are met, you can vary the details of the tongue shape quite considerably. RP and Southern English have a clear [l] in *leap* or *glue* and a dark [ɫ] in *will* [wiɫ] or *ball* [bɔːɫ]. In Southern England outside RP, the primary alveolar articulation of dark [ɫ] is currently being lost, leaving only a [w]-like element, thus *milk*

[miwk], **bald** [bo:wd], *doll* [dow]. This is leading to a reorganization of the vowel system in Southern English, and we deal with this in more detail later.

These modifications are very different from the overlapping assimilations which we discussed earlier, and may indeed have precisely the opposite effect: in *glue* the tongue moves into the [j] position for /l/ before moving into the close back position for /u:/. In the case of *will*, the tongue is in the front close position for /i/, and then has to move back to the [w] position for [l].

In American English, and in Northern England and Scotland, most consonants are fairly dark anyway, and /l/ is dark along with the others, thus *light* [ɫait] *Lancaster* [ɫaŋkastə]. In these dialects there may be little or no difference of colour before and after the vowel. To speakers of other kinds of English, this [ɫ] may seem too dark before the vowel and too clear after it, giving the erroneous impression that the position of clear and dark /l/ has been reversed. The degree to which the back of the tongue is moved into the [w] position is of course variable, and some dialects have darker consonants than others. Actors putting on a Northern or Scottish accent sometimes exaggerate the darkening of the consonants, and this suggests the accent reasonably well for people who are not familiar with it in detail.

Irish English tends to have clear consonants in general, and [l] is clear in both positions. Exaggerated clear [l] is a stock feature of a stage Irish accent. Ulster English varies from the Southern Irish type to the Scottish type, but is unlikely to change the consonant colour much before and after the vowel.

Exercise

Transcribe these words, paying attention to the quality of /l/. Since you are not identifying phonemes, but details of their realization, your transcription should be in square brackets, [ ]. In some cases, /l/ may be subject to the devoicing rule as well as the clear/dark rule.

boil   glade   madly   million   dull   dullard   tell
telling   clue   Lilian   lily   Lil   play

4.4   Vocalization

Some of the most dramatic changes in English over the last centuries have affected combinations of vowel plus /r/. Briefly, what has happened is that short vowels have coalesced with a following /r/ to produce new varieties of long vowel, while long vowels have developed a shwa glide from the vowel to /r/, and this has replaced the /r/ itself. All varieties of English have taken part in this change to some extent, and the differences among dialects concern the degree to which it has been effected. Dialects in which something of a consonantal /r/ remains after a vowel are described as RHOTIC dialects; in non-rhotic dialects this /r/ has completely disappeared.

Some rhotic dialects in Scotland, the South of Ireland and parts of Wales have a tapped /r/, which can on occasion be trilled, especially on stage. But the usual /r/ in English is the alveolar approximant we described in Chapter 3. Whereas the tapped /r/ is necessarily a separate gesture from the preceding vowel, the approximant /r/ can be produced simultaneously with it, if the body of the tongue is held sufficiently open and back. With the tongue in the open back position, the tip can simultaneously be raised towards the back of the alveolar ridge: this is known as R-COLOURING. Post-vocalic /r/ generally occurs as r-colouring in American English, most Irish English, and rhotic dialects of England. With progressive weakening of the colouring, the /r/ gradually disappears.

If you do not have r-colouring in your speech, you can get the feeling of it by practising words like *car, girl* or *court*, or a phrase such as *the early bird catches the worm*, in an American or Irish accent. If all else fails, you can try saying 'gr-r-r-r!' to yourself: the long [r] sound is equivalent to an r-coloured shwa.

Short vowels

Short /i/ and /e/ have taken on a shwa quality before /r/, as in *third* und *Bert*. In most dialects /u, ʌ/ have ended up with the same vowel, but in some Scots dialects /ʌr/ remains distinct, thus *hurt* /hʌrt/. Short /a/ is lengthened and backed to /aː/, and /o/ becomes [oː], as in *part* and *short* respectively.

The subsequent developments take place in recognizable stages. As you read through these next sections, try and work out how far your own variety of English has reached.

> STAGE 1:   /i̥/ and /e̥/ have a common allophone [ə] before /r/. Since there is no principled way of assigning [ə] to /i̥/ or /e̥/ we shall arbitrarily assign it to accented /ə̥/. Our key words can be transcribed /θərd, bərt, part, ʃort, hʌrt/. This is the situation in a number of Scots dialects.
>
> STAGE 2:   /ʌ/ before /r/ takes on the shwa allophone, which is then assigned to /ə/. All allophones are lengthened before /r/, which in turn becomes an r-colouring of the vowel. This is found in much American English, Ulster English, and also in the West Country, where it is known as the 'burr'. Our key words can be transcribed /θərd, bərt, part, ʃort, hərt/ which are phonetically [θəːrd, bəːrt, paːrt, ʃoːrt, həːrd].
>
> STAGE 3:   the r-colouring weakens to the point where /r/ disappears. The vowel allophone is no longer predictable from the environment, and /əː, aː, oː/ are best treated as independent phonemes, thus /θəːd, bəːt, paːt, ʃoːt, həːt/.

In England as a whole, the /aː/ which results from the loss of /r/ is identical to /aː/ from other sources, such as the lengthened /ḁ/ of *father*, thus *farm* /faːm/ and *father* /faːðə/. In the South of England – and in standardized northern accents – this is also the vowel of *path* and *bath*, thus *part* /paːt/ and *path* /paːθ/. In England also, the /oː/ deriving from /or/ is identical to /oː/ from other sources, thus *short* /ʃoːt/ and *Shaw* /ʃoː/.

Long vowels

Whereas short vowels have fused with a following /r/, long vowels have remained separate. Our starting point is a pronunciation in which the articulatory movement for the vowel is completed before the tongue moves on to the /r/.

> STAGE 1:   Once again, there is no particular reason for a tapped /r/ to influence the vowel, and some Scots accents retain the original system, e.g. *here* [hiːr], *poor* [puːr] etc.
>
> STAGE 2:   In dialects with the approximant /r/, the tongue has to change shape. The vowel typically has the tongue

humped upwards, offering a convex surface to the palate; but approximant /r/ has the tip raised, so that the tongue is concave upwards. To make this change of shape takes time, and unless it is carried out very quickly indeed, the intermediate qualities of sound become audible. Since these sound qualities are vowel-like in nature, but not the qualities of any particular vowel, they are usually described by default as shwa. The vowel is thus followed by a 'shwa glide' to the /r/. The traditional name for the process which inserts these glides is FRACTURE or 'breaking'. The fractured forms consist essentially of a long vowel + ə + r. There is a slight complication here, in that the fractured vowel depends not on contemporary pronunciation, but on pronunciation at the time when fracture originally took place. For instance /ou/ has in most environments become /əu/ in RP, but to understand what has happened to the vowel of *more*, we have to start with the fracture of the earlier form /ou/. Here are some typical fractured forms, with common spellings to help you recognize them. For reasons which will become apparent we shall use double letters rather than the colon notation:

ire	aiər	**our**	auər
ere	iiər	**oor**	uuər
are	eiər	**ore**	ouər

STAGE 3: /ə/ fuses with the following /r/ to form an r-coloured shwa; this r-colouring weakens to the point where it disappears altogether, thus producing [aiə, ouə] etc.

You will note that [ə] always follows [i] or [u], and is more open. The addition of the shwa glide technically creates an extra syllable. There are two possible developments. Either the [i, u] can be made closer than surrounding sounds, so that they act as the boundary segment, in which case they are better written [j, w] respectively. This produces forms like *here, four* [hijər, fowər] in stage 2, and [hijə, fowə] in the non-rhotic stage 3. The alternative is SMOOTHING, in which case the [j, w] disappears, thus [hiər, foər], which are the type heard in American English, and [hiə, foə], which are the RP type.

Dialects are not consistent in their treatment of fractured vowels. RP has generally smoothed them, but varies in the case of /aiə/ and /auə/. These can be preserved with the three vowel elements, in which case it is not clear whether they are to be regarded as having one or two syllables. In some kinds of RP, /aɪə/ is smoothed to [aə] and /auə/ to [ɑə], so that *tire* [taə] is very similar to [tɑə], but not quite identical to it.

Fractured vowels sometimes develop in unpredictable ways which are peculiar to themselves. In virtually all varieties of English, /eɪə(r)/ is smoothed to [eə(r)], but in non-rhotic accents other than RP it may lose the final shwa, and become a long half open vowel [ɛ:], thus *there* [ðɛ:]. In Merseyside and Cheshire, and neighbouring areas of the North West of England, and also in the Lagan valley in Northern Ireland, this vowel merges with /ə:/ deriving from /ir, er, ur/, thus *fur, fair* are both /fə:(r)/; *squirt* /skwə:(r)t/ begins exactly like *square* /skwə:(r)/.

Mergers take place more commonly in non-rhotic dialects. Smoothed /oə/ merges with /o:/ from short /o/+r and other origins. In this way, *court* becomes exactly like *caught* /ko:t/, and *shore* like *Shaw* /ʃo:/, *oar* like the accented form of *or* /o:/ and *four* like accented *for* /fo:/.

This is being followed by the merger of smoothed /uə/ and /o:/ so that *sure* becomes /ʃo:/, and exactly like *shore* and *Shaw*. This change is spreading in England even to dialects which resist smoothing, so that in the North traditional [ʃuwə] is giving way to [ʃo:]. It is also irregular in its spread through the vocabulary: some people will change /uə/ to /o:/ in *sure*, but not in *tour* or *poor*, and in this way have /ʃo:, tuə, puə/. There is no way of predicting which form a word will have, and speakers are inconsistent from one occasion to another. There are some general guides, however. A conservative speaker is likely to preserve /uə/ after [j], thus *cure, pure* /kjuə, pjuə/ where another person might have /kjo:, pjo:/ and even *mature* /mətʃo:/. A curious fact is that although the change of /uə/ to /o:/ is in progress in contemporary British English, it can be held up in cases where there used to be [j], so that *sewer* and *lure* remain /suə, luə/ and distinct from *sore, law* /so:, lo:/.

Post-vocalic /l/

The vocalization of post-vocalic /l/ parallels that of post-vocalic /r/. We have seen so far that post-vocalic /l/ is dark in the dialects of Southern England, and that its articulation is becoming incomplete, lacking the alveolar contact essential for a true lateral. The result is a vowel-like glide which we have written [w]. The exact quality of this sound varies considerably; the symbol [w] implies that it is closer than neighbouring vowel sounds, but in fact it may be no closer than the vowel of *lawn* /lo:n/. The glide combines with preceding vowels to produce a new set of complex vowels which are able to merge with other vowel sounds to produce new phonemes. Many dialects are in a state of transition from the old system with /l/ to a new system without; and while they are in this state it is very difficult to make a phonemic analysis. Unless it has advanced very close to the new system, a dialect can usually be analysed as having some kind of post-vocalic /l/.

The vocalization of /l/ has recurred in several dialects, and at different times in the history of the language. It has taken place between /a, o/ and /k/ in *chalk, walk, talk,* and *yolk* and *folk.* The resulting [aw] has merged with /o:/ in /tʃo:k, wo:k to:k/, so that in most non-rhotic dialects these words rhyme with *cork,* while [ow] has merged with the vowel of *cloak* in /jouk, fouk/ to make these rhyme with *coke.*

The change of /al/ to /o:/ also took place finally, where /l/ is spelt ll, e.g. *all, call, hall* /o:l, ko:l, ho:l/. This also happened before /t/, in *salt, malt,* and *halt* /so:lt, mo:lt, ho:lt/, but in some dialects, including those of the North of England, this has been shortened to /o/, thus /solt, molt, holt/. Before /m/, on the other hand, the result is /a:/, as in *calm, palm,* and *almond* /ka:m, pa:m, a:mənd/. *Salmon,* however, has short /a/, /samən/.

These ancient cases are now being reinforced by wholesale /l/-dropping which started in the south east of England, and is now spreading north, and has already become common in the midlands. It is too early to say exactly how the new vowels will affect the structure of the vowel system, but it is likely that the same principles will operate as have operated in the past.

4.5   Sound parallelism

The foregoing sections of this chapter have dealt with the general role of the syllable in the sound patterning of English; in this final section I shall turn to a rather special and aesthetic role of the syllable.

A PARALLELISM is a stylistic device which highlights two or more items which are substantially similar but which differ at some point. To be effective, sound parallelisms need to involve phonemic patterns in structures at least as big as the syllable, rather than just unorganized strings of phonemes.

(i)   The most familiar type of sound parallelism is RHYME, which highlights two syllables with the same closing sequence, but a different opening sequence, e.g. *great/bait* or *send/end*. Like other kinds of sound parallelism, rhyme is usually restricted to a single syllable, but it can sometimes extend over a strong syllable and a following weak syllable, e.g. *roses/noses* or *hooter/scooter*. These 'feminine rhymes' are associated with light and humorous verse rather than serious poetry.

(ii)   In ALLITERATION segments before the syllabic are similar, e.g. *great/grow* or *see/send*. A special case of this is zero alliterating with zero, i.e. in syllables which begin with the vowel, such as *up/on* or *all/each*.

(iii)   Alliteration which includes the syllabic as well, e.g. *great/grazed* or *send/sell*, is a kind of REVERSE RHYME.

Other kinds of parallelism exist, but are not so salient. ASSONANCE involves similarity of the vowel alone, e.g. *great/fail* or *send/bell*; and CONSONANCE involves agreement in post-vocalic consonants, e.g. *great/meat* or *send/hand*.

If all the consonants in the parallelism agree, the result is a PARARHYME. This is a combination of alliteration and consonance. Pararhymes occur quite commonly in everyday words and expressions, and the first half tends to have a close front vowel, and the second half an open one, e.g. *tick tock, zig zag, flip flop, clink clunk* – and its variant *clunk click*, used in advertising to represent the click of a car seat belt – *ding dong, bing bang wallop*. In many cases these examples are onomatopoeic noise words. Most pararhymes are monosyllabic, but note *crinkle crankle* and *crinkum crankum*, and also the BBC television characters the *Wombles of Wimbledon*.

A well-formed parallelism has points of difference as well as the similarities. A word is not normally considered to parallel itself, e.g. *long* is a doubtful rhyme for *long*. This is also true of homophones, i.e. different words which are pronounced the same, e.g. *meat* and *meet*, or *read* /red/ and *red*.

If you were asked to think of a rhyme or some other kind of parallelism, you would probably look for an example in literary language, particularly poetry. But as our examples above have shown, they certainly occur naturally in everyday language. When new words, phrases and slogans are coined, their impact is increased if they contain a parallelism, and e.g. *bigwig* and *brain drain* contain a rhyme, *War on Want* alliteration, and *Third World* and *Third World First* assonance. Vowels alliterate in the phrases *each and every* and *up and over*.

In Cockney 'rhyming slang', a word is replaced by a rhyming phrase, and the rhyming word of that phrase may be omitted, so that e.g. *mate* becomes *china plate* and subsequently just *china*, so that a person can be addressed as *my old china*. These examples are incomprehensible to anyone who does not know the connection, e.g. to interpret *Ooh, my plates!* one has to know that *plates* is short for *plates of meat*, which rhymes with *feet*. Rhyming slang apparently began as a thieves' slang, and making speech unintelligible would have been the whole point of it. Nevertheless, some examples have spread beyond Cockney to British English more generally, e.g. *to use one's loaf* is widely used in the sense 'to think'; in fact *loaf* is short for *loaf of bread* which rhymes with *head*.

Sound parallelism is valued for its own sake in everyday language. In literary language, on the other hand, and especially in poetry, it needs to play some kind of constructive role, if it is to be taken seriously. When we evaluate sound parallelism, we can keep to the phonetic level, and e.g. argue whether or not *home* rhymes with *bone*, or whether an 'eye-rhyme' such as *move/love* is acceptable. Alternatively we can assess the relationship of the parallelism to other levels of language. Even in a nursery rhyme, parallelism may be more than just fun and a play on sounds, and may be integrated into the verse structure, e.g.:

> Sing a song of sixpence   A pocket full of rye:
> Four and twenty blackbirds Baked in a pie.

Alliteration holds the first half line together, and links the two halves of the second line; rhyme binds the two lines together to form the couplet.

More than this, the writer must give the impression that the parallelism has arisen by accident. Of course, if he is writing within a pre-arranged scheme of rhyme or alliteration, then in reality he is obliged to choose words to fit: but the verse suffers if any hint of this is conveyed to the reader. Consider for example the final stanza of the Dundee poet William McGonagall's *The Sprig of Moss*:

> And God that made a way through the Red Sea,
> If ye only put your trust in Him, He will protect ye,
> And light up your path, and strew it with flowers,
> And be your only Comforter in all your lonely hours.

Although the existence and description of sound parallelism in this and following extracts is objective and can be related to observable phonetic facts, the evaluation is necessarily a subjective matter, and so I shall say how I react to them, and you are free to agree or disagree with me. The reference to the Red Sea (the escape of the Israelites, the drowning of the Egyptians, etc) has nothing whatever to do with the rest of the poem, and the phrase has presumably been brought in to rhyme with *ye*. On a dark night I want my path lit, but not strewn with flowers: presumably *flowers* is brought in to rhyme with *hours*. If you agree with me that this is rather feeble, note that there is nothing wrong with the rhymes themselves, and that the problem lies in the relation between sound and meaning.

Our reaction to rhymes depends in part on our other reactions to the verse. Compare these opening stanzas from poems by two Northern English poets, the first from Wordsworth's *Daffodils*:

> I wander'd lonely as a cloud
> That floats on high o'er vales and hills,
> When all at once I saw a crowd,
> A host of golden daffodils;
> Beside the lake, beneath the trees,
> Fluttering and dancing in the breeze.

Most of the rhyme words – hills, daffodils, trees, breeze – are words that would be used quite naturally in the description of a scene of daffodils in the Lake District. One does not normally talk of a 'crowd' of flowers, but if they are fluttering and dancing, it is not difficult to see a likeness to a crowd of people. Compare the opening lines of the Blackburn poet William Billington's *Rooas o't' River Side* ('Rose of the River Side'):

> Bi yon bonk at t' nook o't' wood,
> There runs a river clear,
> An' theer a little, sweet rooasbud –
> A bonny lass lives theer;
> Hoo's th'owd mon's boast, an' th' young mon's toast –
> Her mother's pet and pride!
> Her name's a slip o' poesy,
> It's t' Rooas o't' river side.

If this were in standard English, one might ask why the water is 'clear' other than as a rhyme for *theer*, or whether the wood /wud/ is an essential part of this poem other than as a rhyme for *bud* /bud/. However, the poet is facing fundamental problems in writing verse in the Lancashire dialect, using local words (e.g. *hoo* 'she') and manipulating spelling to suggest local pronunciation. To anyone familiar with it, this stanza successfully conveys the flavour of Lancashire speech (although of a much more archaic kind than is heard today: Billington lived from 1827 to 1884). To evaluate it as dialect verse one has to use different criteria than for standard literary verse, and to find fault with the rhymes would be silly and pretentious.

Different criteria are also required for light and humorous verse, and obscene verse. Short monosyllabic words are easier to rhyme than long polysyllables: you can find more rhymes for *maid* than for *Mexico* or *pterodactyl*. Whereas it is easy to imagine a context in which *maid* occurs naturally with *glade*, it is very difficult to think of a context in which *Cairo* would co-occur with its rhyme *gyro*. In such cases the rhyme is bound to be forced. Instead of subtly disguising the rhyme in the fabric of the poem, the poet deliberately sets out to make an unlikely or outrageous rhyme. Consider this (bowdlerized) version of a well-known schoolboy limerick:

> There was a young man from Devizes,
> Whose ears were of different sizes,
> The one was so small, it was no use at all,
> But the other was huge and won prizes.

If you approach this as literary verse, you might criticize the contrived rhyming of *Devizes, sizes,* and *prizes*. But to make such an outrageous rhyme is the whole point and fun of the poem.

Exercise

Study the sound parallelisms – including not only rhyme, but also assonance, alliteration, etc. – in the following extracts. What contribution do they make to the total impression made by the language of the poem? Is this contribution the same in all three cases? If possible, do this exercise in discussion with a group of people, rather than on your own.

(1)   In Xanadu did Kubla Khan
       A stately pleasure dome decree
       Where Alph, the sacred river, ran
       Through caverns measureless to man
       Down to a sunless sea.
                          (S. T. Coleridge: *Khubla Khan*)

(2)   In a coign of the cliff between lowland and highland
       At the sea-down's edge between windward and lea,
       Walled round with rocks as an inland island
       The ghost of a garden fronts the sea.
       A girdle of brushwood and thorn encloses

The steep square slope of the blossomless bed
Where the weeds that grew green from the graves of its
    roses
Now lie dead.
(Swinburne: A Forsaken Garden)

(3)   Is out with it! Oh,
              We lash with the best or worst
      Word last! How a lush-kept plush-capped sloe
          Will, mouthed to flesh-burst,
  Gush! – flush the man, the being with it, sour or sweet,
  Brim, in a flash, full! – Hither then, last or first,
        To hero of Calvary, Christ's feet –
Never ask if meaning it, wanting it, warned of it – men go.
(G. M. Hopkins: The Wreck of the Deutschland, 8)

CHAPTER 5
Rhythm

The use of the word 'rhythm' as the title for this chapter is likely to conjure up a variety of images relating to different rhythmical phenomena. We talk of the 'rhythm' of the tides and the seasons, the 'rhythm' of the heart and the pulse, the 'rhythm' of dance and music, and even of the 'rhythm' of architecture. These are powerful metaphors, and what they have in common is the regular repetition of some kind of pattern, some parts of which are 'strong' and others 'weak', and some 'long' and others 'short'.

However, just because a pattern is regularly repeated in non-speech rhythms it does not follow that speech rhythms must also consist of regular patterns. We are using the term 'rhythm' in a different, specialized sense, and the ground of the metaphor shifts from one sense to another. We shall investigate patterns of long and short, and strong and weak in speech; and if any kind of regularity turns up it is an added bonus, not something to be expected as a matter of course.

What is loosely called a 'long' phoneme or syllable is more precisely 'lengthenable'; the speaker may not actually make it very long on every occasion, but it can in principle be drawn out significantly beyond the minimum time needed to produce it. A 'short' phoneme or syllable cannot be lengthened in this way. The long/short distinction is not stable over time, however, and historical developments can recategorize a 'short' item to a pattern more like a 'long' one. Now unless we are very careful, we are going to be discussing short 'long' items and long 'short' items, and this is a recipe for confusion. Instead of 'length', let us use the term WEIGHT. HEAVY items are lengthenable, LIGHT items are not. 'Heavy' and 'light' are extremes on a continuum, and some items are intermediate. 'Heavy' items are conventionally marked with the macron (−) and 'light' items with the breve (˘).

There are several levels of rhythm in speech. The lowest level concerns patterns of duration among segments in the syllable. The next level is that of syllables in the accent group. Accent groups combine to form longer phrases, and phrases combine to form the larger chunks of discourse.

5.1 Vowel duration

In Chapter 1 we introduced the colon to mark what is for convenience described as a 'long' vowel. These marks make sense for people from England, particularly the North of England, but elsewhere they may be rather confusing. Historically English has a set of 'long' vowels and a set of 'short' vowels, and as the names imply, the 'long' ones have generally greater duration than the 'short' ones. However, there are several factors which together govern the duration of vowels, and these cut across the historical 'long'/'short' distinction. In RP, the 'short' vowel of *jam* /dʒam/ may actually be rather longer than the 'long' vowel of *heap* /hiːp/.

The term 'vowel length' is thus rather misleading: what we are really talking about is vowel 'weight'. Vowels marked with the colon are heavy, and those without are light; other things being equal, heavy vowels are longer than light vowels. The actual duration of a vowel also depends on its environment, vowels being longer before voiced consonants than before voiceless ones, and longer before fricatives than before stops. Yet another factor is vowel height, i.e. the position of the vowel on the scale from open to close: open vowels are as a rule longer than close vowels. These three factors operate in all varieties of English, but they vary in their relative importance.

Differences in vowel duration are an important ingre- dient in the low-level rhythmical differences among vari- eties of English. Northern English rhythm is conservative, with weight remaining predominant. Although environ- ment and vowel height do have some effect, we can as a general rule say of Northern English that heavy vowels are long, and light vowels are short. Southern English responds much more readily to environmental differences, while outside England, e.g. in Scotland, vowel height is a more important factor.

To examine the effects of environment, consider the following set of words:

heat   heed   hit   hid

If you speak a kind of English in which vowel height over-rides the other factors, all four words are likely to have phonetically short vowels, the distinction between /iː/ and /i/ being preserved by a difference in the vowel quality. Otherwise, /iː/ is likely to be longer in *heed* than in *heat* and /i/ longer in *hid* than in *hit*. These differences may be too small to be noticeable in Northern English, but more marked in the south of England, where the shortened /iː/ in *heat* is quite likely to be shorter than the long allophone of /i/ in *hid*. The open vowels of

hat   had   hot   hod

may all be lengthened to some degree, at least outside the north of England, and more so before /d/ than /t/.

Unless these differences in duration are considerable, you may have difficulty in deciding which of a pair of vowels is the longer. If so, here is a simple experiment which, as it were, tests rhythmical rules to breaking point. Try slowing the words down, and saying them at a half or a third of normal speed. If you do this with the vowel of *halve* – which has a heavy vowel in all varieties of English – you will find that you can draw out the vowel and move to /v/ only at the very end. On the other hand, in *hit* – which has a light vowel in all varieties of English – you will find you cannot prolong the vowel, and move almost immediately to /t/. If you try this on the test words above, you will find that they differ in the point at which you feel impelled to close the syllable with the consonant.

The effect of these rhythmical rules is that vowels have allophones which differ in duration. The longer allophones of light vowels may be subject to the same sort of develop-ments as the heavy vowels, in which case the durational differences are accompanied by differences in vowel quality. The shorter allophones can be expected to be more conservative.

Examples of this occur in the case of /ai/ and /au/. In Canada and parts of the northern USA, and also some English dialects such as Liverpool, /ai/ occurs as [əi] before voiceless consonants, and as [ai] before voiced ones, e.g. *bite* [bəit] but *bide* [baid]. Similarly /au/ sometimes occurs as [əu] before a voiceless consonant, e.g. in Liverpool English *mouse* [məus] but *loud* [laud].

When a light vowel is lengthened, it remains clear in most cases which phoneme the lengthened allophone belongs to; for instance a lengthened [e:] before /g/ in *leg* still clearly belongs to the /e/ phoneme. In other cases, the allophones of different phonemes become indistinguishable, and this can bring about significant differences in the phoneme system. The development of /a/ or /o/ before one of the voiceless fricatives /f, θ, s/ has led in this way to considerable disagreement among dialects.

In Northern English, and most American English, any lengthening of the vowel in *class* and *off* has been insufficient to cause reassignment of allophones, and so these dialects still have /klas, of/. But in the South of England, particularly the South East, lengthened /a/ has become identical to allophones of the /a:/ phoneme, and so have been reassigned to it; thus *pass, mast, path, bath, laugh* /pa:s, ma:st, pa:θ ba:θ, la:f/. Similarly the lengthened allophone of /o/ has been reassigned to /o:/, e.g. *cough, off, cross, cloth lost* /ko:f, o:f, kro:s, klo:θ, lo:st/. However, whereas the /a:/ forms have been generally accepted as part of RP, the parallel forms with /o:/ have fallen out of fashion and are regarded as rather quaint and amusing. They are used by older RP speakers, and in working-class accents of the Home Counties. In just a few words lengthened /o/ is also reassigned to /o:/ before a voiced consonant, e.g. *gone, god* /go:n, go:d/; this too is quaint in RP but survives as a working-class form, and is reflected in the humorous spellings *gorn* and *Gawd*. In contemporary RP the vowel of *god* is sometimes lengthened to make the word sound rather like *guard*. Sporadic lengthening also occurs in American English, where for instances *dog* may be /do:g/ rather than /dog/ as in British English.

For the lengthening to take place, the fricative has to belong to the same syllable. It sometimes fails when the fricative is on the syllable boundary. Thus *pass* has /a:/, but *passage* /pasidʒ/ (/p<a>s<i>dʒ/) has /a/; *chaff* /tʃa:f/ has /a:/, but *chaffinch* /tʃafintʃ/ (/tʃ<a>f<i>n>tʃ)/ has /a/. As a general rule, if a grammatical ending is added to a word, the lengthened allophone – and hence the heavy vowel phoneme – remains, thus *laugh* /lɑːf/ and *laughing* /lɑːfiŋ/.

Exercise

Transcribe these words, paying particular attention to the vowels spelt **a** or **o**:

grass   gas   passenger   bath   crass   nasty   vast
often   broth   hot dog   froth   frothy   cross   crossing

In the cases we have examined, an original light or 'short' vowel is recategorized as a heavy or 'long' vowel. The reverse also take place, but less commonly. As we might expect, the vowel involved is the intrinsically shorter close vowel /uː/; what is more surprising is that the shortening takes place even in environments in which we would expect a lengthened allophone. The spelling **oo** originally represented a heavy vowel, but in the vast majority of English dialects this vowel has been shortened to /u/ before /d/, e.g. *good, hood* /gud, hud/. In *blood* and *flood* the shortening took place early enough for /u/ to change to /ʌ/, thus /blʌd, flʌd/. In words like *room, roof, tooth*, there is dialect variation between /ruːm, ruːf, tuːθ/ and /rum, ruf, tuθ/. Before /k/, most dialects have shortened the vowel in *book, cook, took* to /buk, kuk, tuk/, but not in *spook* which remains /spuːk/. The old vowel remains in the area of Liverpool, Manchester and Leeds in the pronunciation /buːk, kuːk, tuːk/.

In contemporary English dialects, the shortening of /uː/ before /k/ tends to follow the simplification of /juː/ to /u/ after /l/, but to precede the change of /u/ to /ʌ/. In this way there is considerable variety in the pronunciation of the three words, *Luke, look* and *luck*:

	LUKE	LOOK	LUCK
STAGE 1:	ljuːk	luːk	luk
STAGE 2:	luːk	luːk	luk

STAGE 3:   lu:k   luk   luk
STAGE 4:   lu:k   luk   lʌk

Stage 1, with the original forms of all three words, is probably obsolete. Stage 2, with the loss of [j] after /l/, makes *Luke* identical to *look*; stage 3 has shortened the vowel of *look* to /u/. Stages 2 and 3 are typical of the speech of Liverpool, Manchester and Leeds. Stage 4 has the /u/ of *luck* changed to /ʌ/, and this is the stage reached by RP.

Exercise

Think of other examples of words spelt **ook** or with /u/ or /ʌ/ before /k/. Which stage has been reached in your variety of English? Or does the pronunciation of these words follow a pattern different from the ones given here?

Vowel duration and syllable duration

Consonants, like vowels, have long and short allophones, but we seem to be much less sensitive to this. When estimating the duration of a syllable, it is very easy to confuse the duration of the syllable with the duration of the vowel. If a syllable as a whole is lengthened, and the vowel is not lengthenable, then the surplus time is transferred to the following consonant.

We suggested above that vowels are longer before voiced consonants than before voiceless ones. More precisely, it is that part of the syllable beginning with the vowel that is lengthened. Thus in *kilt* and *killed* it is the sequence /il/ as a whole that varies in duration. Since close /i/ cannot be lengthened much, the most noticeable difference is in the /l/, thus [kilt, kil:d]. Similarly /an/ varies as a whole in the pair *Kant/canned*; in Southern English /a/ can be lengthened somewhat and the extra time is distributed over /a/ and /n/, thus [kant, ka.n.d] (where the single dot represents a small degree of lengthening), and in Northern English, where /a/ is not leng·henable, the words contrast more in the duration of /n/, thus [kant], [kan:d]. A characteristic of Northern rhythm is that clipped light vowels are followed by long consonants, as in *jam* [dʒam:].

5.2 Accent

Weight deals with long ('heavy') and short ('light') items. We shall now turn to ACCENT, which controls 'strong' and 'weak' events. The syllables of a word are not all of the same status, some being more prominent than others. In some cases a syllable stands our just because it contains sounds which are inherently prominent, such as an open vowel, or a sibilant; but the more interesting cases are those which the speaker deliberately emphasizes. The term 'accent' refers to prominence given to a syllable by means of a change of pitch.

Accent is also known as 'stress'. This term concentrates on the increased physical effort which is needed to emphasize a syllable, and the resulting peak of loudness which is perceived as a rhythmical 'beat'. Some linguists have taken this to be so important that they have tried to use loudness as a measure of 'stress'/accent. This cannot in fact be done, as 'stress' is only one of several factors which determine the loudness of syllables in context, and in some cases the 'stressed' syllable is measurably softer than the 'unstressed' one. However, if we take words out of context, and pronounce them in their 'citation form', we can assume that accented syllables are accompanied by an increase of loudness.

If there is just one accent in a word the pitch rises to a peak on the accented syllabic and then falls to low again. This has the effect of making that syllable more salient than surrounding unaccented syllables. For instance, toDAY is accented on the second syllable; the pitch is at a mid level on /tə/, but then it jumps to a peak on /ei/ and falls to low. In YESterday, the pitch quickly reaches its peak on /e/, and falls over the next two syllables (see page 98). Some words have alternative accent positions, e.g. progress is accented on the first syllable if it is a noun, i.e. PROgress, but on the second syllable if it is a verb, i.e. proGRESS (see page 99).

The fall to low can be indicated in transcription by means of the falling arrow (\), thus /tə\dei, \jestədei/; on the other hand, if we are using ordinary spelling, and do not need to indicate other phonetic details, it is simpler to indicate the accents by capital letters, as we have done above.

Exercise

Mark the accented syllable in the following words:

bucket   aloud   blackboard   window   defy   picture
alarming   below   billow   suddenly   spectrography
punctiliously

Say the words aloud to yourself, and listen for the raised pitch on the syllables you have marked.

The segments of accented syllables are produced with greater care and articulatory precision than those of unaccented syllables. This has a number of consequences, including the ASPIRATION of voiceless stops, and the REDUCTION of the vowels of unaccented syllables.

Aspiration

Following the release of syllable initial voiceless stops /p, t, k/, the air which has built up behind the closure is allowed to escape before the voicing is switched on. Immediately before the vowel, the turbulent rush of air thus caused – or the 'aspiration' – sounds like an intermediate [ʰ], e.g. *pen* [pʰen], *metallic* (mətʰalik], *rococo* [rəkʰoukou]. This fills the gap that would in other cases be filled by a devoiced approximant, in e.g. *priest* [pɾi:st] or *quit* [kwit] (where the little circle below the character indicates devoicing). After a voiced stop less air is released, and voicing commences more quickly. In this environment approximants are fully voiced, e.g. in *brick* [brik] or *glade* [gleid].

To demonstrate aspiration for yourself, compare *pig* and *big* [pʰig, big], *ten* and *den* [tʰen, den] or *call* and *gall* [kʰo:l, go:l]. If you say these examples with your hand in front of your mouth, you may be able to feel the puff of air after the voiceless stops: this is of course missing after the voiced ones.

The amount of aspiration is variable, and is much greater when the syllable in question is initial than when it is medial; voiceless stops in unaccented syllables may also have a slight degree of aspiration, but this is much less than

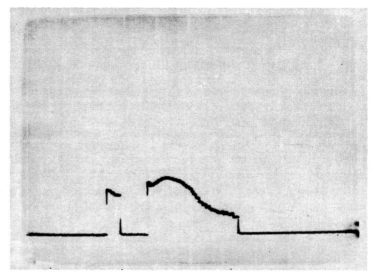

Pitch contour for *today*

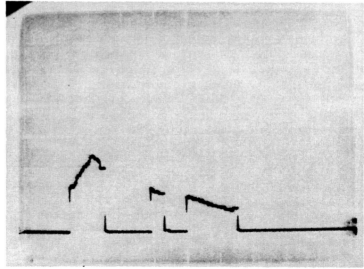

Pitch contour for *yesterday*

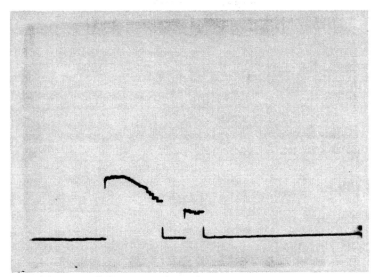

Pitch contour for *progress* (noun)

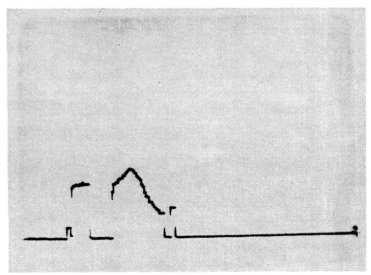

Pitch contour for *progress* (verb)

in accented syllables. Aspiration also varies from one dialect to another, and is generally more marked in RP than in Northern English.

Something similar to aspiration can sometimes be observed at the very end of an utterance. When the speaker stops speaking, he or she abandons the specially controlled kind of breathing used for speech, and returns to normal physiological breathing. A final stop may thus be followed by a high flow of air: this has nothing to do with aspiration, but is sometimes confused with it.

/h/ and /w/

Related to aspiration is the pronunciation of /h/. Historically /h/ was pronounced only at the beginning of an accented syllable, thus *history* /histəri/ but *historian* /isto:riən/. This is why, in old-fashioned written style, you will still sometimes see a phrase like *an hotel*: the first unaccented syllable of *hotel* lost the /h/, and so the indefinite article had to be *an* rather than *a*. Most people now pronounce the /h/, and so the phrase is naturally changed to *a hotel*. The /h/ is still not pronounced when it is unaccented and comes in the middle of a word, e.g. in *annihilate* or *vehicle* (but compare *vehicular* where it is accented). There are also a number of grammatical words – including *he, him, who* etc – which drop /h/ when they are not accented.

This dropping of unaccented /h/ must not be confused with the unpronounced *h* in words of French origin e.g. *hour* and *honour* pronounced /auə, onə/. The spelling **h** was borrowed in the written form, but the sound /h/ was lost in pronunciation in French, before the words arrived in English. Many words which used to belong to his category are now being pronounced with /h/, including *humble, humility* and *human*. *Herb* is generally pronounced with /h/ in British English, but Americans more commonly preserve the traditional form.

Initial /w/ is also sometimes dropped, but not to the same extent as /h/. *Will* and *would* can drop it when unaccented. The /w/ is dropped in *answer*, and in a number of place names, such as *Alnwick* /anik/ and *Norwich* /noritʃ/. Spelling pronunciations are taking over in the case of many proper names, e.g. *Cromwell* is now almost universally

/kromweɫ/, and older forms including /w/-less /krʌmɫ/ have disappeared.

Glottal onset

If an accented syllable begins with a vowel, the vowel itself may begin with a glottal stop. That is, the vocal folds come together and hold back the air stream for a short time while the articulators move into position for the vowel, and then the vocal folds release the air, moving directly into the voicing position. This gives the vowel a very clear, sharply defined onset instead of allowing the quality of the vowel to build up in a gradual or slurred fashion. As this glottal stop is an aspect of the accentuation of the syllable, and not strictly a phoneme of the language, it should be left out of phonemic transcriptions, but it can be marked in narrow phonetic transcriptions; thus *egg* /eg/ can be phonetically transcribed [ʔeg], and *Alice* / \ alis/ can be phonetically transcribed [\ ʔalis]. However, just because it is not a phoneme in English, you may be quite unable to hear it: no matter how carefully you listen, all you will probably hear is a vowel with a sharp onset.

Glottal onset in used in many – but by no means all – varieties of English, and it is most naturally used initially after a pause. In other environments it may be considered a mannerism by some people, e.g. *reaction* [ri\ʔakʃən], or *the upshot* [ði\ʔʌpʃot].

Vowel reduction

The vowels of accented syllables are produced with their full quality, whereas those of unaccented syllables may under certain circumstances be REDUCED to /ə/ or /i/. In *phoTOgrapher*, for instance, where only the second syllable is accented, all unaccented vowels are /ə/, /fətogrəfə/; in *believe* most varieties of English will have /i/ in the unaccented first syllable, thus /bili:v/.

The quality of /ə, i/ is variable, especially in final position. Shwa (/ə/) generally has an ill-defined quality, and is little more than a voiced gap between consonants. But final /ə/, in RP and the South of England, may have a quality in the same region as /ʌ/, so that there is some similarity in the two vowels of *BUtter* [\ˌbʌtʌ]. In much of the North of England a closer variety occurs, but in Liverpool it is front and in the same region as short /e/, so that there is a similarity in the vowels of *BEtter* [\ bete]. Final reduced /i/, in conservative RP and much of the North of England, is close in quality to accented short /i/, so that the two syllables of *CIty* /\ siti/ have similar vowels. In other dialects it is becoming more like accented /iː/, thus [\ siti:].

Non-final /i/ is generally undergoing a change to /ə/ before a consonant, thus conservative *beLIEVE* [bi\ liːv] or *reAlity* [ri\ aliti] are giving way to [bə\ liːv] and [ri\ aləti]. Most varieties of English have probably changed /i/ to /ə/ in endings like *-ness* and *-less*, so that *GOODness* /\ gudnis/ or *HOPEless* /\ houplis/ are now rather old-fashioned.

The diphthong /ou/ patterns rather like a reduced vowel at least in final position. Some words which have /ou/ in the standard varieties may have /ə/ in other dialects, e.g. *fellow* /felou, felə/, *pillow* /pilou, pilə/, *window* /windou, wində/, *potato* /pəteitou, pəteitə/ etc.

Syllabic consonants

When shwa is followed by one of the approximants /m, n, ŋ, l, r/ it tends to combine with it to form a 'syllabic consonant'. Consider words like *BUtton* /\ bʌtn/ or *BOttle* /\ botl/. Although these contain only one phonetic vowel, they would generally be considered to have two syllables. In the second opening sequences /tn, dl/ the approximant is the most open segment, and therefore the syllabic, thus /\ b<ʌ>t<n/, /\ b<o>t<l/.

Consider now the words *WOOden* /\ wudn/ and *MIddle* /\ midl/. The stop /d/ is formed in the same way as /n/ except that the velum is raised for /d/ and lowered for /n/: to get from /d/ to /n/ all you have to do is to lower the velum and allow air into the nasal cavities. This 'nasal release' is the mechanism used when /d/ is followed by syllabic /n/ without an intervening vowel. In the case of /dl/ the /d/ differs from /l/ in having a complete seal between the sides of the tongue and the teeth: to move directly from /d/ to /l/ this seal has to be broken. This mechanism is known as 'lateral release'.

5.3 The accent group

The rhythm of a word depends on the position of the accent. Weak unaccented syllables are grouped round the accented syllable to form rhythmical units of the next higher order. These units are referred to by various names, including, 'rhythm group', 'measure', and 'foot'. None of these terms is really satisfactory. The term 'foot' in particular is best reserved for the corresponding unit of English verse. For want of anything better, we shall simply call this group of syllables an 'accent group'. For the moment we can regard an accent group as the same sort of thing as a word.

A LEADING syllable comes before the accent, e.g. the first syllable of *beFORE* or *forGET*; a TRAILING syllable comes after, e.g. the second syllable of *PARlour* or *HENry*. As in the case of the syllable, items before the peak are rushed, and the tempo slows down after the peak: leading syllables tend to be shortened, whereas trailing syllables may be drawn out.

Leading syllables

As a consequence of shortening, leading syllables are particularly subject to reduction, e.g. *police* /pəli:s/, *bravado* /brəva:dou/, *correct* /kərekt/. If the leading syllable is a verbal prefix, it is reduced in the normal way in RP and most other varieties of English, thus *admire* /ədmaiə/, *consume* /kənsju:m/, *examine* /igzamin/. In Northern English these prefixes tend to be unreduced, cf /admaiə, konsju:m, egzamin/, etc.

In the case of less common words, there may be variation in the reduction of the leading syllable. The first syllable of *Augustine* may occasionally be unreduced, thus /o:gʌstin/, but the reduced /əgʌstin/ is probably commoner. *Australian* usually has an unreduced first syllable in British speech, /o:streiljən/ or /ostreiljən/, but Australians themselves reduce it, thus /əstreiljən/.

The extreme case of reduction is vowel loss, so that for example, the first syllable of *police* may be shortened and – particularly in British English – reduced to the point where it is not clear whether there is a shwa there at all, resulting in /pli:s/. Similarly *banana* becomes /bna:nə/, *potato* becomes /pteitou/ and *tomato* becomes /tma:tou, tmeitou/. Now whereas the resulting /pl/ in *police* is a legal cluster at the beginning of a syllable, /bn, pt, tm/ are not. In popular speech, these words have jocular forms in which the illegal clusters are simplified, thus /na:nə, teitə, ma:tə/. (Although *bananas* is used as an adjective meaning 'crazy', the corresponding noun seems to be /na:nə/ 'crazy person' with the obligatory loss of the initial /b/.)

Accented syllables

It is often taken for granted that accented syllables are lengthened. It is indeed true that some syllables are longer when they are accented than when they are not, consider e.g. the syllable *trans-* in the noun *TRANSfer* and in the verb *transFER*. But this does not mean that all accented syllables are long; they may be short and clipped; as in *HAppen*. The duration of the accented syllable depends on its weight, and on the number of trailing syllables.

A LIGHT syllable is typically short, and has one of the vowels /i, e, a, o, ʌ, u/ immediately before the segment at the syllable boundary; a HEAVY syllable is typically long, and either contains a heavy vowel or else it has an approximant in the closing sequence before the segment at the syllable boundary. To test syllable duration, you can do an experiment similar to the one we used above for vowel duration. If you draw out the word *TRANSfer*, you can linger on the vowel and then on /n/ before you move on to the trailing syllable. This is typical of a heavy syllable. In *HAppen*, you find that you have to move almost immediately on to the trailing syllable: this is typical of a light syllable.

Heavy and light syllables have different rhythmical properties. The duration of a heavy syllable is influenced by the boundary segment, so that it is longer before a voiced consonant than before a voiceless one. If you compare *renting* and *rending*, you may observe that /n/ varies in duration in much the same way as it does in *rent* and *rend*. Similar variations occur in *hamper/Humber* or *anchor/anger* or on the vowel itself, as in *Eton/Eden, ochre/ogre* etc. Before the voiced consonant the accented syllable may be longer than the trailing syllable; but before the voiceless consonant, it is likely to be about equal in duration, or even shorter.

Compare now *bitten* and *bidden*. These words have light accented syllables, and in this situation the accented vowel cannot be lengthened (at least in RP and varieties of English closely related to it.) Unlike a heavy vowel, a light vowel is not influenced by the boundary segment, so that the /t/ or /d/ does not influence the duration of /i/. The two words *bitten* and *bidden* are rhythmically very similar, both of them having a trailing syllable longer than the accented one.

The distinction between light and heavy syllables is relevant for the rules specifying legal words and accent groups in English: they cannot end with an accented light syllable. A word can end with /i/, but this is the reduced /i/ of *merry* /meri/, not the accented /i/ of *bit* /bit/. You will never find an English word ending in one of the vowels /e, a, o, u/.

Exercise

Identify the accented syllables in the following words, and classify them as light or heavy.

> hammer bingo grumble bottle houses paper

Is the accented syllable longer or shorter than the trailing syllable, or about equal in duration? Is the duration of the accented syllable affected by the type of segment at the syllable boundary?

English spelling sometimes indicates the weight of the accented syllable. A double consonant indicates that the preceding accented syllable is light, as in *cutting* and *cutter*. An exception to the general rule is **c**, which instead of being doubled is followed by **k** e.g. *kicking*. (The consonant is not actually doubled in pronunciation.) A single consonant suggests a heavy syllable, e.g. *bacon, music*. Although these are now just oddities of the spelling, they reflect phonetic changes in Medieval English, when some light accented syllables were lengthened, e.g. *even* /iːvn/, which had short /e/ in Old English, now has /iː/. The older short vowel is preserved in the traditional Northern forms of some words, e.g. *water* /watə/, *father* faðə/, *open* /opn̩/, and *broken* /brokn̩/.

Before a single trailing syllable, a heavy syllable may be long; before two trailing syllables it tends to be shorter. In some words an original heavy vowel has been recategorized as a light vowel, and the syllable shortened accordingly. For instance, *holiday* /\holidi/, originally a compound of *holy* and *day*, has light /o/ before the two trailing syllables, whereas *holy* itself has heavy /ou/ before one trailing syllable. There are several adjective/noun pairs in which a heavy vowel in the adjective corresponds to a light vowel in the noun before two trailing syllables, thus *sane/sanity, serene/serenity, divine/divinity*, etc.

Trailing syllables

A trailing syllable, unlike a leading syllable, may be quite long, especially if the vowel is /ou/ or unreduced, as in *bellow, cargo* or *Hansard*, or if the vowel is followed by a lengthenable consonant. We have already discussed syllabic nasals and syllabic /l/ as in *button* or *bottle*; syllabic consonants typically form trailing syllables, and are generally longer than when they are non-syllabic. The duration of a final reduced vowel varies considerably among varieties of English, and from one historical period to another.

In Medieval English, some final reduced vowels were completely suppressed by a process known as 'apocope' /ə\pokəpi/. For instance, the Old English word *cwene* lengthened its accented syllable and then lost the final vowel to produce /kwi:n/ 'queen'. In most cases the suppression of the weak vowel took place after the fossilization of the spelling, where it is still represented by the letter **e**, e.g. *bake, make* etc. In these cases the letter **e** came to function as a sign of length in the preceding vowel. It was added to words which had never had more than one syllable, e.g. *home*, and is still used for newly coined words, e.g. *phoneme*.

Apocope does not now operate in English, but a final /ə, i/ is kept in some dialects. A characteristic feature of RP and certain urban varieties, on the other hand, is lengthened shwa in *never* /nevə/ or a long /i/ in *coffee* /kofi/.

This perhaps explains a curious phenomenon which we reported earlier, namely that final reduced /i/ is becoming more like /iː/ in some varieties of English. We also noted that the diphthong /ou/ patterns rather like a reduced vowel in final position: this was occasionally transcribed /u/ by some older phoneticians, e.g. *window* /windu/ where we would now write /windou/.

Two or more trailing syllables have an effect on each other. There is a tendency for the second to last vowel to be shortened to the point where it disappears altogether, so that the word loses a syllable. Thus *family* /famili/ becomes /famli/; *factory* /faktəri/ becomes /faktri/ and *every* /evəri/ becomes /evri/. This process is known as 'syncope' /ˈsiŋkəpi/. In the South of England, words ending in-**ary** are subject to syncope, thus *secretary* /sekrətri/, *January* /dʒanjuri/, *necessary* / nesəsri/; in America and the North of England the penultimate vowel may be /e/, cf. /sekrəteri, dʒanjueri, nesəseri/. The rule of syncope is cyclical, i.e. it can apply several times as long as its conditions are still met. Thus *temporary* /tempərəri/ becomes /tempəri/ and even /tempri/. Note that the usual effect of syncope is to bring together a consonant plus /r/ or /l/: in the case of *every* this group, namely /vr/, would not otherwise be tolerated in a single syllable or at an internal boundary of an accent group.

The operation of this rule can be traced a long way back in English: medieval examples include *bedlam* from *Bethlehem*, *Bennet* from *Benedict*, and *Austin* from *Augustine* (accented in this case on the first syllable). The town of *Pontefract* was formerly known as *Pomfret*, but the syncope of the second vowel and other forms of reduction have now been reversed by spelling pronunciation.

Syllable division

Whereas a heavy syllable seems to include the segment at the boundary, a light syllable does not. This raises the question of how an accent group should be divided into syllables, and which syllable the boundary segment belongs to. But first, it is as well to consider whether this is a sensible question to ask. A sequence of syllables with its peaks and troughs can be compared to a mountain range, where it is easy to identify the mountain tops and valley bottoms, but meaningless to ask which mountain a particular valley belongs to.

In some cases there is no apparent problem, as only one division would leave legal syllables, thus e.g. *wal+rus* or *lamp+post*. However, these are special cases where originally separate words are run together, a prefix or suffix has been added, or a vowel has been lost from the middle of a word. In the normal case, it is possible to identify the boundary segment, but arbitrary to assign it either to the preceding or following syllable, e.g. in the case of *spanner* both /spa+nə/ and /span+ə/ would divide it into legal syllables.

In order to account for the allophones and other processes which depend on syllable boundaries, we shall find it convenient in practice to group the boundary segment with the following syllable, thus /spa+nə/. A distinction is often made between OPEN and CLOSED syllables. An open syllable ends with the vowel; a closed syllable has at least one segment in the closing sequence. Thus *high* and *tea* are open syllables, and *bread* and *jam* are closed syllables. If the boundary is placed before the boundary segment, the first syllables of *bacon* and *butter* are open, and the first syllables of *banking* and *bungle* are closed.

You may feel that the terms open/closed and light/heavy overlap so much that one pair must be redundant. All light syllables are open, and most heavy syllables are closed. If we treat falling diphthongs like /ai, ou/ as vowel plus glide, i.e. /aj, ow/, then any heavy syllable containing them is also closed. The only remaining heavy open syllables would be those ending with a long monophthong /a:, o:, ə:/, in words like *shah* /ʃa:/ or *law* /lo:/, or one of the centring diphthongs /iə, eə, uə/. Non-rhotic dialects have many words in this class with **r** in the spelling, e.g. *here* /hiə/, *there* /ðeə/, or *car*, *for* /ka:/, /fo:/; but in rhotic dialects these are of course closed syllables ending with /r/, /hiər/, /ðeər/, /ka:r, for/.

The distribution of allophones of /l/ confirms our decision to group a boundary segment with the following syllable. In *weld*, the post-vocalic /l/ is dark, and remains so in *welding* where /d/ is on the boundary; in *yell* /l/ is dark, but in *yelling* it is the boundary segment, and becomes clear. This suggests that it is a syllable initial /l/.

The situations in which the duration of a vowel is affected by the following consonant are also those in which the vowel quality is affected by a following /r/. A long vowel is fractured in this case, e.g. *Mary, fury* /meəri, fjuəri/ etc. A short vowel, on the other hand, is unaffected by a /r/ following at the syllable boundary, e.g. *mirror, ferry, marry, borrow, hurry* /mirə, feri, mari, borou, hʌri/. Where -**y** is suffixed to a word ending in -**r**, it is not always clear whether the vowel should be affected or not. For instance, given *star* /sta:/, you may not be certain whether to pronounce *starry* /stari/ or /sta:ri/; given *fur* /fə:/, *furry* could be /fə:ri/ or /fʌri/. We can expect variation among speakers in such cases.

Certain dialects do not conform to the general pattern. In the Pennine districts of Lancashire and Yorkshire, /e/ and /o/ become [ə] in this position, e.g. *ferry, lorry, bury* [fəri, ləri, bəri]. In some kinds of American English, /e/ becomes identical to fractured /eə/ and even /a/, so that *merry* becomes like *Mary* and even *marry*.

5.4 Augmented syllables

In our earlier discussion of the structure of the syllable, we restricted ourselves to the simple types which contain an opening sequence optionally followed by a closing sequence. We must now take account of the more complex cases in which the basic syllable is augmented by additional consonants following the loss of a vowel, particularly at the beginning or end of an accent group. The resulting structure is treated by speakers of English as a single syllable, and consonants are run smoothly together, even though they are not properly ordered in opening and closing sequences.

As we have seen, the vowel can be lost from a leading syllable, e.g. in *tomato, potato* / tma:təu pteitəu/. The first consonant is now added to the onset of what was previously the second syllable. Although /tm, pt/ are not normally legal onsets, they certainly do occur as a result of this process of syllable loss. Augmented clusters of this kind can become a model for clusters in new words, possibly words borrowed from other languages. For instance, since /tm/ occurs in *tomato*, it can also occur in the word *tmesis* /tmiːsis/.

Augmented clusters may eventually be simplified again, although the process may take several generations, and indeed thousands of years. The initial /kn/ of knee, for instance, is distantly related to the *genu-*; of *genuflect*: first the weak vowel was elided, bring the velar stop into a cluster with /n/, and eventually the stop was elided to simplify the cluster once again. The cluster survived long enough to be fossilized in the spelling. The word *knife* was borrowed into French as *canif* 'penknife'; the insertion of an extra vowel suggests that the French had difficulty with the cluster, as we do now. Similarly, the spelling of *gnaw* represents the old cluster /gn/ which has been simplified in pronunciation to /n/. These /kn, gn/ clusters have survived in modern German; for instance the German word *Knabe* 'boy' – corresponding to English *knave* – is still pronounced with /kn/.

An initial sequence can also be augmented by /s/. These clusters are of considerable antiquity, and their origin is obscure:

sp	st	sk		sm	sn
spr	str	skr			
spl		skl			
skw					

There are also one or two marginal possibilities, such as /sf/ as in *sphere*, but this occurs only in borrowed words.

In final position /s/ can also be used as an augment, e.g. /ps, ks/ occur in *apse* and *axe*, and again the whole cluster is considered to belong to a single syllable. There is, however, an important difference in that most augmented final clusters are brought about by the addition of morphological endings to a word. These endings have several phonemic shapes, and so we cannot refer to them in phonemic transcription. We shall instead identify them by their spellings.

There are three main groups of final augments:

(1) **th**, as in *health* or *fifth*, which forms a noun from an adjective, or an ordinal numeral from a cardinal numeral.

(2) **ed**, the regular past tense marker, and

(3) **s**, which includes among its functions
    (a)   the regular **s**-plural marker e.g. *songs,*
    (b)   the marker of the third person singular of the present tense, e.g. *sings,* and
    (c)   the possessive marker, e.g. *John's (book).*

(1) **th**

In many cases the addition of **th** is not a problem as it is added to a more open consonant, e.g. *health, length* /leŋθ/ or *ninth.* These are legal monosyllables. But when it is added to a stop, as in *width, depth* or *eighth,* it strictly begins a second opening sequence, as the fricative /θ/ is more open than a stop.

The addition of **th** can determine the allophone of the preceding phoneme. Alveolar consonants become dental in this position (the dental sign is [⌐] below the character). Thus compare *eight* [eit] but *eighth* [eitθ], *broad* [bro:d] but *breadth* [bredθ], *ten* [ten] but *tenth* [tenθ], and *heal* [hi:l] but *health* [helθ]. Practice making these words, and see if you can feel the different position of the tongue tip, further back for the normal alveolar allophone, and near or actually on the teeth for the dental one. Note that in the case of /l/ the variation between alveolar and dental is quite independent of the clear/dark variation in RP: /l/ is dark in both *heal* and *health.*

(2) **ed**

The form of the past tense marker depends on the ending of the verb stem:
    (a) after /t, d/ it takes the form /id/ as in *loaded* /loudid/. Since this has a separate vowel it does not augment the preceding syllable.
    (b) After a voiceless consonant other than /t/ it takes the form /t/, e.g. *hoped, jumped* /houpt, dʒʌmpt/.
    (c) Otherwise it takes the form /d/. e.g. *rubbed, jammed* /rʌbd, dʒamd/.
Cases (b) and (c) build up final clusters such as /pt, bd/ which would not be legal in the basic syllable.

(3) **s**

(a) f the word ends with a sibilant, i.e. one of he set /s,

z, ʃ, ʒ, tʃ, dʒ/ then the ending is /iz/. Like the /id/ variant of **ed**, this adds a syllable to the word, e.g. the plural of *horse* /hoːs/ is /hoːsiz/ and the third person singular present of *squelch* /skweltʃ/ is /skweltʃiz/.

(b) after a voiceless consonant other than /s/ the ending is /s/, e.g. the plural of *cat* /kat/ is /kats/ and the plural of *month* /mʌnθ/ is /mʌnθs/: this ending complicates the syllable structure.

(c) otherwise the ending is /z/, e.g. the plural of *dog* /dog/ is /dogz/ and the plural of *band* /band/ is /bandz/: this also complicates the syllable structure.

Morphological augments provide a model for morphologically simple words. For instance the word *apt* is morphologically simple but has the ending /pt/ which is similar to that of *wrapped*. Similarly *lapse* has the same ending as *laps*, and *quartz* the same ending as *quarts*. The augmentation rules can be applied several times, so that e.g. *sixths* is made up of *sik*+**s**+**th**+**s**. Again the morphologically simple types are modelled on the type with endings, thus *mulct* is parallel to *milked*, and can take the **s** ending as *mulcts*; *text* is parallel to *vexed* and can take the **s** ending as *texts*. In fact some syllables are so complex that native speakers have difficulty with them: in a test carried out in Liverpool, people asked to read the word *text* from a card produced /tesk/ and /teks/ and other simplified forms of the target /tekst/.

When **ed** or **s** are added to a vowel, they would appear to be identical to any other syllable final /d/ or /z/. We might expect the preceding vowel to have the allophone that occurs before /d/ or /z/, making *sighs* a perfect rhyme for *size*, and *sighed* for *side*. In fact, in different circumstances in different dialects, we sometimes find the 'final' allophone in this position. In some dialects, particularly in Western Scotland and the Scots areas of Ulster, *tied* has the 'final' allophone, making it different from *tide*, and *rows* for the same reason is distinct from *rose*.

In advanced RP and related varieties, the 'final' allophone [iː] of reduced /i/ occurs before **ed** and **s**, e.g. *buried* [beriːd] or *cities* [sitiːz]. Although shwa has a corresponding 'final' allophone in many dialects, it does not pattern in the same way, so that the 'final' allophone occurs in *matter*, but not in *matters* or *mattered*.

In old-fashioned RP, *studied* has [i], thus [stʌdid], and is identical to *studded* with /id/ added to *stud* [stʌd]. In more advanced varieties these words are kept apart by changing 'final' /i/ to /iː/. In addition, the vowel of *studded* may be changed to shwa, thus [stʌdəd]. This is part of a more general shift of /i/ to /ə/ which was mentioned above, and which is also found in the plural /iz/ becoming /əz/ as in *houses* /hauzəz/.

In most words we can take for granted that the morphological augment is simply added to what is already there. The exception is that a voiceless fricative is voiced before the plural ending in certain words, e.g. *wife* /waif/ has the plural *wives* /waivz/, and *house* /haus/ has *houses* /hauziz/. This rule is breaking down: *paths* /paːðz/ and *baths* /baːðz/ are becoming rather old-fashioned, and many people now say /paːθs, baːθs/. Even after /f/ there is variation between *roofs* and *rooves*, or *dwarfs* and *dwarves*.

5.5 Phonaesthemes

When we discussed onomatopoeia, we saw how sounds can under the right conditions have expressive power. It is also the case that syllables or parts of syllables can be used expressively. For instance, the opening sequence /g/ seems to suggest something to do with 'light' or 'brightness'', e.g. *gleam, glimmer, gloom, glare, glisten* etc, and in the same way /fl/ suggests rapid movement, e.g. *fly, flee, flood, flow, flop*. Here /gl/ and /fl/ may be termed PHONAESTHEMES.

In order to explain what a phonaestheme is, we have to turn first not to sound but to meaning. Just how detailed is our understanding of the meaning of a text? We expect to understand the meaning of the sentences, and the words in those sentences (as long as we do not ask too closely what is meant by words like *the*, or *of*). But below the level of the word, meaning becomes rather vague and hazy.

Some words can be divided into smaller grammatical units called 'morphemes', e.g. *foolish* divides into *fool-* + *-ish*, and *dialectal* into *dialect-* + *-al*. In these cases we can say something of the meaning of the morphemes, or at least explain their role, e.g. *-ish* and *-al* form adjectives from corresponding nouns. In other cases we can identify a morpheme, but it is difficult to give it a clear meaning, e.g. the meaning of the morpheme *gen* is very vague in words like **gen***erator*, **gen***tle*, **gen***erous*, **gen***eric* and *oxy***gen**; it is also difficult to specify the meaning of the *-ceive* which occurs in re**ceive**, *de***ceive**, *con***ceive**, *per***ceive**, etc. Even a knowledge of Latin is not much help here.

If the meaning of morphemes can become obscure, this is also true of their phonetic shape. When they are reduced in unaccented syllables, or transferred in loan words from one language to another, the status of morphemes can become unclear. For instance, you are unlikely to identify the *ga-* of *gather* with the *y-* of the Chaucerian word *yclept* 'called', or with the *com-* of *common*, but these are historically the same morpheme.

In our examples *gleam, glimmer, gloom*, the initial *gl-* is almost certainly a 'dead' morpheme, of which we have only a vague idea of the meaning, and which is reduced phonetically to the point where it just forms part of another syllable. The rest of these words *-eam, -immer, -oom* may also have consisted of well defined morphemes at one time. But these words cannot now realistically be divided into morphemes at all. This grammatical uncertainty can be translated into uncertainty about meaning: although you know what the word *gleam* means as a whole, you may associate the meaning 'light' specifically with *gl-*. In this way it may seem that the syllable onset /gl/ is conveying meaning directly.

However, as in the case of onomatopoeia, a phonaestheme is expressive only when the meaning allows it to be: /gl/ suggests no light in *glottis, globe* or *Glenda*, and /fl/ suggests no movement in *flat, florist* or *flute.*

Exercise

Consider the following possible phonaesthemes. Do they suggest any area of meaning to you, and is this true of all the words in the list? If you can, find three or more additional examples for each list.

(i)   /l/
paddle   waddle   giggle   little   tumble   ladle   mumble
chuckle   puddle   toddle   meddle   fumble

(ii)   /st/
stand   stiff   steep   stalk   stork   stew   staff   stump
statistics   steady   stumble   stone

(iii)   /sw/
swirl   swell   swindle   sweep   swop   swan   swoop

(iv)   /dr/
drip   drop   droop   drag   dragon   drowse   draw   drill

Can you think of any other phonaesthemes?

General Exercise on Chapter 5

This is another group exercise. Read carefully through
Lewis Carroll's *Jabberwocky*.
 (i)   Pick out all the nonsense words and transcribe them
       phonemically. Do they look like possible English
       words? Do they conform to the rules for legal sylla-
       bles and accent groups? Humpty Dumpty gives a
       number of tips on pronunciation and meaning in
       chapter VI of *Through the Looking-glass*.
(ii)   Can you find any phonaesthemes in the poem? Before
       claiming a phonaestheme you should first consider the
       possibility of onomatopoeia and sound parallelism.
       Also, some of the nonsense words contain common
       English morphemes: do not confuse these with phon-
       aesthemes.

JABBERWOCKY

'Twas brillig, and the slithy toves
Did gyre and gimble in the wabe,
All mimsy were the borogoves,
And the mome raths outgrabe.

"Beware the Jabberwock, my son!
The jaws that bite, the claws that catch!
Beware the Jubjub bird and shun
The frumious Bandersnatch!"

He took his vorpal sword in hand:
Long time the manxome foe he sought –
So rested he by the Tumtum tree,
And stood awhile in thought.

And as in uffish thought he stood,
The Jabberwock, with eye of flame,
Came whiffling through the tulgey wood,
And burbled as it came!

One, two! One, two! And through and through
The vorpal blade went snicker-snack!
He left it dead, and with its head
He went galumphing back.

"And hast thou slain the Jabberwock!
Come to my arms, my beamish boy!
O frabjous day! Callooh! Callay!
He chortled in his joy.

'Twas brillig, and the slithy toves
Did gyre and gimble in the wabe;
All mimsy were the borogoves,
And the mome raths outgrabe.

Words and Phrases

A phrase is made up of one or more accent groups, and each accent group contains one or more words. In this chapter we shall investigate the role of accent in building up phrases, and the effect on individual words of inclusion in a phrase.

6.1 Word accent

It is notoriously difficult to predict the accented syllable or syllables in an English word. Contrary to what might at first appear, however, accentuation is not entirely capricious, and there are general principles at work.

The accentuation of a word depends on whether it belongs to the native 'Germanic' or the borrowed 'Classical' part of the vocabulary. The rule for Germanic words is basically very simple: they are accented on the first syllable, e.g. *NEver, FAther, HEAven, SEven,* etc. In this way the accent acts as a marker of the word boundary. Many Germanic words are monosyllables anyway, so that the question of where the accent falls does not arise in the first place.

An important corollary of the 'Germanic rule' is that if a Germanic suffix is added to a word, it does not affect the position of the accent, e.g. *singing* is accented on the same syllable as *sing,* and *friendly* on the same syllable as *friend.* This also applies to words of Classical origin, so that e.g. *conSEcutively* is accented on the same syllable as *conSEcutive.* There are, however, signs that this rule is beginning to break down: for instance, the addition of **-ly** can alter the accentuation of *necessary, voluntary* and *primary,* so that the adverbs become *necesSArily, volunTArily* and *priMArily.*

Exercise

Transcribe these words, noting the effect – if any – of the addition of the suffix. All the suffixes will be of the 'Germanic' type, and all except the last add a syllable:

like	likeness	duke	dukedom
late	lately	bush	bushes
necessary	necessarily	primary	primarily
voluntary	voluntarily	educate	educated
negotiate	negotiating	rate	rates

There are just a few exceptions to the general Germanic rule. Words which begin with the prefix **a-**, e.g. *abroad, ashore*, etc. are accented on the second syllable; this prefix derives historically from the preposition *on*, and like other prepositions before a noun phrase, it is unaccented. Certain verbal prefixes, such as **be-, for-, with-,** are similarly not accented, e.g. *beGIN, forBID, withSTAND*, presumably because when the rule first came into operation, the prefixes were not really felt to be part of the verb. The prefix on the corresponding noun, however, is sometimes accented, e.g. compare the verb *foreSEE* and the noun *FOREsight*.

The different accentuation of nouns and verbs is developing further in modern English, and is affecting non-Germanic words. Verbs of two syllables of Latin origin are typically accented on the root, e.g. *conVICT*, while the corresponding nouns are accented on the prefix, cf. *CONvict*. Other examples include *transfer, permit, progress, export, survey* and *protest*. It would be historically more accurate to say that these words were formerly accented on the root, and that the accent has shifted on to the prefix first in the noun, and later in the verb. Some 'conservative' nouns e.g. *deBATE* and *ocCULT* are still accented on the root, while some 'advanced' verbs, including *to PERfume, to COmment* and *to PREfix*, are accented on the prefix. Note also that in longer words unaccented vowels tend to be reduced in nouns before the corresponding verb, thus *delegate* is /deləgət/ as a noun, and /deləgeit/ as a verb, and *compliment* is /komplimənt/ as a noun, and /kompliment/ as a verb. The accentuation of these noun/verb pairs can arouse strong feelings: some people object to the accent on the prefix of *REsearch* and to the accent on the root of *comMENT*. The former is an 'advanced' pronunciation, and the latter is very 'conservative'.

The position of the accent in words of Classical origin depends partly on the weight of the syllables of the word, and partly on the final suffix. The rules are very complex, and are breaking down in modern English, with many irregularities as a result. For instance, while *ADjective* is accented on the first syllable, the very similar word *obJECtive* is accented on the second. A full coverage is beyond the scope of this book, and we shall deal only with the major principles.

Accent is assigned from right to left, starting at the end of the word, and working towards the beginning. As a rule of thumb, accent falls on heavy syllables: a heavy syllable is accented unless it is immediately followed by another heavy syllable, and a light syllable is accented only before an unaccented syllable. An inflectional ending such as **-us, -a, -um, -o** or **-i** is left out of account, rather like a Germanic suffix, so that a preceding light syllable is not accented. For example, in *aROma* and *CInema* the **-a** is left out of account; in *aroma* the heavy /rou/ is accented while in *cinema* the accent is passed from the light second syllable on to the first.

Exercise

Account for the position of the accent in the following words. Ignore the inflectional ending, and identify the weight of the last syllable of the stem. The first one has been done for you.

> *tetanus*: the ending is **-us**, and the preceding syllable is light, so the accent passes back to the first syllable, thus *TEtanus*.

vibrato	cantata	America	conundrum
emphasis	malaria	broccoli	thesis

Since the position of the accent depends in many cases on the weight assigned to a vowel, it follows that if different vowels can be assigned to a word, the accent will vary accordingly. For instance, if the second vowel of *trachea* is taken to be /i̯/, it is unaccented, and the word is pronounced *TRAchea* /ˈtreikiə/; but if it is treated as long /iː/, the word is pronounced *traCHEa* /trəˈkiːə/. *Uranus* is pronounced /juˈreinəs/ or /ˈjuːrənəs/; *Medici* /ˈmeditʃi/ is often pronounced /məˈdiːtʃi/ by English people. Similar variation is found in non–Classical words: *Hiroshima* is anglicized as either /hiˈroʃimə/ or /hirəˈʃiːmə/.

The accentuation of Classical words is complicated by a rather curious rule which seems to operate as part of the process of borrowing: we tend to avoid accenting them on the last syllable. The endings of words like *liberty, personal, glorious, resident* will be recognized by Latin scholars as accented syllables in Latin (e.g. *liberty* derives from *liber-TAtem*). Although these endings now have reduced vowels in English, they retain the property characteristic of accented syllables of blocking the accent on the syllable immediately preceding. The accent therefore falls two syllables to the left, and hence *LIberty, PERsonal, GLOrious, REsident.*

Polysyllabic words

Polysyllabic words may be long enough for more than one accent to be assigned by the 'Classical' rule. Consider, for example, *PHOtoGRAphic, GEoLOgical, EMphySEma, DUoDEnum, CAliFORnia, COrioLAnus, ARchaeOlogy,* etc. In these words the third syllable is accented, the second syllable is unaccented and another accent falls on the first syllable.

Related words can have different accent patterns owing to the loss of accent on the last syllable. Compare for instance *PHOtoGRAphic* and *PHOtograph:PHOtoGRAphic* has two accents, the second being 'protected' by the suffix **-ic,** while in *PHOtograph,* the syllable **graph** is final and loses its accent. Note also *PLEsioSAUrus* where the accent on **-sau(r)** is protected by the ending *-us,* and *PLEsiosaur* where it is not. Syllables which lose their accent in this way may nevertheless retain their full vowel quality; this is sometimes described as 'secondary stress'.

Strictly speaking, it is not the last syllable which is subject to accent loss, but the last morpheme. Some final morphemes contain two syllables, and in this case both of these are deaccented. Example of this include **-acy, -ary, -ory** and **-mony**, e.g. *LIteracy, SEcretary, SAnitory, MAtrimony*. The vowels of these morphemes are in most cases reduced, but unreduced forms of some suffixes are found in some varieties of English. For instance, in Northern English **-ary** may be pronounced /eri/, e.g. *secretary* /↗sekrəteri/, and in American English **-mony** is often /mouni/, thus *matrimony* /↗matrimouni/. British and American English differ in the pronunciation of *laboratory* partly according to whether **-ory** is reduced or not, thus /lə↘borətri/ or /↗labərəto:ri/. Since these two-syllable morphemes tend to end in **-y** they are easily confused with the one-syllable **-y** ending. The most notorious example of this concerns the word *controversy*. The 'conservative' pronunciation takes **-versy** as the morpheme and it may be reduced or unreduced, thus /↗kontrəvəsi/, /↗kontrəvə:si/; but the more 'advanced' pronunciation treats **-y** alone as the final morpheme, which gives rise to /kən↘trovəsi/.

There are a number of exceptions to the 'final morpheme' rule and these are typically words borrowed relatively recently from French. Examples include *CIgaRETTE, coMEdiENNE, MIllioNAIRE, MAyonNAISE, COnnoisSEUR*, etc. In these words the final syllable retains its accent. Most of these can be recognised from the spelling: some end in an alveolar consonant and have the consonant letter doubled and followed by **e** (e.g. *cigarette*), while in others the last syllable is spelt with two vowel letters and a final silent **e** (e.g. *millionaire*).

Exercise

Mark the accents in the following words, and if you can, account for the position of the accents. Watch out for the loss of accent on final syllables.

computational	dialect	leucocyte
sesquipedalian	contrapuntal	epidermis
protozoa	phonological	hominoid
lymphoblast	telegraphic	anhydrous
heliotrope	polyanthus	vinaigrette
tetrahedron	Marseillaise	verisimilitude

6.2 Onset and nucleus

The TONE GROUP or 'tone unit' consists either of a single accent group, or of several accent groups run together in an unbroken rhythmical sequence. It can contain a single word e.g. *baNAna, PAthoLOgical,* or a phrase, e.g. *FISH and CHIPS, MAry SMITH, JACK and the BEANstalk,* etc. The last accent in the tone group is termed the NUCLEUS. If the tone group has two or more accents, the first one is the ONSET. The nucleus is generally considered to be the most important accent, and in typical cases it is the most prominent, being louder and longer and possibly reaching a higher maximum pitch.

In the case of a single accent, the pitch rises to a peak on the accented syllable, and then falls back to low, following a hump-shaped contour. See this contour on the word *no* on page 123.

The contour which results from the combination of two accents as onset and nucleus varies fom one variety of English to another. In Scotland and Ireland, America and some English conurbations such as Merseyside, the hump of the onset is followed by the hump of the nucleus. But in RP, and most dialects of England, the contour of the onset is modified. There may be little or no dipping in the pitch between onset and nucleus, so that the pitch rises to a peak on the onset, stays at more or less the same level until the nucleus, and then falls to low. See the pitch contour for the phrase *No I won't* on page 123: the pitch rises to a high level on *no,* and falls to low on *won't.*

By convention pitch movements are described according to what happens after the accented syllable. The RP-type onset is said to have a 'level tone' and the nucleus a 'falling tone'. The level onset and falling nucleus is the pattern that is used by default, i.e. when there is no reason to do anything else. If you cite a phrase out of context, e.g. by reading it from the printed page or from a blackboard, the default pattern is the one you are most likely to use.

Exercise

Mark the position of the nucleus in the following phrases, and also of the onset if there is one:

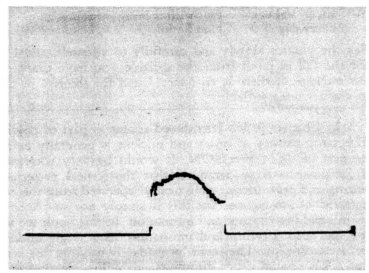

Pitch contour for *no* (a falling tone)

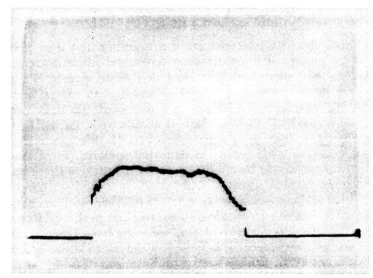

Pitch contour for *No I won't*

bacon and eggs	for the time being	at present
every day	John Smith	London Road

Say the phrases slowly and carefully to yourself, and listen for the fall in pitch from the syllable you have marked as the nucleus. If there is an onset, listen for the rise in pitch to the accented syllable.

In Chapter 5, we introduced accent as part of rhythm. The pitch pattern of onset and nucleus is generally held to be part of INTONATION. It would be very convenient if language was so arranged that rhythmical patterns of timing and prominence were neatly separated from the pitch patterns of intonation, but this is simply not so. Accentuation straddles rhythm and intonation. In this book we shall use the term 'rhythm and intonation' as a single undifferentiated concept. The term 'prosody' is used in this sense, but it has several other meanings, including specifically the rhythm of verse. Another cover term used particularly by American writers, is 'suprasegmentals'.

The intermediate accent rule

If more than two accents are run together in a tone group, any accented syllables between onset and nucleus are liable to lose their accent in all but low deliberate speech. We have so far been marking accented syllables with capital letters, leaving unaccented syllables in lower case. To draw attention to a syllable that has lost its accent by a particular rule, we shall enclose it in square brackets []. We can only use this notation with words in ordinary spelling, as otherwise the brackets could be confused with the brackets that enclose phonetic transcriptions.

Let us start with the word *NAviGAtion* with accents on the first and third syllables. If we add the prefix **CIRcum-**, and say the word very slowly, we now have three accents, *CIRcumNAviGAtion* But if we say the word more quickly, the accent in the middle seems to disappear, leaving only the onset and nucleus, thus *CIRcum[na]viGAtion*. In exactly the same way, if we take a phrase like *TEN THIRty FIVE*, which has three accents when spoken slowly, we find that the accent in the middle disappears when the phrase is spoken more quickly, thus *TEN [thir]ty FIVE*. This rule operates regularly in certain set phrases, such as *the A[b]C,*

the B[b]C, a DIRty [old] MAN, a FISH and [chip] SUpper.
In a small number of cases, a word deaccented by this rule
may have a special reduced form, e.g. *many* can be pronounced /mni/ in the phrase *HOW [ma]ny TIMES.*

The rule explains otherwise rather puzzling changes in
the accentuation of longer words. Examine carefully the
following examples:

an INdependent WITness	enTIREly indePENDent
AFternoon TEA	SAturday afterNOON
EIGHteen NINEty	NINEteen eighTEEN
the UNknown SOLdier	iDENtity unKNOWN
PRINcess MARgaret	an AUStin prinCESS

Each of the words that occurs in both columns has two
accents in isolation, thus *INdePENDent, AFterNOON* etc: in
context the accent that happens to come in the middle is
lost, e.g.:

an INdePENDent WITness	→	an INde[pen]dent WITness
enTIREly INdePENDent	→	enTIREly [in]dePENDent

A number of place names are subject to this same pattern:

BIRken[head] MARket	NORTH [bir]kenHEAD
BEL[fast] LOUGH	EAST [be]FAST
the BER[lin] WALL	the CIty of [ber]LIN

In the case of the two-syllable place names, with a potential
accent on each syllable, native speakers of English may be
at a loss to say how they would normally pronounce the
words out of context. Unless the word is spoken very
slowly, the accent to the left is likely to be lost, e.g.
[ber]LIN.

Exercise

Transcribe the following phrases as they would be before
and after the operation of the intermediate accent rule:

nineteen eighty four	the M.P. for Norwich
a tale of two cities	the ferry across the Mersey

If you study recordings of natural speech, you will find
many cases where the intermediate accent rule has clearly
applied, and other cases where it clearly has not. You can

also expect to find a third category, for which you are unable to decide whether the rule has operated or not. Accent suppression is not all-or-none; it is a process that can apply to a greater or lesser degree. It is inevitable, therefore, that there will be a number of unclear cases. A raised dot or small circle immediately before the relevant syllables is sometimes used to indicate partial accent suppression, e.g. *CIRcum°naviGAtion, PAleo-°anthroPOlogy*.

6.3 Weak-forms

When words grouped to form phrases, GRAMMATICAL words (words belonging to classes with closed membership) are treated rather differently from LEXICAL words (words belonging to classes with open-ended membership). Examples of grammatical words are articles, prepositions, pronouns and conjunctions, and lexical words are words such as nouns, verbs and adjectives and most adverbs. Although all words are accented when pronounced in isolation, in context lexical words are accented unless there is a reason to deaccent them, but grammatical words are often deaccented anyway.

Some unaccented grammatical words become 'clitics', i.e. they are treated exactly like the unaccented syllables of single words, and are attached as leading or trailing syllables to accented words. A leading clitic is a 'proclitic' and a trailing clitic is an 'enclitic'. Clitics may be reduced, and lose some of their consonants. In the following examples, the single words are rhythmically similar to the corresponding phrases:

/fəget/	*forget*	/fədet/	for debt
/riəlistik/	*realistic*	/wiəlisniŋ/	we are listening
/seldəm/	*seldom*	/selðəm/	sell them

These reduced forms, such as /tə/ for *to* or /ə/ for *a*, are known as WEAK-FORMS. The processes of reduction are much the same as in single words.

Vowel reduction

In most cases the vowel is reduced to /ə/. Words thus affected in RP include:

verbs:	am are, was; have, has, had; do, does; can, could; must; would; shall, should;
pronouns:	them, us;
prepositions:	at, for, from, of, to
conjunctions:	and, as, but, than, that.

Outside RP there are many more words which can have the reduced vowel, and some of these are now archaic in RP. For instance, RP speakers tend not to use weak personal pronouns such as /jə/ for *you* or *your* and /mə/ for *my*. These are still found in regional varieties of English, and also old-fashioned RP; the form /jə/ is fossilized in the pronunciation of *How do you do?* as /hau djə duː/ (or as /hau dʒə duː/ by the coalescence of /d/ and /j/). Outside RP, *I* and *they* have weak-forms with /ə/, thus /ə, ðə/, and *I* has the weak-form /a/ in the North of England. In some dialects outside England, the preposition *on* has the weak-form /ən/.

Other words including *we* and *she,* have /i/ as the reduced vowel, thus /wi, ʃi/. In advanced varieties, where the 'final' allophone of reduced /i/ is indistinguishable from the /iː/ of the accented forms /wiː, ʃiː/, it would be simpler to say that *we and she* do not have weak-forms at all. In non-final position, unaccented /i/ may be subject to further reduction to /ə/, and this gives rise in some non-RP varieties to such forms as /əm/ for *him* and /ət/ for *it*. In this same category we must include the special case of *the,* which on those rare occasions when it is accented is pronounced /ðiː/ but which is normally reduced to /i/ before a vowel, e.g. *the end* /ði end/. Before a consonant /i/ is further reduced to /ə/, cf. *the man* /ðə man/.

Words ending in /uː/ may have partially reduced forms ending in /u/ finally or before vowels, thus *who, to, you* /(h)u, tu, ju/.

h-dropping

In accordance with the general principle that /h/ is pronounced only at the beginning of an accented syllable, grammatical words beginning with /h/ have weak-forms without /h/. Words thus affected include *have, has, had; he, him, his, her; who.* However, when people are on their best linguistic behaviour, they sometimes put the /h/ on the weak-form. RP speakers are said to pronounce the /h/ initially after a pause, but not otherwise: in other words, *he* has an /h/ in the sentence *He does* /hi dʌz/, but not in *Does he?* /dʌz i/.

The dropping of /h/ from weak-forms has a long and respectable history. The word *them* appears to have a rather odd weak-form usually spelt *'em*. In fact, *them* has a regular weak-form /ðəm/, and *'em* is from quite a different source. Until about the time of Chaucer, the word for 'them' in the South of England was *hem*: the accented form of this word has been replaced by *them*, but its /h/-less weak-form /əm/ survives. The word *it* is another interesting example. You may have noticed that – at least in the dialects of England – the word *it* cannot normally be accented. The word began with /h/ in old English and was spelt *hit*; the accented form has become obsolete, and the current word *it* is its weak-form. It is anomalous to accent *it*, just as it would be for any other weak-form.

Initial /w/ is dropped in *will and would*. *Would* is reduced first to /wəd/ and then to /əd/; *will* is rather unusual in that /i/ reduces to /ə/, although the intermediate stage /wəl/ does not normally occur, so that /əl/ is the only weak-form of *will*.

Exercise

Identify the words with weak-forms, and decide which weak-form is likely to occur in the following cases:

What was he doing?	Have they started?
A dozen will do.	When would you go?
John had been before.	Look at me!
She broke her leg.	We want to see them.
He had egg on his face.	You can do the others for me.

6.4 Boundaries

A number of phonetic patterns are associated with the boundary between adjacent words. Because of the possibility of augmenting syllables, very complex clusters can be built up, e.g. *sixth spring* with /ksθspr/. This is a tongue-twister even for the native speaker, and it is not surprising that means have developed of simplifying such clusters.

Elision

A /t/ or /d/ may be ELIDED or 'dropped' when it occurs in the middle of a consonant cluster, usually when the next consonant begins the following word. The /t/ in this case follows a stop or fricative, and the /d/ follows an approximant:

soft	/soft/	but	*soft pillow*	/sof pilou/
kept	/kept/	but	*kept quiet*	/kep kwaiət/
old	/ould/	but	*old man*	/oul man/
jammed	dʒamd/	but	*jammed shut*	/dʒam ʃʌt/

Note too the special case of *ask* which elides /k/ before **ed,** thus *ask* /aːsk/ but *asked* /aːst/ and (*he*) *asked Sheila* /aːs ʃiːlə/. Final /d/ normally drops only before a consonant, but in the case of the weak-form of *and* it can drop even before a vowel, e.g. /ən oːl/ *and all*.

In some cases the elided consonant leaves a trace behind. In the phrase *tinned salmon* /tind samən/, /n/ occurs before syllable final /d/, and is consequently lengthened, thus [tinːd]: when /d/ is elided the lengthening of /n/ remains, thus [tinː samən]. Even so, the operation of this process is not very clear to native speakers of English, and considerable confusion is caused in writing as a result. Are potatoes which have been mashed and creamed 'cream potatoes' or 'creamed potatoes'? Is something very new 'brand new' or 'bran new'? Is the town in Warwickshire 'Sutton Coldfield' or 'Sutton Coalfield'? Most of us probably have to stop and work cases like this out from time to time. Some can be solved by substituting a word beginning with a vowel, in this way avoiding the consonant cluster. Is a six-year-old child 'age six' or 'aged six'? If we change *six* to *eight* it becomes clear: 'Kevin aged eight' is clearly right, and 'Kevin age eight' is rather odd. But mistakes are very common, even in public notices. For instance, the arrivals board at a British airport has a column headed *Expected Times*, and right next to it another column headed *Schedule Times*. The phrase /ʃedʒuːl taimz/ is of course interpretable in two ways – 'times that are scheduled' or 'times given in the schedule' – but when it is parallelled with *expected*, presumably *scheduled* times is what is intended.

Exercise

Identify the places where elision can take place in the following phrases. Transcribe the words first as they would be pronounced out of context, and then retranscribe them to show the operation of the elision rule. The first one has been done for you for illustration:

roast beef	/rəust biːf/ → /rəus biːf/

roast beef	stuffed tomatoes	chained together
rolled gold	kind to hands	a child's voice

Assimilation

When a sound anticipates some feature of the pronunciation of a following sound, or continues some feature of a preceding sound, it is said to 'assimilate' to that sound. The alveolar consonants /t, d, n/, for instance, tend to assimilate to a following labial or velar consonant, and anticipate the place of articulation:

that boy	/ðat bɔɪ/	becomes	/ðap bɔɪ/
one girl	/wʌn gəːl/	becomes	/wʌŋ gəːl/
Red Cross	/red krɒs/	becomes	/reg krɒs/

The sibilants, /s, z/ assimilate to the place of articulation of /ʃ, ʒ/:

nice shape /nais ʃeip/		becomes	/naiʃ ʃeip/
boys' shoes /bɔiz ʃuːz/		becomes	/bɔiʒ ʃuːz/

Sporadic assimilation occurs when /θ, ð/ precede or follow /s, z/, e.g. *both sides* becomes /bəus saidz/, and *How's that?* ('howzzat') becomes /hauz zat/. In some varieties of English the cluster /ðz/ may be simplified in the word *clothes* to /kləuz/. But this is not predictable: *fourth Sunday* does not become /fɔːs sʌndi/, and *maths* is not simplified to /mas/.

A rather different kind of assimilation is found in Yorkshire English: a voiced obstruent is devoiced before a voiceless consonant, thus *rib cage* /rib keidʒ/ becomes /rip keidʒ/ and *bedside table* /bed said teibl/ becomes /bet sait teibl/. This is very localized however, and is one of the ways in which a Yorkshire accent can be distinguished from a Lancashire one. There is no trace of this rule in RP.

Rules of assimilation apply after elision, and in fact the elision may provide the conditions for assimilation to operate. Thus *handbag* may be pronounced /hambag/:

	/hand bag/
(by elision)	/han bag/
(by assimilation)	/ham bag/

Similarly, *largest share* /lɑːdʒəst ʃeə/ becomes /lɑːdʒəs ʃeə/ by elision and then /lɑːdʒəʃ ʃeə/ by assimilation. *Must* having been reduced to /məst/ can by this process end up as /məʃ/, e.g. *I must show you* /ai məʃ ʃou juː/.

The assimilation rules apply cyclically, e.g. after they have applied once, they can apply again if the right conditions still hold or have been set up. In *pint mug* /paint mʌg/ the /t/ can assimilate to the following labial, and the resulting /p/ can cause the assimilation of the preceding /n/ to /m/, hence /paimp mʌg/:

pint mug	/paint mʌg/
(by assimilation, pass 1)	/painp mʌg/
(by assimilation, pass 2)	/paimp mʌg/

You may not be able to hear the /p/ in this phrase, but it will certainly leave a trace behind in the shortening of the preceding vowel and the nasal. *Pint mug* is rhythmically quite different from *pine mug*.

Assimilation creates a problem for phonemic analysis. If, for example, you are asked to identify the phonemes of *hot pie,* should you analyse it /hot pai/, i.e. before assimilation, or as the assimilated form /hop pai/? The point is that the assimilation rule changes one phoneme into another: it does not really make sense to ask which one it is. Furthermore, because assimilation is a process, it may be carried out only partially. If you speak slowly and deliberately, and much more carefully than you normally would, you may produce words in their unassimilated forms. In rapid conversation you are more likely to assimilate fully. In between these extremes are overlapping forms, e.g. in *that girl* you might start the velar movement for /g/ while you are still making /t/; in *gunman* /gʌnmən/ you may bring your lips together for /m/ while you have still got your tongue tip in position on the alveolar ridge for /n/. When you sit and think about assimilation and practise examples, you are more likely to produce careful overlapping forms than the full assimilations. Full assimilation is more common in some varieties of English than in others.

Exercise

Transcribe the words in the following phrases in their citation forms. Check for consonants that can elide, and then carry out rules of assimilation as many times as appropriate. Rewrite the phrases at each stage. The first one has been done for you.

closed shop	/klouzd ʃop/
(by elision)	/klouz ʃop/
(by assimilation)	/klouʒ ʃop/

closed shop	clothes shop	fan club	ground floor
Aunt Mary	lined paper	don't go	lost sheep

Hiatus

Elision and assimilation take place when consonants cluster at the boundary. A problem of a different order arises when two vowels come together across the boundary. The transition from the one vowel to the other is known as HIATUS (/haiˌeitəs/ from a Latin word meaning 'gap'). English avoids the hiatus as far as possible by using glides to link the syllables together, the selection of the glide depending on the nature of the first vowel.

(i)   after a vowel in the close front area, the glide is [ʲ]:

try /trai/	+ *again* /əgen/	becomes [trai ʲəgen]
free /fri:/	+ *ale* /eil/	becomes [fri: ʲeil]
Monday /mʌndi/	+ *evening* /i:vniŋ/	becomes [mʌndi ʲi:vniŋ]

(ii) after a close and back vowel, the glide is [ʷ]:

do /du:/	+ *ask* /a:sk/	becomes [du: ʷa:sk]
how /hau/	+ *old* /ould/	becomes [hauʷould]
go /gou/	+ *under* /ʌndə/	becomes [gouʷ ʌndə]

These linking glides are executed very rapidly, and are not very prominent, and to indicate this they are written small and above the line. Examples with the glide alone contrast with cases in which the first word ends with a close vowel and the second begins with the ordinary phoneme /j/ or /w/. In the latter case the glide is much longer and stronger. Compare

new age	[nju:ʷeidʒ]	with	*new wage*	[nju:ʷweidʒ]
three ears	[θri:ʲiəz]	with	*three years*	[θri:ʲjiəz]
two eights	[tu:ʷeits]	with	*two weights*	[tu:ʷweits]
high oaks	[haiʲouks]	with	*high yokes*	[haiʲjouks]

In some kinds of RP – the kind of RP that even some RP speakers would regard as affected – the single glide is very weak, and the articulators do not travel very far towards the palate or the velum. The two syllables are smoothed together and the result sounds something like [njueidʒ], [haouks], etc.

You will have noticed that whenever we have transcribed the glides, we have put them in square brackets. It is one thing to describe them phonetically, but we are not prepared to commit ourselves on their phonemic status. They come between phonemes, but are not phonemes themselves. Consequently they do not belong in a strictly phonemic transcription.

The only other vowels that can end a word are /a:, ɔ:, ə:, ə/. In most cases these have a post-vocalic /r/ in rhotic dialects, and have **r** in the spelling. In non-rhotic dialects this /r/ is not normally pronounced except when the next word begins with a vowel. This is called the 'linking /r/'. E.g.:

far	/fa:/	but	*far and wide*	/fa:r ən waid/
for	/fɔ:/	but	*for and against*	/fɔ:r ən əgenst/
here	/hiə/	but	*here and there*	/hiər ən ðeə/

In some cases the conditions for the pronunciation of linking /r/ are set up by the loss of /h/, e.g. in *He showed her his etchings* the /r/ of *her* is dropped if the /h/ of *his* is pronounced, but it is restored once the /h/ is dropped, so that the sequence *her his* becomes /ə:r iz/.

In non-rhotic dialects, this [r] is not a true phonemic consonant, but simply a glide to avoid the hiatus. It is also used when there is no **r** in the spelling:

Shah	/ʃɑ:/	and	*Shah of Iran*	/ʃɑ:r əv irɑ:n/
law	/lɔ:/	and	*law and order*	/lɔ:r ən o:də/
India	/indiə/	and	*India Office*	/indiər ofis/

This 'intrusive' [r] takes speakers of rhotic dialects by surprise, and seems very strange to them. Some people object very strongly to it, even though – if they but realized – they use it themselves. It is an established feature of British English, and must be counted as a characteristic of contemporary RP.

Double consonants

In the special case where two identical consonants come together, we get a double consonant. Unlike some other languages, such as Italian or Swedish, English does not tolerate double consonants inside a morpheme, but they certainly do occur across morpheme and word boundaries. In most cases the duration of the first consonant is held for the duration of the second, e.g. in *ten nuns* /ten nʌnz/ the duration of [n] is much longer than in *ten onions* /ten ʌnjənz/. There is only one alveolar articulation, and it would not be normal to release the first /n/ before starting the second, i.e. it is [ten:ʌnz] rather than [ten] followed by [nʌnz]. In the case of a stop, the holding phase is prolonged, so that the first has no release, and the second no closing phase, e.g. *black car* [blak:ɑ:] or *big girl* [big:ə:l]. The double consonant may be the result of assimilation, e.g. *that cat* /ðak kat/, or *this shirt* /ðiʃ ʃə:t/.

Exercise

Trace the form of the following phrases step by step from the citation forms of the individual words to the expected pronunciation of the whole phrase:

cracked cups	raw eggs	wet paint
high up	a car engine	no others
Veronica Edwards	pit closures	blind mice

6.5 'Binary' verse

Some of the points made in this chapter, particularly concerning the accentuation of phrases, are relevant to the study of English verse. We shall make a distinction – which to the literary critic may seem an artificial one – between what we shall call 'literary' verse, and the more ancient tradition of 'binary' verse, which is now less prestigious and used mainly in nursery rhymes, greeting card verses, proverbs, advertising jingles and so on. We shall discuss 'binary' verse here, and defer discussion of 'literary verse' until the next chapter.

You may not think of some of the examples of 'binary' verse as verse at all. Here for instance is a children's nonsense rhyme:

DIP dip STAtion   CORpoRAtion
HOW many BUSes   IN the STAtion.

Each verse – or 'half-line' – contains two beats, and in most cases the 'beat' is an accent, and the two accents pattern as onset and nucleus. Two verses, or two tone groups, form the whole line. The 'binary' structure can optionally be taken further: two lines can form a couplet (as in this case), and two couplets can form a quatrain. At the lower level there may be a single weak syllable between beats (as in the case of three of the four verses here) so that two syllables are associated with each beat.

Here are some more examples of this kind of verse:

HUMPty DUMPty   SAT on the WALL;
HUMPty DUMPty   HAD a great FALL.
ALL the king's HORses   and ALL the king's MEN
COULdn't put HUMPty   toGEther a[gain].

MADE you LOOK,   MADE you STARE,
MADE the BARber   CUT your HAIR.

a NEW BROOM	SWEEPS CLEAN.
EMPty VEssels	make MOST SOUND.
MAny HANDS	make LIGHT WORK.
DRINka PINta	MILka DAY.

you'll NEver get a BEtter bit of BUtter on your KNIFE.

Superficially, this kind of verse seems to have a very powerful rhythm which imposes itself on the reader: it is almost impossible to avoid the strong thumping beats when you read it aloud. However, it is a self-evident fact that the visual marks of the text have no rhythm, and any rhythm there might be is supplied by the reader.

If our examples have two beats per half line, that is because the reader processes the text to make it that way. For instance, if the verse *all the king's horses* were treated in the normal way and read very slowly – as nursery rhymes usually are – it could have three accents, but the intermediate accent rule is invoked to reduce the number to two. On the other hand, the phrase *in the station* might under normal circumstances lose the accent on the preposition *in* and so have only one accent, but this rule is blocked to leave the desired number. If there is no suitable syllable available to form the onset, an unaccented syllable after the nucleus can be pressed into service to provide a beat, as in the last line of *Humpty Dumpty*. (We have marked this with square brackets.) If this verse has a fixed number of beats, it is because the accent rules of English are manipulated to achieve the desired number.

Although the desired number of beats is fixed, there may on occasion be alternative ways of getting them. In the example

EMPty VEssels   make MOST SOUND

I have operated a rule (which we have not discussed) that deaccents a verb between subject and object. Perhaps you do not like my version of this proverb, and you may prefer

EMPty VEssels   MAKE most SOUND

If so, your preference is to use the intermediate accent rule to get down to two beats. However thumping the rhythm may seem, it is not even tied to particular syllables.

Binary verse may seem to use an exaggerated but otherwise normal speech rhythm. It is in fact – in the best sense of the word – an artificial stylization of it. Let us call the stylized pattern the METRE. When binary verse is recited, it is normal practice to abandon the normal rules of the language, and read according to the metre.

If accentuation rules can be manipulated to fit one metrical pattern, then perhaps by manipulating the rules in a different way, a different metre can be obtained. Binary verse is sometimes written in such a way that it can be recited at half speed, in which case a set of secondary beats emerges between the primary beats. Take for example:

SING a [song] of SIX[pence]   a POcket [full] of RYE []

FOUR and [twen]ty BLACK[birds] BAKED [in] a PIE []

If you read this rapidly, putting a beat only on the syllables in capitals, you have the same kind of pattern as we have discussed above. However, when it is sung, or recited by children in the conventional sing-song manner, intermediate beats are placed on the syllables in square brackets. Those in the middle of the verses – *song, full, twen-, in* – would in normal circumstances be suppressed by the intermediate accent rule, while those on *-pence* and *-birds* would not be accented anyway. Again the only explanation is that the reader manipulates the accent rules to get the required number of beats.

The empty brackets at the ends of the lines of our example call for some comment. At these points there is no weak syllable to take the secondary beat, and there is simply a gap in the metrical pattern. You will probably pause briefly at these points when you recite the rhyme. The resulting pattern with four beats in the first half line, and three in the second followed by a 'silent beat' is conventionally known as BALLAD METRE. For convenience the half lines are written out as full lines, e.g.

SIMple SImon   MET a PIEman
GOing [to] the FAIR []

or to take a more serious example:

It [is] an ANcient MAri[ner],
And he STOPpeth ONE of THREE. [ ]

"By thy LONG grey BEARD and GLITtering EYE,
Now WHEREfore STOPP'ST thou ME?" []

Note how the accentuation rules are manipulated here. In the first line there are insufficient accents to make up the four, and so *is* and even the reduced syllable of *mariner* are given a beat. In the third line there are too many accents, and so the accent on *grey* – intermediate between *long* and *beard* – is suppressed in the usual way. You may feel that forcing the language into the metrical scheme is rather naive and childish, and indeed, poets have put a lot of effort in trying to avoid enslaving the rhythm to the metre.

When you read verse aloud, you sometimes experience a conflict between the natural rhythm and the metre. The metre seems to invite you to accent syllables contrary to the normal rules of accentuation. For instance

The boy stood on the burning deck

seems to invite the reading

The BOY stood ON the BURning DECK

and yet you know as a speaker of English that it would be rather odd to accent the preposition *on* here, and that precedence should be given to the verb *stood*. You may as a result read the line

The BOY STOOD on the BURning DECK.

The first version identifies the metrically strong syllables, and performs a SCANSION of the line. The second version predicts which syllables would be accented if the line were read as ordinary English, and not verse. When you read this kind of verse aloud, you can read according to the metre, or following the second version, which is commonly described as 'reading according to the sense'. Or, more likely, you will do something in between, trying not to lose either the metre or the sense entirely. If you are reading light or humorous verse, or obscene verse, or the words of a popular song, you will probably follow the metre, and not bother too much about the sense:

'twas IN the MONTH of LIver[pool],
in the CIty OF juLY;
the RAIN was SNOWing HEAvi[ly]
and the STREETS were VEry DRY.

(since we are using capitals for accented syllables, we have removed them from the beginning of the line, and from the proper name *July*.) If the verse is intended to be taken seriously, you would probably try to follow the sense more closely, and avoid accenting prepositions and conjunctions, or putting a strong beat on an unaccented syllable at the end of the line.

Exercise

(1) This extract from Milton's *L'Allegro* is written with four beats to the line. Is this 'binary' verse of the kind described above? Do the lines divide naturally into half-lines, and if not, why not?

Haste thee nymph, and bring with thee
Jest and youthful Jollity,
Quips and Cranks, and wanton Wiles,
Nods, and Becks, and Wreathed Smiles,
Such as hang on Hebe's cheek,
And love to hang in dimple sleek;
Sport that wrinkled Care derides,
And Laughter holding both his sides.
Come and trip it as ye go
On the light fantastick toe,
And in thy right hand lead with thee,
The Mountain Nymph, sweet Liberty.

Make a recording of someone reading the passage aloud. How many accents can you hear in each line, and how well do they match the expected metrical beats?

(2) The *Poetic Gems* of the nineteenth century Dundee poet William MacGonagall have given later generations much unintended amusement. Consider this opening extract from *The Tay Bridge Disaster*:

Beautiful Railway Bridge of the Silv'ry Tay!
Alas! I am very sorry to say
That ninety lives have been taken away
On the last sabbath day of 1879,
Which will be remember'd for a very long time.

'Twas about seven o'clock at night,
And the wind it blew with all its might,

And the rain came pouring down,
And the dark clouds seemed to frown,
And the Demon of the air seem'd to say-
"I'll blow down the Bridge of Tay."

To what extent does this conform to the 'binary' type of verse?

Does the metre have any similarities to that of Milton's poem?

CHAPTER 7

Accentuation

When we produce a phrase, we accent some words and leave others unaccented. Taking a common-sense view of the matter, it might seem self-evident that the words we pick out to accent are the most important words. In practice, this is not how it works at all. We have already seen how words are deaccented because they come in the middle of a tone group, or because they are grammatical words. In the first place, we do not positively assign accents, but get rid of them: the accents of a phrase are those that are left after the rules have applied. Secondly, although it is usually unimportant words that lose their accents, importance is not taken into account, and sometimes the key word of a phrase or sentence is deaccented.

In informal written texts, such as tabloid newspapers and private correspondence, words are sometimes highlighted by means of capitals, underlining, italics or boldface, e.g.

In our view, this is NOT the way to do it.

The impression is given that the highlighted word is in some way particularly important. In reality, the word *not* here is just the one that carries the last remaining accent, after *the way to do it* has been deaccented. We shall be discussing in this chapter some of the rules that cause deaccentuation.

Note that whereas the usual informal practice is to highlight the whole of the word, we are here putting only the accented syllable in capitals. Secondly, we shall use square brackets to mark words which have been deaccented, e.g. instead of

Even the PRESIDENT wears them.

we would write

Even the PREsident [wears them].

7.1 The rhythm of phrases

The rhythm of phrases is not fixed in advance, but is at least in part under the control of the speaker. Accent groups may be run together in an unbroken rhythm, or they may be rhythmically kept apart. In a phrase of more than two accents, some accents may form a natural internal group, e.g. in a phrase of three accents, the middle accent may be more closely connected with the first than the third, or vice versa. In *a pound of Cheshire cheese, of Cheshire cheese* forms an internal group of this kind, while in *after dinner speeches, after dinner* forms an internal group.

In both cases, the whole phrase can be run together as a single tone group, in which case *Cheshire* or *dinner* are subject to the intermediate accent rule. But if they are internally divided, the position of the break is indicated by giving the preceding accent group level pitch, and by lengthening it or even inserting a short pause. In the first case, if *a pound* is isolated in this way, the pitch rises on *pound* just as for an onset, but this is an onset without a nucleus. In the second case, if *after dinner* is separated from *speeches*, it has an onset on *after* and the level tone on *dinner* in the position of the nucleus. The level tone acts as a 'non-final' signal, but it is not clear whether it is really an onset or a nucleus. In recent years there has been increasing agreement that it is a LEVEL NUCLEUS, and we shall mark it (→), e.g.

a →POUND   of CHEshire ＼ CHEESE.
AFter →DInner   ＼ SPEEches.

The symbol ＼ precedes the word with the falling nucleus.

Inside a tone group, the distinction between intermediate leading and trailing syllables is neutralized, and all intermediate unaccented syllables are treated as trailing. In a single word, such as *INdePENdent* or *PHOtoGRAphic*, there is no way of inserting a rhythmical break, and no particular reason to group the second syllable with the first rather than the third, and in this position the second syllable patterns as a trailing syllable. When the accents are rhythmically separated, intermediate syllables are treated more clearly as leading or trailing. Consider this pair of sentences:

Take Grey to London.
Take Greater London.

When you are presented with these as a contrasting pair, it is quite natural to make them as different as possible. To do this, you might group *Grey* with *take*, and separate it from *to London*, in which case *Grey* is long and *to* is a short leading syllable. In the second example, *Greater* groups with *London*, and the syllables of *Greater* are more equal in duration.

Just because we are able to make such examples different, it does not follow that we always do so. It is very difficult to think up a situation in which they could possibly be confused, and in real life it is rarely necessary to keep the two rhythms strictly apart. The sentence /teik greitə lʌndən/ is not really ambiguous in practice, and no great harm is done if all three accents are run together, and both phrases made identical. In any case, rhythmical differences are less important for correct interpretation than the context.

The rhythm of phrases containing the conjunction *and* varies according to how the items are grouped, and in this case the rhythmical differences may be significant. Given a construction of the form *X and Y*, there may be a reason to run Y together with X, or to separate it from X in order to link it with items that follow. Consider the rhythmical treatment of *and* in a list of names such as *John and Margaret Hughes*:

JOHN and →MARgaret . . .   ＼HUGHES
→JOHN . . . and MARgaret   ＼HUGHES

If *John and Margaret* is run together without a break, treating *and* as a trailing syllable, the likely interpretation is that John's name is also Hughes, and that John and Margaret are probably a married couple. On the other hand, if we insert a rhythmical break, and make *and* a leading syllable, *John and Margaret Hughes* are regarded as separate individuals, and John's surname is unknown. In the phrase *John and Joan and Jeff,* you can manipulate the rhythm of the *and*s to indicate whether John or Jeff – if either – is Joan's partner.

For a more elaborate and extreme example, consider the following possible exchange:

A: What did they give you for dinner?

B: Well, we had soup and a roll and T-bone steak and onions and chips and peas and a bottle of wine and apple pie and custard and cheese and biscuits and coffee and a chocolate mint and a brandy.

In order to make sense of this menu, you have the interpret the occurrences of *and* in different ways. Items linked together in the real world – on the same plate! – will be linked and run together rhythmically, while those separated in the real world will be separated with a rhythmical break. In the latter case, *and* remains a leading syllable. The wrong rhythm will suggest such unlikely gastronomic delights as peas with wine, or custard with cheese.

Any kind of grouping can be highlighted in this way. This includes, as a special case, the grammatical structure of a sentence. Grouping can be used to resolve a syntactic ambiguity, e.g. in the phrase *old men and women* the women are old if *women* is grouped with *men*, but if it is rhythmically separated, the age of the women is unspecified. In everyday conversation, examples like this are likely to remain potentially ambiguous, and rhythm is brought in only to clear up a misinterpretation.

'Isochronous stress'

A widely held view of the rhythm of English phrases is that they have 'isochronous stress', i.e. that 'stressed' syllables are spaced equally in time. English is said to be a 'stress-timed' language. The idea goes back to the work of Joshua Steele, who in 1775 had the apparently excellent idea of trying to represent speech rhythm by means of musical notation, dividing stretches of speech into 'cadences' equivalent to musical bars, each of them beginning with a strong syllable. He set up an extremely interesting and stimulating hypothesis, but since it has not been confirmed by contemporary measuring instruments, the case must be regarded as not proven.

The apparent psychological reality of isochrony can be demonstrated very easily. All one has to do is to take a long phrase, and produce it without grouping the accents, and without suppressing any of them by the intermediate accent rule. When linguists make up sentences, and even record them on measuring instruments, they may actually utter them in this artificial way. But it does not follow that people speak naturally like that.

We shall not adopt the isochronous stress hypothesis in this book for several reasons. The unfortunate result of using musical notation is that the properties of music have been confused with the rhythm of English. The division of phrases into bars (now usually called 'feet'), beginning each one with the 'stressed' syllable, completely disregards the difference between leading and trailing syllables. The notion of 'stress' is very vague, and can refer to an accented syllable, a syllable which has lost its accent, or even – when all else fails – a pause. The notion of equal timing is also vague, the rhythmical beats coming at intervals varying from about a third to over half a second. People are relatively insensitive to differences of this kind, and are willing to treat considerably different intervals as perceptually equal. Given the vagueness and generous tolerances, it is neither surprising nor interesting that a candidate can usually be found in roughly the right place to stand as the regular rhythmical beat.

7.2 Contractions

The neutralization of the distinction between leading and trailing syllables can bring about a clash between the rhythm of a phrase and its grammatical structure. For instance, the sentence *John is a doctor* divides grammatically into the subject *John* and the predicate *is a doctor*, and *John has got a Jaguar* divides into *John* and *has got a Jaguar*. This being so, one might expect *is* and *has* to pattern as leading syllables, but inside the tone unit they pattern instead as 'trailing' syllables, added as an ending to the previous word, thus *John's a doctor*, *John's got a Jaguar*. The phonetic shape of the weak-form depends on the ending of the previous accent group, and it may lose its vowel, as in these two

cases. Vowelless weak-forms are known as CONTRAC-
TIONS.

Most contractions are of finite verbs. The vowel is lost
after a pronoun subject from *am, have, had, will, would*, e.g.
I'm hoping /aim houpiŋ/, *they've gone* /ðeiv gon/. With the
exception of *am* these also drop the vowel after the word
who and certain other WH-words e.g. *those who'd won* /ðouz
u d wʌn/ but *Who am I?* /hu: əm ai/. *Has* and *is* lose the
vowel more readily, after any subject or WH-expression,
and pattern like the syllable augment **s** (discussed above in
section 4 of Chapter 5): the /z/ is devoiced after a voiceless
consonant, e.g. *What is he doing?* /wot s i du:iŋ/, and the loss
of the vowel is blocked after a sibilant, e.g. *Alice has come*
/alis əz kʌm/. Alongside these genuine contractions, note
the case of *'re* for *are* in e.g. *we're*: we drop the letter **a** in
spelling, but in the pronunciation /wiə/ the reduced vowel
survives as /ə/.

Apart from the verbs, there remains only one further
vowelless weak-form in standard usage, namely the *'s* form
of *us*, which occurs in e.g. *let's go* /let s gou/. This form is
used only in the first person imperative, when *let us go* is
equivalent to 'come on'; it cannot be used for the second
person imperative, where *let us* is equivalent to 'allow us'.
The contraction is also avoided in liturgical usage: a priest
is more likely to say *Let us pray* with /əs/ than *Let's pray*.

Vowelless weak-forms were commoner in earlier
periods of English. In Shakespeare you will see *his* written
's. *'Tis, 'twas* and *'twere* survive in verse rather than prose
or ordinary spoken usage (these also occur in the leading
position rather than between onset and nucleus). In Lancashire and Yorkshire, the definite article is often vowelless,
and has a variety of forms, including [t] and [ʔ] or [tʔ], and
is conventionally spelt *t'* e.g. [av jə si:n ʔlasiz] *have you seen
t' lasses?*. The alveolar stop is subject to assimilation, e.g.
[im pʔ bek] *in t' beck*, or [tə kʔ ka:] *to t' car*.

Some grammatical words lose a consonant between
onset and nucleus, e.g. the past infinite marker *have* and the
preposition *of* can drop final /v/ before a consonant. Thus
you should have come becomes /ju: ʃud ə kʌm/ and *John o'
Gaunt* is pronounced /dʒon ə go:nt/. The pronunciation /ə/
for *of* is particularly associated with expressions of measure

or quantity, such as *a cup of tea* /ə kʌp ə tiː/, and similarly
a piece of string, a pound of butter, a pint of beer, a gang of yobs
etc. The loss of /v/ is reflected in the special spellings *a cuppa*
and *a pinta*.

Exercise

Identify the words in the following sentences that would be
reduced to weak-forms, and which of these can be written
as contractions. Then transcribe the sentences, paying
particular attention to the phonetic shape of the weak-
forms.

  (i) You can go when you have finished.
 (ii) To impress her he would do anything.
(iii) Would you like a glass of milk?
 (iv) I wonder who will be paying for all this.
  (v) They have decided that they are better off than us.

Contractions are recognized as a normal feature of
colloquial English, since they can be written down. But
most weak-forms do not have an accepted written form,
and their existence is not generally recognized. Indeed, there
is a literary convention whereby written equivalents of
weak-forms are used as a sign of an uneducated speaker. For
instance, if a speaker in a novel or a play were to say *She cried
'n' cried 'cos she'd lost 'er hat*, the intention of the apostrophes
would be to indicate that the pronunciation is in some
respect defective. In fact, the reductions indicated have
nothing to do with education or careful speaking at all, and
/ʃi kraid ŋ kraid kəz ʃid lost əː hat/ would be an unremarkable rendering of that sentence in RP. The literary convention is quite misleading, and part of a wider convention
whereby funny spellings are used to suggest non-standard
dialect. Perhaps it is in response to this convention that
beginners sometimes assume that they never use weak-
forms other than contractions in their own speech, or that
only non-standard varieties of English use them, or that RP
is uncontaminated by them. In reality they are an essential
rhythmical ingredient of fluent English speech.

Not

There are two ways of negating finite verbs in English. The first has *not* /nɒt/ added to the weak-form of the verb, thus *we are not, I am not* /wi ə nɒt, ai m nɒt/. Let us call this the NOT form. In most cases there is an alternative, the N'T form, with the full form of the verb, and a contraction of *not,* /nt/ written *n't*, e.g. *hasn't, doesn't, didn't,* etc. Southern English prefers the N'T form wherever it exists, but Northern English uses both, with a subtle difference of meaning, e.g. *she won't go* is not quite synonymous with *she'll not go.* The use of the N'T form is sometimes contrary to what one might intuitively expect, e.g.

A: Would you like to go again? B: no, i CERtainly WOULDn't!

In an emphatic denial, one might expect the speaker to accent the negative particle; in fact the nucleus comes in the same place as in an emphatic confirmation, cf. *yes, i CERtainly WOULD.* (In these last two examples, the word *I* is written without its customary capital letter, as it is unaccented.)

The Northern English N'T forms follow a rule which deletes the last consonant of the verb before the addition of /nt/, with the result that these forms have only one syllable. In this way *is* becomes /int/, and *did* becomes /dint/. *Am not* /ant/ is identical to *are not*, and also – by the loss of /h/ – to *have not, has not* and *had not.*

The standard English forms are a mixture, some of them following the 'Northern rule', others preserving the final consonant. Where this rule has applied in the standard forms, the vowel has been lengthened, as in *shan't* and *can't.* *Won't* derives from *wol*, an obsolete form of *will; don't* is also in this group but its form is irregular and its origin obscure. The non-standard *ain't* presumably also derives by loss of the final consonant followed by vowel lengthening.

We can also expect to find a mixture in regional varieties of English, and the declarative forms do not necessarily match the interrogative forms. For instance it is common in Liverpool English to have *it isn't* /it iznt/ with /z/, but *isn't it?* /in it/ without. As this last example also shows, *n't* drops its /t/ in certain circumstances. Since /n/ and /t/ are both alveolar, they are subject to assimilation to a following velar or labial place of articulation, e.g. *he hasn't been* /i hazm(p) biːn/. In Scottish speech, the negatives may be quite different from the standard forms, e.g. *didnae, isnae* etc. and the interrogative type as in *Will ye no come back again?*

Exercise

In interrogative constructions, the spoken N'T form is written out as the NOT form in formal written English, and word order may be different in the spoken and written forms, e.g. compare the formal written *did she not go?* and the colloquial *didn't she go?* Identify and transcribe the colloquial forms of the following examples:

(i) Would you not like to know?
(ii) It is my turn now, is it not?
(iii) Was not the door open?
(iv) Have you not been drinking? You had better let me drive, had you not?
(v) Will you not come back again?

7.3   The compound rule

When two words are compounded, usually to form a compound noun, any accents in the second word are suppressed. (Historically, this is a special case of the 'Germanic' rule that puts the accent at the beginning of the word.) For instance *a BLUE BOttle* is a phrase with two accents, 'a bottle that is blue', whereas the compound *BLUE[bottle]* referring to the large fly of that name has lost its accent on the second element *bottle*. Compare also *a COtton DRESS* 'a dress made of cotton' with *a COtton [merchant]* 'a merchant who deals in cotton' and *an ENGlish TEAcher* 'a teacher who is English' with *an ENGlish [teacher]* 'one who teaches English'. In many cases the compound has a special meaning which cannot be inferred from its parts, thus *LEAther[jacket]*, *BLACK[bird]*, *GREEN[fly]*, *HOUSE[wife]*, *COAL[man]*. Note that we are using the brackets to mark the whole of that part of the phrase which is deaccented by the rule, and this may include more than one syllable. In the case of e.g. [jacket], the second syllable would be deaccented anyway by the rules which determine the accentuation of the word *jacket*. You will also note that the rule applies in the same way irrespective of whether the compound is written as one word, as two or more words, or even with a hyphen e.g. *FRYing-[pan]*.

Certain collocations of words automatically become compounds. This is true, for instance, of political parties, e.g. *the conSERvative [party]*. The rule applies irrespective of how familiar or new the collocation might be: the *SOcial demoCRAtic [party]* had a compounded name before fighting its first general election. We would even compound the name of a new invented party, e.g. *the HOME rule for WIgan [party]*. (In this last example, *rule* has also lost its accent coming as it does between *HOME* and *WIgan*.) The 'soirée' kind of party, on the other hand, is not usually compounded, cf. *the CHRISTmas PARty, the OFfice PARty*, etc., (but cf. *a hallowE'EN [party]*). Stories on the other hand become compounds, e.g. *a GHOST [story], a SHAggy DOG [story]*.

Exercise

Decide whether the following examples are treated as compounds or not. Identify the position of the nucleus, and of the onset if there is one.

a fountain pen	ice cream
a couldn't–care–less attitude	farmhouse cheese
a box of matches	a matchbox

To help you understand the accentuation of these phrases more fully, here are two points to note:

(i) the intermediate accent rule can combine with the compound rule in a single phrase: this applies above to our examples *SOcial [de]moCRAtic* and *HOME [rule] for WIgan*.

(ii) the compound can apply more than once in the same phrase, e.g. a story about *the conSERvative [party]* is a (*conSERvative [party]*) [*story*].

Meaning and importance play no role in the compound rule. For instance in *Where's the TELephone [directory]?*, the speaker is looking for a directory not a telephone, but is nevertheless obliged by the English language to accent *telephone*.

The dynamic predicate rule

Study the position of the nuclear accent in the following examples:

The KEttle's boiling.	The RAIN'S stopped.
My COffee's cold.	The MILK'S come at last.
A GUN went off.	The SHIPyard's gone bust.
THREE of the PLANES crashed.	TERM'S starting again.

As in the case of compounds, the nucleus seems to come in the wrong place. If a sentence draws attention to a significant event or change of state, one might expect this to be accented, e.g. that the kettle is BOIling, or that the shipyard has gone BUST. What in fact happens is precisely the opposite: the key phrase actually loses its accent, and we can indicate this in our square bracket notation e.g. *the TRAIN [crashed]*. (No satisfactory explanation can be offered for this rule at the present time, and it just has to be accepted as one of the curiosities of the sound patterning of English.)

The change of state is essential. In *the HOUSE [is on fire]* the house has changed from its previous state of not being on fire. In *the HOUSE is up the HILL*, by contrast, there is no change of state, and the predicate is accented in the usual way. *the HOUSE [is up the hill]* would belong to a world in which houses, like Burnham Wood, were able to move.

The dynamic predicate rule is used strategically in conversation to indicate that an event or change of state is necessary, or that something is wrong: *the DOOR's [open]* may be interpreted not as a statement about the door, but as a command to shut it, and *the WAter's [too cold]* is likely to be something more than a description of the water, e.g. it might indicate a refusal to go swimming.

Exercise

Mark the following expressions, which are mostly noun phrases, with what you would consider the most usual pattern of accentuation. Make a recording of them, and listen for the fall from the nucleus, the rise to the onset if there is one. As far as you can, account for the position of the accents.

the Greater London Council
the Rank Organization
All's Well That Ends Well
there's a fly in my soup
the Oxford English Dictionary
a disk operating system
the crime prevention officer
the United States of America
the British High Commission
the Campaign for Nuclear disarmament

a Man for All Seasons
George Bernard Shaw
the Canterbury Tales
New York City
the fire brigade
what the butler saw
the Sidney Opera House
double yellow lines
the latest opinion poll

7.4 Recovering information

When phrases and sentences are produced in context, not all their content is entirely new. Some items do not need to be spelt out in full, and can be taken for granted or reconstructed from fragmentary references. This RE-COVERABLE information is replaced by a substitute such as a pronoun or the pro-verb DO, or it is omitted (ELLIPTED) entirely. A substitute is as a general rule left unaccented, and we shall mark it [ ]. Consider the following (very odd) question and answer:

A: WHO painted the mona LIsa?
B: da VINci painted the mona LIsa.

The problem with B's reply is that it is a citation form, taking no account of the context. By accenting *LIsa*, B gives the impression that this is a piece of NEW information, when in fact this is already GIVEN in A's question. The whole of the phrase *painted the Mona Lisa* is given and recoverable, and just *da VINci* would be an adequate reply to A's question. In any case, given items would not normally be accented. Now compare a second question and answer:

A: WHAT did da VINci do?
B: da VINci painted the mona LIsa.

In this case *da Vinci* is the given information. In very informal speech the subject might be ellipted, and in more formal usage it might be replaced by an unaccented pronoun, thus *he PAINTed the mona LIsa.*

Exercise

Here are several more possible versions of B's reply: your job is to reconstruct the question that they answer. Some will answer the questions given above, but other questions are also involved. To make the examples clearer, capital letters are used only for accented syllables.

   (i)   da vinci PAINted the mona lisa.
  (ii)   da VINci did.
 (iii)   the MOna LIsa.
 (iv)   PAINted the mona LIsa.
  (v)   da vinci painted the MOna LIsa.
 (vi)   yes he DID.
(vii)   he PAINted it.
(viii)   yes THE mona lisa.
 (ix)   no da VINci painted the mona lisa.
  (x)   da VINci

It is sometimes claimed that anything can be accented in an English sentence. This is true, as long as you can think up a possible context in which it would occur.

Constants and variables

In the majority of cases grammar and accentuation work in co-operation: the items that are replaced by a pro-form or ellipsis are also the ones that would be deaccented. But on occasion grammar and accentuation move in different ways. Consider this odd sentence:

> It's not that ALan doesn't like KATE: she CAN'T STAND him.

She and *him* are recoverable information, referring back to Kate and Alan respectively; if they are deaccented, they leave *can't* and *stand* as onset and nucleus. But this would also indicate that they keep the same order, i.e. that *she* referred back to Alan, and *him* to Kate. In this case our example does not really make sense.

In fact, accentuation does not strictly depend on the distinction between given and new, but on whether the slot containing the item in question is CONSTANT or VARIABLE. A constant is an information slot which is not changed, modified or challenged in any way; a variable is a slot which is filled either with new information, or with given information which is changed, modified or challenged.

In our example, the subject slot is the first filled with *Alan* and this is changed to *she*: the subject slot is consequently a variable. Similarly the object is a variable, changing from *Kate* to *him*. The subject and object must therefore be accented, even though they are replaced by pronouns. On the other hand, we might say that the verb *doesn't like* means more or less the same as *can't stand*: the verb can thus be treated as a constant, and therefore unaccented. A more realistic version of our example sentence would be

> it's not that ALAN doesn't like KATE: SHE can't stand HIM.

Parallelism

A parallelism compares and contrasts words or phrases which have some items in common, but also vary at some point. The items in common are constants, and the item that varies is the variable. The constants are deaccented. For example

> A: i want a BLUE LIGHTbulb.
> B: sorry, we've ONLY got CLEAR ones.

Here *clear* (*lightbulbs*) parallels *blue lightbulb(s)*, and in the second case the accent falls on the variable *clear*, and the noun from the normal rule for constants and variables. The parallelism rule, however, has two interesting properties: first, it operates inside a word, and secondly a constant can be deaccented the first time it is mentioned.

The following examples are closely based on actual cases observed on radio and television. They are taken from interviews, and can be regarded as natural spontaneous speech:

> SOME of these unemployed teenagers are [unemploy]aBLE.
> The GOvernor is in effect the [govern]MENT.

On their own the final words of these sentences are of course pronounced *unemPLOYable, GOvernment*. But in the context they are paralleled with *unemployed* and *governor* respectively, so that *unemploy-* and *govern-* are constants: the accent is consequently shifted on to the syllable containing the variable. Taken out of context, these pronunciations are very odd indeed, but the kind of parallel context in which they occur is by no means uncommon in everyday speech. Given another example from a political speech:

> . . . . . . [employ]ERS' contriBUtions, ...

you can probably infer without any difficulty that the speaker must have been talking immediately before about [employ]EES.

For an illustration of the deaccentuation of a constant on its first mention, consider the way we conventionally begin jokes about an Englishman, and Irishman and a Scotsman:

> Well, there was an ENGlish [intelligence agent], an IRish
> . . .

This can only continue

> . . [intelligence agent], and a SCOttish [intelligence agent].

You might expect that in a joke about intelligence agents, the key phrase *intelligence agent* would be very important and therefore accented. The relevant fact is that *English intelligence agent* is paralleled with *Irish intelligence agent* and with *Scottish intelligence agent*, and this makes *intel-*

ligence agent a constant and therefore a candidate for deaccentuation. From the addressee's point of view, the deaccentuation of *intelligence agent* the first time it is mentioned is a clear indication that it is a constant in a parallelism, i.e. that more intelligence agents are going to be referred to. It would be very odd to start the joke

> Well, there was an ENGlish [intelligence agent], an IRish [priest], and a SCOttish [doctor].

This would absurdly suggest that intelligence agents, priests, and doctors were the same sort of thing. It might still be amusing, but for different reasons.

Exercise

The accentuation of English numerals varies in ways which might seem unpredictable until you understand what is going on. Account for the changing accentuation of the numeral in boldface in the following examples:

$8 + 6 = $ **14**   13, **14**, 15 . . .   4, **14**, 24, 34, . . .
$2 \times 12 = $ **24**   21, 22, 23, **24**, . . .   **24**, 34, 44, . . .

If you listen to broadcast football results, you can usually tell after hearing the first part whether it is a home win (i.e. the first team mentioned wins), an away win, or a draw. Make up a table of imaginary results, giving only the score for the home team, e.g.

Liverpool	1	Arsenal	??
Spurs	0	Everton	??

Read the results out to a partner, and see if he or she can guess the score for the away team. The interesting ones here are the draws: in what ways can we indicate in advance that the away team must have the same score as the home team?

Ellipsis

The ellipsis of a word or phrase can have an effect on grammatical words which would otherwise be attached to it.

Consider the kind of context in which they are reduced to
weak-forms:

auxiliary verb	+ infinitive:	that will do
auxiliary verb	+ past participle:	he has gone
auxiliary verb	+subject:	has everyone?
BE	+subject:	Who are you?
BE	+ complement:	I am the taxman
preposition	+ noun phrase:	to charity
conjunction	+ clause:	(he said) that she knew
article	+ noun phrase:	the doctor
title	+ name:	Saint Michael

In each case a word in the category to the left of the plus
sign can be reduced when followed by an accented item in
the category to the right. If there is no such item, then the
grammatical word cannot be reduced. Compare *I want to
go* and *I want to*. Before the infinitive *go, to* is reduced to
/tə/; but when *go* is missing, *to* must have its full form. That
is not to say that it is accented: it is both unaccented and
unreduced. The elliptical type might occur in the second of
the following cases:

A: What are you going for? B: (i) because i WANT to [go]
                                                (ii) because i WANT to [ ]

In B's first reply, *go* is deaccented as it is given in the question, and *to* is reduced immediately before it. In the second
case, where the infinitive *go* has been ellipted, *to* must retain
its full form /tu:/. The unreduced grammatical word is a
sign that something has been ellipted.

    In other cases, the grammatical word is unreduced
when for some reason it is placed after the word or phrase
it is expected to lead to. In *For whom?*, *for* is in the leading
position to *whom* and consequently reduced; but if *for* is
shifted to the end, i.e. *Who for?*, it is no longer leading, and
not reduced, thus /hu: fɔ:/. If normally leading grammatical
words are in final position, they have either been shifted,
or else something has been ellipted. This is the origin of the
textbook rule that weak-forms cannot be used finally. This
is perfectly true, but it does not identify the reason; and in
any case many non-final grammatical words cannot be
reduced either.

Exercise

In the following examples, decide which grammatical words are likely to be reduced, and which are not. If you can, give an explanation. Recover any items which have been ellipted.

  (i)   Has anyone got a box of matches? – Yes, I have.
 (ii)   You do not have to join, but I feel you ought to in fact.
(iii)   What was that you said it was, Angela?
(iv)   He is looking for a box to keep his tortoise in for the winter.
 (v)   What do you want to know where it comes from for?

Explain the following:
   If John was three and Mary /wəz tuː/, how old was Mary?
   If John was three, and Mary /woz tuː/, how old was Mary?

7.5 'Literary' verse

In the last chapter, we investigated the binary structure of popular verse. We now turn to 'literary' verse. A characteristic of much literary verse is that it has an apparent movement of its own, which can be described informally as going 'de-dum de-dum de-dum'. We have already called the corresponding pattern in binary verse the METRE. When you read literary verse aloud, you probably feel obliged to read according to the sense, and this creates a tension as the metre clashes with the rhythm of your reading.

    Now just because it would be extremely naive to read according to the metre, it does not follow that the metre should be ignored, or that we can pretend that it is not really there. When we describe the movement of literary verse, we have to take account both of the metre and of the rhythm of a sensible reading. Take for example these well-known lines from Shakespeare:

    Shall I compare thee to a summer's day? (Sonnet XVIII)
    To be, or not to be: that is the question. (*Hamlet*, III i 56)

You can probably 'feel' a metrical structure with five beats to the line:

shall I comPARE thee TO a SUmmer's DAY?
to BE or NOT to BE that IS the QUEstion.

When you read these lines, you probably remain aware of this metre, but you do not allow it to determine the way you recite the verse. These lines are rhythmically similar to

should i rePEAT it in aNOther WAY?
to DIET or NOT to diet: THAT is their PROblem.

and you may accordingly recite

shall i comPARE thee to a SUmmer's DAY?
to BE or NOT to be: THAT is the QUEstion.

Rhythm and metre are not necessarily fixed. The rhythm depends on your response to the sense. The reading suggested above puts three accents on the one line and four on the other, but you can doubtless think of a way of reading them with a different number of accents, or with the accents on different syllables. You can also vary the way you run words together, or separate them with pauses. Your recognition of the metre depends on your ability to make the syllables of the line conform to some kind of 'de-dum de-dum' pattern.

Feet

We need to be more explicit about the 'de-dum de-dum' or sometimes 'dum-de dum-de' pattern of the metre. 'Dum' represents a metrically strong syllable, the ICTUS, and 'de' a metrically weak syllable or syllables, the REMISS. Ictus and remiss together make up the metrical FOOT.

Several types of foot are recognized in traditional studies of metre, the main ones being the following:

IAMBIC: the iambic foot, or *iambus*, is of the form 'de-dum', with the remiss first and the ictus second.

TROCHAIC: the trochaic foot, or *trochee* /trouki:/, is the reverse of the iambus, and is of the form 'dum-de', with the ictus first and the remiss second.

ANAPAESTIC: the anapaestic /anəpestik/ foot, or *anapaest* /anəpi:st/, is like the iambus but has two syllables in the remiss, i.e. 'de-de-dum'.

DACTYLIC: the *dactyl* is the reverse of the anapaest, having two weak syllables in the remiss after the accented syllable, i.e. 'dum-de-de'.

There is obviously some connection between the foot and the accent group, and ictus corresponds to accent as remiss corresponds to leading and trailing syllables. Let us assume for the moment that feet match as accent groups exactly. In the iambus and anapaest, remiss syllables are in leading position, e.g. *alone, for me, her desire, to the skies.* Feet of this kind are described as having 'rising rhythm'. Trochaic and dactylic feet have trailing syllables in remiss, and 'falling rhythm', e.g. *seven, seen them, merrily, warned of it.* There is a long-standing controversy whether the true iambus is weak-strong or short-long; but this is not a real issue, as insofar as the foot matches the accent group, the iambus has a leading syllable (i.e. both short and weak) in the remiss and a long accented syllable in ictus position.

It is possible to find lines of English verse in which accent groups and metrical feet do make a perfect, or near-perfect, match of this kind. Here, for instance are two iambic lines from *Paradise Lost*.

> And swims or sinks, or wades, or creeps, or flyes: (II:950)
> Through wood, through waste, o're hil, o're dale his roam. (IV:538)

Apart from the pauses, these have a perfect 'de-dum de-dum' movement. This is very far from the norm in English verse, and is actually a very special effect. Note how each weak syllable is a leading syllable, and each ictus syllable is long and accented. Compare the trochaic metre of this line from *The Lady of Shalott*:

> Willows whiten, aspens quiver

where the syllables in remiss are trailing syllables, and follow fairly short accented syllables. However, much more typical of English verse as a whole is this stock example of an iambic line from Gray's *Elegy*:

> The curfew tolls the knell of parting day

If you intuitively divide this line up into phrases, and group the unaccented syllables as leading or trailing, as they would be according to the normal rhythmical rules of English, the divisions will be something like this:

the CURfew / TOLLS / the KNELL / of PARting / DAY

in which case not all the accented syllables (cf. the first and the fourth) are long, and not all weak syllables are short. You can of course read this with a strong 'de-dum de-dum' movement.

the CUR/few TOLLS / the KNELL / of PAR/ting DAY

with a regular short-long short-long pattern, but this is certainly not there 'in the text'. If you see this pattern in the line, that is because you yourself have supplied it. First, having read thousands of lines of English verse, you recognize this line as belonging to the 'iambic pentameter' type with five beats; and secondly, you have chosen to read it according to the metre rather than the sense.

To read 'according to the metre', you have to read the whole line without any internal grouping, and without removing any accents by the intermediate accent rule, or other accent suppression rules. These are the very conditions which we noted above for producing 'isochronous stress' in English as a whole: interestingly enough there is a traditional view in English metrics that a regular rhythm is what distinguishes the rhythm of verse from that of prose. The metre may be regular, but unless somebody reads according to the metre, the rhythm of the recitation is unlikely to be.

What we tentatively described above as 'rising rhythm' and 'falling rhythm', are strictly RISING METRE and FALLING METRE. In most cases the distinction is determined very simply by the first and last syllables of the line. If the first syllable is a leading syllable and the last syllable is accented, then the line as a whole has rising metre; if it begins with an accented syllable and ends with a trailing syllable, the line as a whole has falling metre. We can test this idea by rewriting some lines. Let us take the first two stanzas of *The Lady of Shalott*:

> On either side the river lie
> Long fields of barley and of rye,
> That clothe the wold and meet the sky;

> And thro' the field the road runs by
> > To many-tower'd Camelot;
> And up and down the people go,
> Gazing where the lilies blow
> Round an island there below,
> > The island of Shalott.
>
> Willows whiten, aspens quiver,
> Little breezes dusk and shiver
> Thro' the wave that runs for ever
> By the island in the river
> > Flowing down to Camelot.
> Four gray walls, and four gray towers,
> Overlook a space of flowers,
> And the silent isle imbowers
> > The Lady of Shalott.

In the first stanza, all lines except the second, seventh and eighth begin with a syllable that is unlikely to take the ictus, and all lines end with an accented syllable, or at least one that readily occupies the ictus position. As a result, the stanza is predominantly rising, and this effect carries over into the problematic lines, such as *Gazing where the lilies blow*, so that these also appear to be rising, but with a missing initial syllable. The second stanza is markedly different, having falling metre as a result of the lines which begin with an accented syllable, and end with a trailing one. (The lines ending /auəz/ are of course ambivalent: if /auə/ is treated as a triphthong, they end with the accented syllable, but if it is treated as a disyllabic sequence /awə/ then they end with the expected trailing syllable.) This effect so carefully constructed by Tennyson would be destroyed if we rewrote the initial lines of the stanzas:

> Either side the River Humber.
> Fields of barley without number, . . .
>
> The willows whiten, aspens quake,
> The little breezes dusk and shake . . .

The first pair of lines are now 'falling', and the second pair 'rising'.

When literary verse is recited, the rhythm is determined at least in part by the normal accentuation rules which you use to read any text aloud. At the same time, if you react to a text as metred verse, you will be aware of the metre as a simultaneous but distinct kind of organization. A tension is created as you read according to the sense, and avoid following the metre slavishly. If you get several people to read a piece of verse aloud, you can expect their readings to vary: some will follow the metre fairly closely, while others will give a freer rendering determined more by the general rules of speech rhythm.

This tension is important to make the verse interesting. If there is no tension, the verse becomes turgid, and very tiresome to read. Sixteenth-century dramatic verse can be monumentally dull for this reason, and here is an example from Norton and Sackville's *Gorboduc*, Act II. Accented syllables are capitalized, and unaccented syllables left in lower case; unaccented syllables in the ictus position are put in square brackets, and accented syllables in the remiss are put in parentheses.

> i SAW, mySELF, the GREAT prePARed STORE
> of HORSE, of ARmour, [and] of WEApon [there]:
> ne BRING i [to] my LORD rePORted TALES
> without the GROUND of SEEN and SEARched TRUTH.
> lo, SEcret QUArrels RUN aBOUT his COURT,
> to BRING the NAME of YOU, my LORD, in HATE.
> (EACH) MAN, al[most], can NOW deBATE the CAUSE,
> and ASK the REAson [of] so GREAT a WRONG,
> why HE, so NOble [and] so WISE a [prince],
> is, [as] unWORthy, REFT his HEri[tage],
> and WHY the KING, misLED by CRAFty MEANS,
> diVIded THUS his LAND from COURSE of RIGHT.

You may find a different way of reading this passage, but it is difficult to avoid accenting nearly every ictus, or to accent many of the syllables in remiss.

If you have occasion to comment on the movement of a line of literary verse, it may not be clear whether you should describe the rhythm or the metre. If you describe the rhythm, you miss the very aspect of the movement that makes it verse; and to describe the 'de-dum de-dum' of the metre seems just naive. In reality you do not need to make a choice: you need to describe both separately in order to explain what is going on. The danger is that by attempting to describe both at once, you will end up describing a no-man's-land between the two. Eighteenth-century metrists – such as Dr Johnson, in the section entitled *Prosody* at the beginning of his dictionary – were content to describe the metre. In the nineteenth century, perhaps because they were more sensitive to the rhythm of speech, metrists began to take more account of the way a line of verse would be read aloud. While this was a step in the right direction, it confused metre with rhythm, and the relationship between these two has remained a problem in metrics ever since.

Exercise

In his *Melody and Measure of Speech* (1775), Joshua Steele reports an exchange of letters between himself and Lord Monboddo discussing amongst other things the first line of *Paradise Lost*. Steele argued that 'to give the proper expression' the first line should be divided into cadences

| Of | man's | first diso|bedience | and the | fruit

The accented syllable is the first one in the cadence, immediately following the vertical line (|). Note that there is a gap at the beginning of the first and fifth cadences. This has come to be called the 'silent stress'. Steele argued that pentameters 'always require the time of six cadences at least', including pauses. Monboddo argues that 'the five accented syllables are, *man's, dis, be, and, fruit*.'
Who was right, if either?

To contrast rhythm and metre, you can choose a paragraph of *Paradise Lost* at random. Note the regular and relentless 'de-dum de-dum' of the metre (despite the considerable rhythmical variety there are actually only about half a dozen genuinely irregular lines in the whole poem). When you read it aloud, you may feel a constant struggle to keep away from the metre and read according to the sense.

CHAPTER 8

Intonation Structures

Long stretches of language are made up of smaller units. There is no agreed general term for these units, and we shall simply call them 'chunks'. On a superficial inspection, the chunks of language – phrases, accent groups, syllables, phonemes – might seem to be organized into a well-defined hierarchy, with chunks on one level being made up of chunks of the level below, much as an army is divided into brigades, battalions, companies and platoons. In practice, the status of each level is ill-defined with respect to the others, and there is considerable indeterminacy.

The sentence is generally assumed to be a clearly defined chunk which needs no further explanation. We shall base our explanation of intonation on the sentence at this point, and show how intonation is used to convey the internal structure of a sentence.

8.1 The sequence

By a 'sequence' we mean a set or list of items that are ordered in some way. A sentence can be seen as a sequence of phrases and clauses. Some items – such as forms of address, or time phrases – come more naturally at the beginning, while others, especially those which carry the main point or force of the sentence as a whole, come naturally at the end.

Very roughly, the 'force' of a sentence depends on whether it is a statement, a question or a command. If we examine the phrases and clauses in the sentence, we may find that one particular item carries the force of the sentence as a whole:

when I was \/ YOUR age, I was DOing my own \ WAshing.

\/ SUsan, WHERE do you keep your \ CUPS?

if you've \/ forGOtten it, BRING it \ toMOrrow.

The first is a statement, the second a question, and the third a command. In each case it is the second chunk that carries the force. The first chunk sets up the conditions which make it possible to convey the main or 'focal' chunk; e.g. a question is not effectively asked unless the addressee is identified first. The first chunk gives the background or context within which the second is to be interpreted, and may be a precondition for understanding the whole.

The final item has the fall in pitch that we have already introduced. There are several kinds of 'non-final' nucleus, one of which is the level nucleus. There are more elaborate types, and the phonetic forms of these vary from one dialect of English to another. The following description applies to the standard varieties, and some others, but probably not to Scots or Ulster English, or the speech of some English cities, including Liverpool and Newcastle. If this description does not seem to make sense for your kind of English, you should be able to identify corresponding 'non-final' nuclei that do the same sort of job.

Whereas the final nucleus has a 'hump' shape, a typical non-final nucleus takes the form of a 'trough': the pitch drops rapidly to a low level and then climbs back to more or less its previous level. This LOW RISE will be marked (/) at the beginning of the word; thus / toMOrrow indicates that the pitch drops between the first and second syllables, and then climbs up again over the second and third syllables. The hump and the trough can be combined to form the FALL-RISE (\/), which has the effect of forcing the item concerned on the addressee's attention. These contours are illustrated on page 167.

In writing, non-final items tend to be marked off by commas, as we have done in our examples above. Note that we have chosen to mark them intonationally with the fall-rise.

When items in the sentence are presented in the expected order, with the background first and the focal item last, non-final items have a rise or fall-rise in pitch, and the final item has a fall.

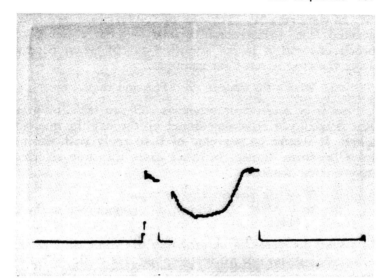

Pitch contour for *tomorrow* (low rise)

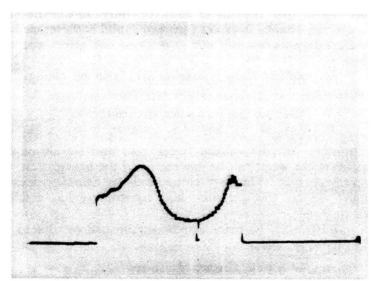

Pitch contour for *tomorrow* (fall-rise)

In the everyday exchange of conversation, we take for granted the background against which a sentence is produced, and it is not specified except when necessary. Take the case of time for example:

> A: What's for dinner?   B: Fish and chips.

Unless it is made clear otherwise, B can take for granted that A is enquiring about dinner on the day the question is asked. It would be perverse of B to reply with the menu for Christmas dinner. In other cases the time referred to may not be obvious:

> A: What are you thinking of doing?
> B: well, AFter $\diagdown\diagup$ DInner, i'm going down to the CAT and $\diagdown$ FIddle.

In asking his question, A probably has some time reference in mind, but has not made it explicit. He could be referring to 'this afternoon', 'today', 'during the summer vacation', or even 'when you've got your degree'. B is obliged to choose a time reference, and indicates it at the beginning of his reply. (Of course, B may be fully aware that A is enquiring about his career intentions, and is therefore being deliberately awkward; but that does not affect the issue here.)

An explicit time reference may also be changed, by narrowing down the previous reference:

> A: What are you doing this weekend?
> B: Well, on $\diagdown\diagup$ SAturday, i'm going to my $\diagdown$ MOther's.

'Saturday' is part of the 'weekend', and so although B answers the question, he has modified the background time reference first. The first chunk *well on Saturday* does not itself answer the question, and accordingly has a falling-rising tone.

References to place can be established or altered in a similar way, thus:

> A: What's the weather like there?
> B: well, in the $\diagdown\diagup$ DEsert of course, it's extremely $\diagdown$ HOT.

> A: What's it really like in the North of England?
> B: well, in $\diagdown\diagup$ LANcashire, we live in $\diagdown$ CAVES, you know.

Notice the use of *well* to introduce the time or place phrases, and assist the intonation in signalling the modified reference.

Other non-focal items include conditions, sentence adverbials, and the topic. Conditions are relatively straight forward:

if it's ⌄⁄ RAIning, put your ⟍ MAC on.
ifi'd've ⌄⁄ KNOWN she'd be there, i'd've stayed ⟍ aWAY.

(In the second example the sequence *if I'd've* is common enough in speech, but looks rather odd in writing as we do not allow two contractions to come together. In this particular case, the weak-forms cannot be expanded: both *if I had have* and *if I would have* are ungrammatical in English.)

Sentence adverbials give an indication of how the message is to be taken; in some cases they are little more than a hint of what is to come, and giving the addressee time to adjust:

A: How am I getting on?
B: ⌄⁄ FRANKly, you're wasting your ⟍ TIME.

A: Have my tickets arrived?
B: FORtunately for ⌄⁄ YOU, they ⟍ HAVE.

Related to sentence adverbials are reporting phrases containing verbs of saying and thinking:

he ⌄⁄ SAID he was going on ⟍ STRIKE.
she ⌄⁄ TOLD me that she'd ⟍ PAID for it.
i ⌄⁄ THINK there may be a bus in a ⟍ MInute.

The reporting phrase is highlighted by the fall-rise, and this raises the possibility that the report is not true.

The 'topic' is in many cases the subject of the sentence, but is more generally the point of departure, something the speaker intends to comment on:

the TROUble with ⌄⁄ YOU is that you're TOO ⟍ NOsey.

what ⌄⁄ I want to know is WHERE the ⟍ MOney's gone.

he ⌄⁄ sucCEEDS by TRAMPling on everyone ⟍ ELSE.

In these statements, the first chunk contains the less informative part of the sentence.

In many cases, the background item is an adverbial phrase or some kind of subordinate clause, and the focal item is the main clause. This is not, however, the case if the main clause is the topic:

> A: When did you start looking after yourself?
> B: well, i was DOing my own $\diagdown\diagup$ WAshing, when i was $\diagdown$ YOUR age.

Here the informing item is the time phrase *when I was your age*, and the main clause *I was doing my own washing* is modifying *looking after yourself.*

We have treated the sentence so far as a simple sequence of phrases or clauses. If you examine B's reply in our last example, you will see that it consists of one sentence, but contains within it *I was doing my own washing* and (less obviously) *I was your age* which look like 'sentences' in their own right. Intonation patterns in a similar way, indicating the structure of the smaller 'sentences' as well as the overall sentence. Although intonation rules are very simple, the intonation pattern of a complete sentence can be very complex owing to the 'nesting' of intonation structures in the overall structure.

8.2 Lists

A list of items – even two items joined by *and* – constitutes an independent structure inside the sentence. We have already looked at some lists, including *John and Margaret Hughes* and the menu in the first section of Chapter 7. To examine the intonation of lists, we shall first take lists out of context, and secondly remove any problems of meaning by deliberately choosing a banal list.

Let us therefore start with a list of vegetables. Items in the list can be linked by giving a level nucleus to all items except the last:

> $\rightarrow$ CAUliflower, $\rightarrow$ BROccoli, $\rightarrow$ CAbbage, $\rightarrow$ SPROUTS, and $\diagdown$ KALE

Each of these entries could be longer chunks with its own onset and nucleus, so here is a list of vegetable varieties:

ALL the year → ROUND, NINE star → peRENnial, MAY → exPRESS, PEER → GYNT, SCOTCH ⟍ CURLED.

A closed list ends with the final fall; an open lists ends with a 'non-final' signal to indicate that it is incomplete.

The list can be presented in this way if it is already formed in the mind of the speaker, and if the addressee can take it in rapidly. If the speaker has to think of each item in turn, or if the items are so unfamiliar that the addressee needs to take them one at a time and process them individually, then a looser connection is required, and more elaborate non-final markers, such as the rise and fall-rise, will be used:

    ⟋ CAUliflower, ⟋ BROccoli, ⟋CAbbage, and ⟍ KALE.

A complex list may contain sublists, e.g.:

    cabbage, kale, sprouts; peas, beans; carrots, parsnips, onions.

Each of these sublists is a sequence in its own right. In writing, the sublists can be marked off with semicolons, and the individual items with commas. If the low rise corresponds here to the comma, we need an even more elaborate marker to correspond to the semicolon, namely the fall-rise:

⟋ CAbbage	⟋ KALE	⟍⟋ SPRoutS
⟋ PEAS	⟍⟋ BEANS	
⟋ CArrots	⟋ PARsnips	⟍ Onions.

For a rather more interesting list, consider now the opening paragraph of *A Tale of Two Cities*:

It was the best of times, it was the worst of times, it was the age of wisdom, it was the age of foolishness, it was the epoch of belief, it was the epoch of incredulity, it was the season of Light, it was the season of Darkness, it was the spring of hope, it was the winter of despair, we had everything before us, we had nothing before us, we were all going direct to Heaven, we were all going direct the other way – in short, the period was so far like the present period, that some of its noisiest authorities insisted on its being received, for good or for evil, in the superlative degree of comparison only.

Here we have a list of clauses, the end of the list being marked with the dash. The crudest technique for reading it aloud would give the last clause a fall, and all the others a level or rising nucleus. But that would be to treat it as a list and nothing more, rather like a list of unconnected entries in a telephone directory. If you read it as a piece of prose, you will wish to bring out its internal structure, and since it is written in paired clauses, you might give the first clause of each pair a rise and the second a fall-rise. This would clearly indicate that each pair or list of clauses is a sublist of the whole list; but it would be a rather pedantic and 'heavy' reading. A third possibility would be to concentrate on the antithesis of the members of each pair, giving the first a rise and the second a fall; this would of course abandon any attempt to bring out the structure of the list as a whole. While you are mentally arranging the list structure, you might wish also to convey the fact, for example, that paired items are also paralleled, and this affects the position of the final accent in each item.

Note that the intonation rules can be manipulated in various ways to bring out the structure of the text. There is no one 'correct' version, but some versions are more pleasing than others. It is quite impossible to predict in detail exactly how a given speaker is going to read out a given text on a given occasion. When you discuss the rhythm and intonation of a written text, you can only identify some of the more likely possibilities, and choose what you consider the most desirable version. If you get someone else to read out a text for you, you can almost predict that he or she will produce a version that you would have never thought of.

Exercise

Get different people to read the Dickens extract aloud, preferably recording it. (If you record it, do not allow your readers to hear each other reading.) How do they tackle the list of antitheses? Do they use one of the three methods we have described, or do they do something quite different? Since the list is so long, it may become monotonous if the same method is used throughout; you may find, therefore, that some people start off with one technique and switch over to another half way through.

8.3 Stops and starts

In simple cases, the sentence consists of just a single sequence. Consider this example (which like the next few succeeding is taken from *A Christmas Carol*):

> During the whole of this time, Scrooge had acted like a man out of his wits.

The comma marks the end of the first chunk, the time phrase beginning with *during*. This chunk relates the sentence to the previous context, but does not actually present anything new: it is clearly background information, and you will probably give it a rise if you read it aloud. When you get to the comma, the sequence is unfinished, and you expect it to continue. Let us call the end of that first chunk a 'continuation point'. One way of reading the sentence might therefore be

> during the WHOLE of this ∕ TIME, SCROOGE had ∕ ACted like a MAN out of his ╲ WITS.

Compare this more complex example:

> He was about to speak; but with her head turned from him, she resumed.

This sentence contains two sequences, and the first chunk *he was about to speak* could stand as a complete sentence on its own. When I read the sentence aloud, I put a fall on *speak*, as though it were the actual end of the sentence:

> he was aBOUT to ╲ SPEAK; but with her HEAD turned ∕ FROM him, she ╲ reSUMED.

Let us call the end of the first sequence a 'stopping point'.

In some cases a sentence begins with a word or phrase that anticipates a following paired chunk. Some of these pairs are lists; e.g. a *not only* anticipates, a *but also*, a *both* anticipates an *and*, and an *either* anticipates an *or*. For example:

> He was not only very ill, but dying.

where the comma marks a continuation point, and the full stop the end of the sequence. Similarly, the word *so* may look forward to a clause beginning with *that*:

> The quarter was so long, that he was more than once convinced he must have sunk into a doze unconsciously, and missed the clock.

Without the word *so*, the first comma could end the sequence, even though it is early on in a fairly long sentence; in fact the first stopping point occurs at the second comma. Others markers of non-final chunks include subordinating conjunctions e.g. *while, although, because,* and prepositions, e.g. *in, on, over.*

When we read a written sentence aloud, we do much more than just recognize the words: we have to 'interpret the meaning'. We divide it into chunks, and have to convey the whole structure and its parts to the addressee. We may do this inefficiently and hesitate when we get temporarily lost in the text. If we have time to prepare, we can identify potential problems in interpretation, and look for ways of clarifying them. For example an ambiguous sentence might cause us to stumble at first; but having found the correct interpretation, we automatically chunk it so as to exclude the undesired interpretations. The relative lack of hesitation pauses in lectures or on stage is a good indication of a prepared script.

The distinction between background and focal information, and hence between stopping points and continuation points, is not given in the text, but has to be decided by the reader. In some sentences, chunks can be taken in different ways. Consider this further example from *A Christmas Carol*:

> The idea being an alarming one, he scrambled out of bed, and groped his way to the window.

The first comma marks a continuation point, as the first chunk cannot stand as a complete sequence; but the second comma can be interpreted in either way. It can be taken to mark a stopping point, with *he scrambled out of bed* being Scrooge's response to the alarming idea, and in this case *bed* is given a falling nucleus. On reconsideration, you might wish to treat scrambling out of bed and groping towards the window as a list of Scrooge's activities; in this case you would treat the second comma as marking a second continuation point. In order to decide between stopping points and continuation points, one has to scan ahead in the sentence.

The linking of items in sequences is made explicit in speech by rises and falls. The writer has to use grammatical and other means to indicate the relationship between parts of the sentence, and rises and falls in reading aloud reflect the reader's interpretation. Compare these alternative formulations of what might loosely be called the 'same sentence':

> If you do that, you'll get into trouble.
> DO ╱ THAT and you'll GET into ╲ TROUble.

> Although he's over 70, he's remarkably fit.
> he's Over ╲╱ SEventy and he's a reMARkably ╲ FIT.

> While we were going through the tunnel, we ran out of petrol.
> we were GOing through the ╲╱ TUnnel and we RAN out of ╲ PEtrol.

The first member of each pair is the kind of sentence we expect to see written down: it is the more formal, 'prose' version, in which the relationship between the parts of the sentence is made explicit. The words *if, although, while* indicate 'this is the beginning of a non-final chunk', and the comma indicates the end of the chunk. Structures of this kind are described as 'hypotactic'. In the second 'conversational' version, the two chunks of the sentence are simply joined by *and*; this type is called 'paratactic'. The intonation signals that the first chunk ends at a continuation point, and the addressee is left to work out, by examining the sentence as a whole, that *and* is an informal stand-in for *if, although, while*, or some other grammatical word.

Of course, the 'prose' version can also be used in speech, particularly in formal usage (and may be the impression of speech generally given in novels and plays). The conversational version can also be written down, particularly in informal writing. Children naturally use this form when they learn to write creatively; we acquire the formal machinery of prose writing slowly over a long period of time. The 'prose' versions have to be composed more carefully, but they provide clearer signposts to the interpretation; the 'conversational' versions are easier to write, but they leave the reader more work to do in finding the intended interpretation.

A distinction has traditionally been made between a 'periodic' sentence, and a 'loose' sentence. A 'periodic' sentence is usually defined as a sentence in which the sense is not complete until the end of the sentence. This is not a very good definition, since it is true of all sentences. (What would be the nature of a chunk that came between the end of the 'sense' and the full stop?) It is more likely that a 'periodic' sentence is one that avoids internal stopping points; such 'continuously continuative' sentences are characteristic of literary prose. A 'loose' sentence may contain several stopping points, and this gives the language a 'conversational' flavour.

Exercise

Study this example of Dr Johnson's prose, taken from *Lives of the Poets*. Are the breaks between chunks stopping points or continuation points? How does this affect the way you would read this kind of prose aloud, if you were called upon to do so?

> "His prose is a model of the middle style; on grave subjects not formal, on light occasions not grovelling; pure without scrupulosity, and exact without apparent elaboration; always equable, and always easy, without glowing words or pointed sentences . . . What he attempted he performed; he is never feeble, and he did not wish to be energetic; he is never rapid, and he never stagnates. His sentences have neither studied amplitude, nor affected brevity; his periods, though not diligently rounded, are voluble and easy. Whoever wishes to attain an English style, familiar but not coarse, and eloquent but not ostentatious, must give his days and nights to the volumes of Addison."

You can expect to find cases which are simultaneously stopping points at the end of a list, and continuation points in a grammatical structure. How do you resolve the problem in reading aloud?

8.4 Punctuation

The efficiency with which chunks are marked off differs for speech and writing. In writing, we mark off clearly the larger sections of text, such as sentences, paragraphs, sections and chapters; but at levels intermediate between sentence and word, we use punctuation marks sparingly and in a rather inconsistent way to identify just some of the chunks. On the other hand, we consistently use spaces to separate words. In speech we can mark the beginning of a big new chunk, but whether this is a sentence or a paragraph or a chapter is left vague; we do not usually mark off individual words, and we certainly do not leave a gap or pause between them. On the other hand we do tend to give a detailed indication of internal structures intermediate between sentence and accent group. The marking of chunks is thus efficient in speech where it is inefficient in writing, and vice versa. As a rule of thumb, when we read a written passage aloud, we are likely to use spoken boundaries corresponding to punctuation marks, and we have to decide where other, additional boundaries should be placed.

At the level of the sentence and below, written chunks are marked off by punctuation marks, including the comma, semicolon and full stop or 'period'. To any literate person, the use of these marks is all but self-evident, but nevertheless it is difficult to explain exactly what kind of chunk they identify. Perhaps this is why one of the traditional ways of teaching people to punctuate correctly is by examining cases of faulty punctuation.

Exercise

The idea behind this exercise was originally devised over four hundred years ago by the schoolmaster Nicholas Udall, presumably to impress on his pupils the importance of punctuation. The passage is taken from his comedy *Ralph Roister Doister* (III, iv), and is an extract from a letter from Ralph to a widow, Dame Christian Cunstance, proposing marriage:

> "Sweet mistress, where as I love you nothing at all,
> Regarding your substance and richesse chief of all,

For your personage, beauty, demeanour and wit,
I commend me unto you never a whit.
Sorry to hear report of your good welfare,
For (as I hear say) such your conditions are,
That ye be worthy favour of no living man,
To be abhorred of every honest man.
To be taken for a woman inclined to vice.
Nothing at all to virtue giving her due price.
Wherefore, concerning marriage, ye are thought
Such a fine paragon, as ne'er honest man bought.
And now by these presents I do you advertise
That I am minded to marry you in no wise. . . ."

First read the passage aloud in the manner indicated by the punctuation. Then read it again, this time to convey the meaning that Ralph presumably intended. How would you punctuate the passage to indicate this second reading? Udall's own solution is given in scene v (note that if you consult a reliable edition, you can expect to find Elizabethan punctuation conventions here, which look rather odd if you are not familiar with them). You may find the passage rather corny, but Udall certainly makes his point and at length!

This passage is also rather useful to give an idea of the connection between written and spoken chunking. When you read it aloud, how do you indicate the boundaries between chunks? Do you mark off any chunks in speech that are not marked by punctuation in the written form?

In the history of writing, punctuation is of relatively recent introduction. Before the seventeenth century, the chunks marked off by punctuation were assumed to be modelled on the chunks of the spoken language, so that the punctuation suggested the oral delivery. From this period we find attempts to relate punctuation marks to lengths of pause, e.g. the claim that the speaker pauses longer at a colon that at a comma. Thus James Gough in *A Practical Grammar of the English Tongue* (1754):

The Stops or Pauses are Four, viz. Comma, marked (,)
Semicolon (;) Colon (:) Period, or full stop (.)
At a Comma, the Reader should pause while he can privately tell One; at a Semicolon, Two; at a Colon, Three; and at a Period, Four.

Such ideas were never very realistic, but nevertheless they survived long after the marks were given their modern roles. Note that in Gough's second sentence the semicolons in practice mark off the bigger chunks, and the commas the smaller ones.

The role of punctuation as it has developed is not to guide the reader on oral delivery, but to help the reader understand the sentence by marking the main chunks. Once you understand a written sentence, you automatically read it with the correct intonation, pausing and groupings of words. However, a competent reader is able to chunk quite long sentences by just reading the words, and punctuation marks are not really necessary. If you read an older text, e.g. from the seventeenth century, with the original punctuation, you may find your eye coming to rest on commas which mark the end of grammatical chunks which you could perfectly well have identified unaided; far from helping, these redundant marks are merely a nuisance. If we used a punctuation mark corresponding to every chunk boundary in speech, the eye would be constantly interrupted as it scanned the line of print.

In modern usage, heavy punctuation with non-essential marks is considered rather fussy. We still use some rather redundant marks by convention, e.g. to mark off the items in a list like *tall, dark, and handsome*; there is even a 'school' rule that bans the comma before the *and* at the end of the list, but requires it elsewhere. Apart from such strange relics, we put in punctuation marks to prevent the reader from chunking incorrectly, and misinterpreting the sentence. One obvious use is to clarify potentially ambiguous stretches. For instance, here is an extract from a newspaper, reproduced as printed:

> A hundred and twenty years on the Red Cross emblem means many thing (sic) to many people but to all of them it spells hope and practical help.

The beginning of this sentence is ambiguous owing to the lack of punctuation. Is the first chunk *a hundred and twenty years on, a hundred and twenty years on the Red Cross*, or even *a hundred and twenty years on the Red Cross emblem*? By the time you reach the full stop, the structure is presumably quite clear; but if the job had been done properly, there would have been no ambiguity in the first place. If you were reading the sentence aloud, e.g. to disambiguate it for someone else, you would put a rhythmical break after *on* to indicate the end of the first chunk.

Some of the odder prescriptive conventions of English punctuation actually prohibit a comma at a point where a boundary signal is virtually essential in speech. Take for example the following sentence:

> But the vast majority of people in this country, are deeply opposed to violence for political ends.

The subject of the sentence, *the vast majority of people in this country*, is so long that in speech we are likely to mark it off as a chunk on its own. In writing, however, a comma would offend against the convention that a subject must not be separated from its predicate. Similarly, in

> Some people prefer, polyunsaturated margarine.

the phrase *polyunsaturated margarine* might well be marked off in speech as a chunk, but to put a comma after *prefer* would offend against the convention that prohibits commas between verb and object. Even if you were not previously aware of the prescriptive conventions, you will probably agree that the punctuation of these examples looks odd.

8.5 Chunks of verse

In our discussion of the rhythm of verse, we found that metred verse has a kind of organization in addition to that found in ordinary language. Verse may also have its own kind of chunking: verse is typically divided into lines of relatively similar length, and lines may be grouped into couplets and stanzas. In extreme cases, such as the sonnet, the whole poem is composed in a predetermined format.

Lines of verse are conventionally classified according to the number of ictuses or 'beats':

2:	dimeter	3:	trimeter	4:	tetrameter
5:	pentameter	6:	hexameter	7:	heptameter

these 'beats' refer to course to the metre, and not to the rhythm of a recitation. As we have already seen (Chapter

7, section 5), a pentameter can have a variable number of accents when read aloud.

The line of verse may appear to be a very simple structure, but this is deceptive. It is a metrical chunk, and the boundaries between chunks in recitation may not correspond to the metrical lines.

Endstopping and enjambment

Lines may be composed to fit a pre-arranged format. Take for instance the opening of the second of Wordsworth's *Lucy* poems:

> She dwelt among the untrodden ways
> Beside the springs of Dove,
> A Maid whom there were none to praise
> And very few to love:

The stanza is divided into two grammatical chunks which fit neatly into two lines each, and each of these is subdivided into two chunks which fit neatly into the lines. The first line of each pair is a tetrameter, and the second a trimeter. Although the chunks which make up the lines are similar to the chunks of prose and speech, the way these chunks fit together is rather special. If the lines are recast as prose with the same grammatical structure, they would turn out something like this:

> A maid whom there were none to praise and very few to love dwelt among the untrodden ways beside the springs of Dove.

We have of course tidied it up a bit by deleting the word *she*. Note how this is a single sequence; the chunks all end at continuation points, and there is no suitable candidate for a fall in pitch before the end. In the original version, some 'non-final' chunks are postponed until after the expected 'final' chunk. The chunks are made to fit the lines, but this is not like prose since the poet has abandoned the normal conventions for ordering items in the sequence.

Compare the effect of the opening lines of Brooke's *The Soldier*:

> If I should die, think only this of me:
> That there's some corner of a foreign field

> That is for ever England. There shall be
> In that rich earth a richer dust conceal'd:

In this case the order of items in the sentence is more like prose, but the chunks do not fit the lines exactly. The lines all end at some kind of chunk boundary, but the most important boundary, the end of the first sentence, falls in the middle of the third line. This break in mid-line is the CAESURA. The third line also ends at a minor boundary. Lines which end at a major boundary are described as END-STOPPED, while those ending at a minor boundary are RUN ON lines; the effect of running on is called ENJAMBMENT.

It would be mistaken to think of end-stopping and enjambment as discrete categories: lines are more or less run on, depending on the relationship between the breaks at the caesura and the end of the line. The enjambments here are very mild, as the lines do at least end at phrase boundaries. The effect is more startling if the line division breaks up a lower level unit such as an accent group, as happens in Miranda's first speech (*The Tempest*, I iv):

> If by your art, my dearest father, you have
> Put the wild waters in this roar, allay them.

where the weak syllable *have* is separated from the accented syllable *put*.

The tension created between the lack of fit between the chunks and the verse structure is usually resolved at a higher level of organization. Often this is the couplet; there are several examples of this in Keats's *Ode on a Grecian Urn*:

> Sylvan historian, who canst thus express
> A flowery tale more sweetly than our rhyme:

> Heard melodies are sweet, but those unheard
> Are sweeter; therefore, ye soft pipes, play on:

While the enjambment may blur the individual line, it highlights the division of the stanza into couplets. In *The Windhover*, Hopkins uses enjambment to bind a whole stanza together:

> I CAUGHT this morning morning's minion, king-
>   dom of daylight's dauphin, dapple-dawn-drawn Falcon, in
>   his riding
>   Of the rolling level underneath him steady air, and striding

High there, how he rung upon the rein of a wimpling wing
In his ecstasy! then off, off forth on swing,
    As a skate's heel sweeps smooth on a bow-bend: the hurl
      and gliding
    Rebuffed the big wind. My heart in hiding
Stirred for a bird, – the achieve of, the mastery of the thing!

Note how the first line ends actually in the middle of a
word. Hopkins takes enjambment even further than this,
and in *The Loss of the Eurydice* mismatches larger chunks
with the stanza division:

The Eurydice – it concerned thee, O Lord:
Three hundred souls, O alas! on board,
Some asleep unawakened, all un-
warned, eleven fathoms fallen

Where she foundered! One stroke
Felled and furled them, the hearts of oak!
And flockbells off the aerial
Downs' firefalls beat to the burial

Lines 3 to 6 form a chunk straddling the stanza division, and
this is reinforced by the enjambment splitting the phrase
'fallen where she foundered'.

Exercise

The following two poems by Milton are 'Petrarchan'
sonnets, that is, they are divided into a group of eight lines
– the 'octave' – and a group of six lines, the 'sestet'. The
octave is subdivided into quatrains.

How soon hath Time the suttle theef of youth,
Stoln on his wing my three and twentith yeer!
My hasting dayes flie on with full career,
But my late spring no bud or blossom shew'th.
Perhaps my semblance might deceive the truth,
That I to manhood am arrived so near,
And inward ripenes doth much less appear,
That som more timely-happy spirits indu'th.
Yet be it less or more, or soon or slow,
It shall be still in strictest measure eev'n,
To that same lot, however mean, or high,
Toward which Time leads me, and the will of Heav'n;
All is, if I have grace to use it so,
As ever in my great task Masters eye.

                  (Sonnet 7)

When I consider how my light is spent,
E're half my days, in this dark world and wide,
And that one Talent which is death to hide,
Lodg'd with me useless, though my Soul more bent
To serve therewith my Maker, and present
My true account, least he returning chide,
Doth God exact day-labour, light deny'd,
I fondly ask; But patience to prevent
That murmur, soon replies, God doth not need
Either man's work or his own gifts, who best
Bear his milde yoak, they serve him best, his State
Is Kingly. Thousands at his bidding speed
And post o're Land and Ocean without rest:
They also serve who only stand and waite.

(Sonnet 19)

Compare the way the chunks of the text fit into the verse structure in the two sonnets:

(i) Do you think that, from the point of view of meaning, they divide naturally into a group of eight lines and a group of six?

(ii) How closely do the 'chunks' of the sentences match the lines? Are the lines end-stopped or run on? Where are the most important breaks: at the end of the line or at the caesura?

(iii) How closely does the rhythm match the metre when you read the poems aloud? Do you find yourself accenting all and only the syllables with ictus? Or is there a tension between rhythm and metre?

You might also like to consider whether Milton is simply playing games with his reader, or whether the relationship he establishes between text and verse structure has some artistic purpose.

Note the 'periodic' structures of Sonnet 19: in his prose Milton composed enormous sentences of three hundred or more words with no internal stopping points.

CHAPTER 9

Colloquial Intonation

Up to now, whenever we have referred to 'spoken English', it has made relatively little difference whether we examined spontaneous speech or written English read aloud. In reality we have concentrated on reading aloud, and paid scant attention to extempore speech. Whenever we are dealing with a text longer than a short phrase, the distinction is an important one. Different processes are involved in speaking and reciting, and these are reflected in the phonetic form of the text. You can usually tell whether the speaker is talking spontaneously, or reciting a prepared script. In spontaneous speech, the speaker has to think and prepare what to say next, and a large proportion of 'speaking time' is actually silence. Actors are expected to read written language aloud as though it were being delivered spontaneously, and in fact they have an almost impossible job. Owing to stage conventions, it is possible to recognize acting as a third category, alongside spontaneous speech and reading aloud.

9.1 Chunks of speech and writing

In spontaneous speech we compose the text in small chunks, a few words at a time, and have to build up a sentence or a larger text which makes sense to the addressee. Pauses may be put in at chunk boundaries, to allow the addressee to catch up, and they are also inserted when the speaker hesitates to plan what to say next. Hesitation pauses are filled with *er, erm*, or a phrase such as *you know, sort of*. Because speech is judged by the standards of the written language, pause fillers like these tend to be condemned by people who do not understand why they are there. A skilled speaker will make use of some or all chunking pauses to plan ahead.

Our expectations of what sentences and longer chunks of language are like are based on the forms of the written language. This is understandable, since we are much more familiar with long written documents than with accurate transcripts of conversations or extempore speeches. The larger chunks of writing are composed at the writer's own speed, and can be edited and redrafted as often as required before they appear in print. Transcribed speech may look bizarre, inarticulate and incompetent in comparison. Consider this example:

> When I was in er . . . first called up, we were erm . . . very cold, you know, it was in February, and we had to erm . . . I think I went to Margate at first, you know, very cold there . . . marching up and down the prom, you know, and sort of erm . . . and I had terrible neuralgia, because it was so cold, so I had to have tablets for that . . .

The speaker is an intelligent and articulate woman, talking in an informal conversational style, which is quite normal and unremarkable. She is composing and speaking at the same time, and hesitates to think what to say next. When she decides to reformulate a phrase or clause, it is too late to discard the previous draft, as it has already been uttered. As addressee, we know intuitively what to discard, but when these bits of earlier drafts are written down they look decidedly odd. Language delivered in this way with hesitation pauses and false starts is actually easy to understand, because this is what we are used to in conversation.

To make a more realistic comparison of transcribed speech with written language, we must first edit it, by removing the pause fillers and false starts, and by marking the rises and falls:

> WHEN i was \/ FIRST called up, we were VEry \ COLD. it was in \ FEbruary. i think i went to \ MARgate at / FIRST. VEry \ COLD there, marching up and down the / PROM. and i had TErrible \ neuRALgia, because it was so / COLD. so i HAD to have \ TABlets for \/ THAT.

The units which are here marked off with full stops are examples of the structures which we have simply called 'sequences'. They differ from the sequences we have examined so far in that some of them end with a rise, apparently marking a 'non-final' item, while the apparently 'final' fall comes in the middle. This is a problem to which we shall return later. These sequences do not look quite like sentences of the written language, but are probably the nearest analogue in speech to written sentences.

In view of the way it is composed in advance and then edited, a written text is likely to be more concise, expressing the meaning in fewer and more complex words than spontaneous speech. For this reason, a written text that is read aloud can be difficult to follow unless it is delivered slowly.

Exercise

Redraft the passage above as a piece of written language. What can be left out in the final version? What is the minimum number of words needed to convey the meaning? Compare the chunks and pausing places in your version with those of the original.

9.2 Phrase order

In our discussion of the sequence in the last chapter, we assumed that the phrases and clauses of the sentence were ordered in a particular way. The rule that assigns non-final rises and a final fall operates when, and only when, the items are in this expected order.

While this may also be the preferred ordering, at least in written English, there are occasions when it is difficult to reconcile with the requirements of English grammar. Consider the following unlikely exchange:

A: I'm looking for Mrs Johnson.
B: oh, mrs \/ JOHNson has just been \ SEEN by me.

The common topic *Mrs Johnson* is placed in its expected position at the beginning here, but it is very awkward as the subject of the passive construction. Speakers prefer to refer to their own actions as *I did X* rather than *X was done by me*. An alternative with the topic at the beginning of an active construction is just as awkward:

> oh, mrs \/ JOHNson i've just \ SEEN.

A much more natural response would be

> oh, i've just \ SEEN mrs / JOHNson.

This reverses the expected order, and postpones the topic until after the item with the fall. Note that when postponed, it takes its rising nucleus with it.

There is another common use of this 'fall-plus-rise' pattern in conversation. The speaker may wish to get to the point immediately, and postpone background items to the end. Most of the examples discussed in the last chapter can be reordered in this way:

> i'm GOing to my \ MOther's on / SAturday.
> it's PRObably quite \ HOT in the / DEsert.
> put your \ MAC on if it's / RAIning.
> you're WASting your \ TIME / FRANKly.
> he was GOing on \ STRIKE he / SAID.

The only exception seems to be in the case of the vocatives, in which case the postponed item is unaccented:

> the \ BOSS wants to see you, mr robinson.

Because the relationship of the phrases is marked by intonation, there is a choice of order in spoken language. Of course both types can be written down. For instance, suppose that you read the sentence

> I'm going to my mother's on Saturday.

and suppose that the time reference 'Saturday' or 'the weekend' has already been mentioned. It would not make sense to assume that the purpose of saying the sentence was to give the time reference *on Saturday*. If it makes better sense to assume that the main information is contained in *I'm going to my mother's,* you might well read the sentence aloud with a fall on *MOther's* and a rise on *SAturday*.

> i'm GOing to my \ MOther's on / SAturday.

In a sentence like this the reader has a lot of work to do, and this sort of writing would be classed as chatty or conversational.

The general principle of phrase ordering, which puts background information at the beginning of the sentence, and marked off from the main piece of information with some kind of 'non-final' signal, is one that is found in many languages beside English. The alternative ordering, with the background information postponed, is also found in other languages. However, the retention of the 'non-final' pitch movement on the postponed item – common as it is in colloquial English – is not generally found in other languages, and the resulting fall-plus-rise contour may be peculiar to English.

9.3 Meaning and force

The way a sentence is intended to be interpreted does not necessarily correspond to its face value. For instance, the sentence *Your coat is on the floor* is superficially a statement of fact, identifying where the object in question is to be found. In response to the direct question *Where's my coat?* it could be interpreted as nothing more than a statement. However, if it were spoken by a parent to a child, the parent would probably intend the child to pick the coat up. Although it is presented as a statement, its force is that of an instruction. Intonation is often assumed to indicate the force of an utterance, and to do so directly. This is only partly true; intonation is one of several factors that together indicate force, and has the special role of hinting at how directly the message should be interpreted.

The assumption that intonation has a primary role in indicating force arises not from the study of real data, but the kind of stereotypes that suggest themselves if we sit and think about intonation. Among these stereotypes are the claims that statements and commands have falling nuclei, as in B's replies in

A: What is your name? B: JOHN ⟍ SMITH
A: How old are you? B: TWENty ⟍ SEven

and the command issued by a teacher to pupils

HAND it in by ⟍ FRIday.

In the case of questions, we have to distinguish WH-QUESTIONS, i.e. those beginning with a word with initial

wh such as *who, when, where* or a phrase such as *what on earth*, and YES/NO QUESTIONS, i.e. those that can be answered *yes* or *no*. WH-questions are said to have the fall, e.g.

> WHERE have you ↘ BEEN?
> WHAT's the ↘ TIME?

and yes/no questions the rise, thus

> would you LIKE some ↗ COffee?

These stereotypes intuitively make sense to people when they are brought to their attention. They also have the advantage that the corresponding patterns can be found in other languages, so that such examples can actually be 'translated' complete with their intonation. They have the disadvantage that if tested against natural spontaneous speech, they are found not to work very well.

In order to identify the true role of intonation here, we have to examine the relationship between what speakers actually say, and what they intend the addressee to infer. A question such as

> When are you leaving?

could be a genuine enquiry about the addressee's intentions, and in this case the fall is appropriate, thus

> WHEN are you ↘ LEAving?

However it could also be a pseudo-polite way of saying 'I wish you would go'. In order to indicate that a more indirect interpretation is required, a final rise may be used, thus

> WHEN are you ↗ LEAving?

The words of this example indicate a question, but the rise suggests 'this is only background, and incidental to what I am really saying'. The addressee is left to work out the full intention behind the utterance. The rise does not give any indication of what interpretation is intended, but merely how to tackle the problem of interpretation.

Although the overall intention behind this example may be rather rude, the speaker is nevertheless helping in a way with the problem of interpretation by using the rise. He could use the fall, giving no indication of the true intention, in which case it might take the addressee a bit longer to work out that an indirect interpretation is intended. The use of the rise narrows down the set of possible interpretations by excluding the most direct one.

Sentences which on the surface merely convey information may in practice intend the addressee to act upon the information received. For instance

Dinner's ready.

is unlikely to be simply giving information about dinner: it commonly carries the covert instruction 'come and get it'. While the fall on

↘ DInner's ready.

will do the job adequately, the desired interpretation is made much clearer by the fall-rise

↘↗ DInner's ready.

Similarly, if a child is climbing up the furniture and is told

you'll ↘↗ FALL.

the fall-rise makes clear that the message is more than a prediction about the future, and it leads towards the interpretation 'get down'. The person who enters the kitchen and exclaims

those ↘↗ CAKES smell nice.

is not reporting an olfactory response, but is almost certainly hinting 'I'd like one'. The fall-rise in these examples does not carry any 'meaning' of its own, but guides the addressee to the intended interpretation: he or she is expected to take some kind of action in response to the information given.

In the case of commands, the rise can be used for politeness. The imperative command, such as

Go away.
Eat your dinner.

presupposes that the speaker is in a position of authority to issue the command in the first place, and that he or she is exercising that authority. The use of the rise in

GO ↗ aWAY
EAT your ↗ DInner

with the indication 'don't interpret this at its face value' may have the effect of downtoning the command. Of course, if there is no possible interpretation other than as a command, the use of the rise can be seen to be not genuine and therefore possibly patronizing.

In other cases commands would be rather odd if taken strictly at their face value. The carrying out of a command can be taken to be in the interests of the speaker, and contrary to the interests of the addressee. There is therefore something anomalous in the 'commands'

> Have a good time.
> Enjoy yourself.

and the rise or fall-rise is appropriate here:

> HAVE a good ∕ TIME.
> ∨∕ enJOY yourself.

A student knocking on a lecturer's door is thereby seeking permission to enter: it would be very odd in such circumstances to issue a command to enter! The rise or fall-rise on

> come ∕ IN,
> come ∨∕ IN

indicates that it is not to be taken as a command, but as something more like an invitation.

A command also presupposes that the addressee is not already doing what is commanded. There is something anomalous in telling someone who is already hurrying to hurry up. Instructions like

> GET a ∕ MOVE on
> HUrry ∕ UP

typically end with the rise. Into this same category come negative commands. A written notice standing in a lawn reading

> DO NOT WALK ON THE GRASS

is a true prohibition, preventing the action before it starts. Prohibitions are spoken with falls, thus

> DO not ↘ overTAKE.
> DO not collect two hundred ↘ POUNDS.

The negative command

Don't walk on the grass.

on the other hand, is likely to be issued when the addressee has actually already started walking on it: if the command were to be taken at its face value, there would in advance be no possibility whatever of its being obeyed. Negative commands tend to have rises, e.g.

DON'T walk on the ∕GRASS.

We noted above in the discussion of intonation stereo-types that yes/no questions are particularly associated with rises. The reason for this may have less to do with their illocutionary force than with the way we use sentences of this kind. On the surface, a yes/no question asks whether a piece of information is true or false. But it is difficult to think up a yes/no question that does nothing beyond that. We nearly always have an ulterior reason for asking the question, and therefore a reason for using the rise. Thus

Have you got a light?

is a request, and

Do you like ice-cream?

is probably an invitation. On the other hand, in questions which present alternatives, e.g.

Do you want some or not?
Is it a boy or a girl?

the alternatives actually form a list, and so the final item takes the expected fall.

9.4 Social rituals

By 'social rituals' we refer to such acts as apologizing and thanking. These can on occasion be acts which are meant to be taken seriously. For instance, someone who knocks a little old lady over in the street is expected to make a proper apology, and someone who receives a birthday present is expected to make a sincere expression of grati-tude. But these are exceptions rather than the norm in the

way we use *sorry* or *thank you*. More commonly we apologize for some utterly trivial impoliteness in order to avoid
giving offence to the other party; or we thank the other
party out of politeness for some utterly trivial service. To
indicate that these ritual acts are not to be taken seriously,
we can give them a final rise.

In such cases, if the speaker uses the fall, the addressee
has the job of deciding whether the expression should be
taken seriously at face value, or as a mere ritual act. If the
rise is used, it must be the latter. Since it is relatively rarely
the case that the expressions used in these rituals are to be
taken at face value, the use of the rise is very common.

Apologies

A serious apology can be expected to fall at the end, e.g.

> i'm ＼ SORRY.
> i'm TErribly ＼ SOrry.

The rising

> ＼／ SOrry.
> ／ SOrry.

is more likely to be interpreted as a mere politeness. A
polite formula such as

> i DON'T want to make a ＼／ NUIsance of myself, . . .
> i DON'T wish to ＼／ inTRUDE, ...

are ways of making a nuisance of oneself or of intruding
without giving offence.

In other circumstances, e.g.

> ＼／ SOrry, we're ＼ CLOSED.

the rising *sorry* amounts to a polite refusal.

Apologies of a kind are also used to ask for a repeat
in a conversation. The expression

> i BEG your ＼ PARdon.

with a fall, and taken at its face value, is a serious apology.
Of course if this is inappropriate it will be assumed to be
ironic, and could be interpreted as a demand for an apology.
The more common use as a request for a repeat has the rise,

> i BEG your ／ PARdon.

or simply

    ↗ PARdon.

The expression ↗ SOrry can of course also be used in this way.

Thanking

Here we have to distinguish the expression of gratitude for the gift of goods or services on the one hand, from the routine recognition of a minor service on the other. Genuine gratitude requires the fall, thus

    ↘ THANK you.

whereas the rising

    ↗ THANK you.

excludes gratitude as an interpretation. Thus to use the rise on receipt of a birthday present merely recognizes the service of handing it over. The falling type used in circumstances where it is manifestly inappropriate – e.g. to someone who has just sneezed over your dinner – is likely to be taken as ironic, and therefore offensive.

    We would normally expect the meaning of the words used to be compatible with the intonation used. Sometimes they clash, e.g.

    thanks EVer so ∨↗ MUCH.

in which the words suggest effusive gratitude, whereas the intonation indicates that the phrase is being used as a gesture of politeness. In such cases, the addressee is likely to interpret the whole according to the intonation, and disregard the wording. For instance, you may hear shopkeepers saying

    THANK you very ↗ MUCH.

as a matter of routine when taking money from customers: the customer might feel that the shopkeeper ought to be grateful, but that is not necessarily quite what is meant.

    Other equivalent phrases, such as *thanks* or *ta* pattern in the same way as *thank you*. An exception to this is the use of *cheers*. Formerly this was a drinking expression, the

English equivalent of 'prosit', but it has come to be used by young people to mean 'thank you'. This *cheers* only takes the falling pattern; it cannot (yet?) be given the rise.

Greetings

When we say *good morning,* it is rarely the case that we are expressing the wish that the other person will have a good morning. We are more likely to be merely recognizing the reappearance of a familiar face. In most cases, therefore, the rise will be appropriate, thus

> ╱ MORning.

The falling type has a variety of interpretations. It might be used to a superior, or it might be used to start a conversation.

The word *hello*, in origin a call for attention, usually has some kind of rise, thus

> ╱ heLLO.
> ╲╱ heLLO.

If it is given a fall, a more serious interpretation is looked for; you might say

> ╲ heLLO.

when introduced to somebody, or when meeting someone you know, e.g.

> ╲ heLLO, ╱ ALan.

In the case of farewells, a falling

> good ╲ BYE.

is dramatic and final, and conveys a force similar to 'adieu'. It could almost be taken to carry its etymological meaning 'God be with you'. And in addition to 'I don't expect to see you again' it can have the less pleasant meaning 'I don't want to see you ever again'. But in normal cases the speaker expects to see the addressee again, and the rising types

> good ╱ BYE
> good ╲╱ BYE

are expected.

9.5   Intonation and writing

In this chapter we have reviewed some of the resources available in the spoken language to facilitate the correct interpretation of the speaker's message. In everyday conversation we have to make what we say fit its context, and this involves using colloquial intonation patterns. However important these may be in speech, there is no way of encoding them in the written language. We do have, of course, the question mark and the exclamation mark. But the former is used for both wh-questions and yes/no questions, and takes no account of whether the question would be spoken with a rise or fall. And although we may have an intuitive idea how to use the exclamation mark, it is not at all easy to give a clear definition of an exclamation. Whatever an 'exclamation' might be, there is an unwritten rule that the mark has to be used sparingly; liberal use of it may be acceptable in private letters, but in serious writing it is a sign of a naive or inexperienced writer.

The lack of means of representing these resources of the spoken language gives us a useful insight into some of the more subtle differences between written and spoken language. What we cannot represent, we have to do without. In serious writing, we have to compose our sentences so that the written text itself guides the reader to make the intended interpretation. This means that the wording does the job of colloquial intonation: there is not much work for the intonation to do, and it is consequently little more than a citation pattern with no function beyond getting the words across. More conversational texts contain sentences composed more on the lines of colloquial speech; although these are in one sense simpler in that they are more speech-like, the reader actually has to work harder to arrive at the correct interpretation, and then has to use the resources of colloquial intonation to convey that interpretation.

Intonation and phrase order

In speech we give a clear signal when phrases are not in their expected order, but we have no means of doing this in writing. Sentences can certainly be written down with the colloquial ordering, but the reader is left to work out the relationship among the parts of the sentence. When you read aloud a conversational text, you have a lot more work to do than when you read something more prosaic. You have to reconstruct the kind of situation in which the words might have been spoken, and impose a colloquial intonation pattern that would be appropriate in that context. Of course, different people will reconstruct slightly different contexts, and produce different readings of the same text. There is never just one intonation pattern for a text. Take for example:

> At last it was morning. He'd been awake most of the night.

If these sentences are read with a final fall, they are presented as independent and unconnected; the hearer is left to work out the connections between them. The first sentence is not very informative, since all nights end in the morning: the second sentence is making clear the point of the first sentence. The connection can be brought out by putting a rise on the time phrase *most of the night*:

> he'd been ＼ aWAKE most of the ／ NIGHT.

The alternative for the writer is to reorder the second sentence putting the time phrase at the beginning:

> For most of the night he had been awake.

This ensures that the time phrase will be seen as the connector and read with the rise:

> for MOST of the ／ NIGHT he had been ＼ aWAKE.

If you read this aloud, the intonation pattern is virtually redundant as there is little choice. In the colloquial version, by contrast, the intonation plays an important role in conveying the intended interpretation. A sentence so drafted that the intonation is redundant is more clearly in the category of 'prose' than a sentence in which the intonation plays an important role. The prose version is ideal for a text intended for silent reading, but you may also find it rather dry and lifeless when read out.

Exercise

Here is an extract from the script of a pantomime version of *Cinderella*. If you were an actor reciting these lines, what problems would you encounter in the text, and how would you make sure of conveying the correct interpretation to the audience?

> You see, Baron Hardy, Your Majesty, didn't always behave like a frightened rabbit. He was once a man of strong character. He married the haughty Lady Belladonna. She had two daughters by her first marriage – Bella and Donna – who were exactly like their mother in all ways. The Baron had also been married before, to the kindest, gentlest of ladies, who sadly died shortly after the birth of their daughter – Cinderella. As she grew up, Cinderella became exactly like her mother.

Force

In conversation, the speaker can monitor the addressee's response, and if something is insufficiently explicit or misunderstood, it can be repeated or reformulated. The writer does not know who is going to read his text, or what expectations and suppositions the reader will bring to the text, and so he or she needs to be maximally explicit, allowing for a wide range of possible readers. The item that carries the force of a whole sentence will normally be read with the fall, and there is little call in serious writing for the rise to point to an implied meaning.

This applies to the reading of verse as well as prose, but verse is made more complex by the verse structure. We have already discussed the tension that exists between rhythm and metre, and between normal chunking and the chunks of verse. The intonation can also vary as in prose from a 'citation' style to a more 'colloquial' style, although the effect of the verse structure is to inhibit colloquial intonation. To begin with, the accentuation of a line of verse may compromise between colloquial accentuation and the desire to bring out the metre; and since the accentuation forms the skeleton of the intonation pattern, it is difficult to flesh out an artificial accentuation with colloquial pitch patterns.

The need sometimes felt to bring out the verse structure adds another dimension to the variation of intonation in the recitation of verse. If you listen to different actors performing the same piece of Shakespeare, you can expect them to produce very different versions. To some extent this will be due to the differences of interpretation that we discussed above for prose, but they also differ in the treatment of the metrical structure. A question in the dialogue of a play, such as

> Hath a dog money? Is it possible
> A cur can lend three thousand ducats?
> (*Merchant of Venice*, I iii)

happens to be written in iambic pentameters, but it would be quite reasonable in this case to pay little attention to the metre, and read the questions with a fairly colloquial, conversational intonation. When you hear verse recited in this way, it may be difficult or impossible to recognize it as verse at all just by listening to it: you have to refer back to the printed text to identify the lines and the metre. But compare another yes/no question, this time from a sonnet (Sonnet 65):

> Shall Time's best jewel from Time's chest lie hid?

It would be very odd indeed to give this an ordinary conversational intonation, as that would be to treat it as an ordinary conversational yes/no question. Most people will probably bring out the metre here to some extent, and move towards a citation intonation in verse-reading style.

Exercise

In many cases, it is easy to decide whether to treat a passage of verse as 'conversational' or not. Some of Robert Browning's verse does not fit easily into either category. An extended example of this is *Bishop Blougram's Apology*, of which here is the opening paragraph:

> No more wine? then we'll push back chairs and talk.
> A final glass for me, though: cool, i' faith!

We ought to have our Abbey back, you see.
It's different, preaching in basilicas,
And doing duty in some masterpiece
Like this of brother Pugin's, bless his heart!
I doubt if they're half-baked, those chalk rosettes,
Ciphers and stucco-twiddlings everywhere;
It's just like breathing in a lime-kiln: eh?
The hot long ceremonies of our church
Cost us a little – oh, they pay the price,
You take me – amply pay it! Now we'll talk.

Read this passage aloud, and if possible get someone else to do so too. Do you read it as a piece of verse, or as conversation? Identify features of the language that mark it as 'conversational': in what ways do these features make it difficult to read the lines purely as verse? (Do the conversational features create a tension between syllables you would expect to accent in conversation, and those you expect to accent in verse? Or are the up-and-down movements in the pitch of the voice affected in any way?) And conversely, what features of the language mark it clearly as verse, and in what ways does the verse form interfere with a purely conversational rendering?

Direct speech

In the case of direct reported speech, a piece of real or imaginary speech is embedded in the structure of a written prose sentence. The conventional way of reading this aloud assigns a colloquial intonation pattern to the speech as though it were conversation, and leaves the reporting phrase unaccented:

"No", said John.

If you put a fall on *no* here, *said John* will remain low in pitch; but if you put a rise on *no*, this rise will continue through *said John*. This remains true even if the reporting phrase is quite long:

"No", replied the professor anxiously.

However, if it is too long, and you give it the rise, you may get to your highest pitch before the end of the sentence. To patch it up, you will probably break off at some point and start again:

> "No", replied the professor anxiously, holding his briefcase in one hand and his umbrella in the other.

I might well read this

> ╲ NO replied the professor anxiously holding his BRIEF-case in ╲╱ONE hand and his umBRElla in the ╲ OTHer.

Although this is perfectly well-formed from a grammatical point of view and as a piece of written English, it reads very awkwardly. This is because insufficient attention has been paid to the way it would be read aloud.

Exercise

Here are the opening sentences of Chapter 2 of *A Tale of Two Cities*:

> "You know the old Bailey well, no doubt?" said one of the oldest of clerks to Jerry the messenger.
> "Ye-es sir," returned Jerry, in something of a dogged manner. "I *do* know the Bailey."
> "Just so. And you know Mr Lorry."
> "I know Mr Lorry, sir, much better than I know the Bailey. Much better," said Jerry, not unlike a reluctant witness at the establishment in question, "than I, as an honest tradesman, wish to know the Bailey."

Although the language of this extract is superficially simple, it requires considerable skill to read it aloud: in addition to the problem of colloquial intonation, there is the problem caused by direct reported speech. Get one or more people to read the passage to you without preparation. How well do they cope? How far does their performance improve if you give them time to prepare it and then ask them to read it again?

CHAPTER 10

Conversation

In the foregoing chapters, we have studied the formation of the vowels and consonants that make up the substance of words and sentences, and gone on to study the rhythmical and intonational devices which are used to convey the force of those words and sentences to the addressee. Our study of phonetics has in this way been tied to language. If we observe closely a group of people engaged in conversation, it is clear that much more is going on than purely 'linguistic' communication. For instance a nod or a wink, a sigh, a pause or a diplomatic cough may be used to reinforce, modify or even to replace what is said in language. The term PARALANGUAGE is used to refer collectively to communicative activities in conversation which accompany language but which are not themselves part of language.

Paralanguage may be vocal, as in the case of laughs and sighs, etc., or it may involve gestures like nods and winks, or more general movements and postures, so-called 'body language'. Although gesture is used as an accessory to language, it belongs to a kind of communication which human beings share with animals, and which is obviously much older than language. Gesture can be developed to function as a sophisticated alternative to language, as in the case of the sign language used by the deaf. Where gesture is used in communication alongside language, it does more than accompany or amplify it. It is difficult to put into words the meanings of a wink, or of raising the eyes to look at the ceiling; the action of touching pursed lips with the forefinger may be glossed as 'keep quiet', but in a particular context it is likely to have a more specific meaning.

Groups of vocal or non-vocal features combine to form recognizable signals, which are used in a conventional way.

An example of this is leaning over and whispering a secret. Alternatively, these features may involuntarily communicate personal information about the speaker: the speaker's identity, geographical origin and social class, and whether he or she is in a good or bad mood, and even the conditions under which he or she is speaking. Although we can easily distinguish in principle between conventional and involuntary uses of paralanguage, the two are inextricably intertwined in the fabric of conversation.

10.1 Attitude

It is often taken for granted that intonation – where 'intonation' is essentially the rise and fall in the pitch of the voice – is concerned with conveying the speaker's attitude. This assumption arose historically because it became clear that intonation did not reflect those aspects of language that were studied and understood by linguists at the time. It was perhaps understandable that 'attitude' should become a vague cover-term for ill-understood aspects of language. As the scope of linguistics has widened in recent years, some 'attitudes' – including those involving chunking and force – have been rescued from obscurity. If intonation conveys attitude at all, then 'intonation' has to be understood to include not only ups and downs of pitch, but paralinguistic features as well.

'Attitudes' which remain obscure are those concerned with the general area of emotion. Some emotional states are internal to an individual such as sorrow or nausea, while others are externally directed. In the latter case the attitude may be directed towards an addressee, a third party, or towards the message itself. These distinctions are blurred in practice, and lead to miscommunication. The effect of pain may be confused with hostility towards the addressee. Annoyance directed at a third party may sound like annoyance with the addressee, and elicit the response 'Well, don't blame me, it's not my fault!'. A speaker who is bored may give the impression of being bored with the message he is putting across, and so on.

Attitudes can be classed in a rough and ready way as generally 'positive' or 'negative'. The attitude towards another person may be plotted on a scale from 'hostile' to 'friendly' and from 'dominant' to 'submissive'. Hostility is presumably a negative attitude, and friendliness a positive one. Dominance and submissiveness depend on the status relationships of the people concerned: a submissive attitude from a superior is condescending or patronizing, while a dominant attitude from an inferior is 'bumptious' or insubordinate, and both these are in a sense negative. Attitudes towards the message include the degree of sincerity. Sincerity is positive or negative depending on the attitude expressed in the message itself. An insincere apology or compliment may be insulting or ironic, while an insincere insult amounts to friendly banter. Since attitude itself is such a complex matter, we are unlikely to find a simple relationship between attitude and the way it is conveyed in speech.

Before asking how intonation conveys attitude, we must turn the question round. How do human beings convey their attitude? The most efficient means does not use language at all: by observing the speaker's physical gestures, facial expression and posture and we have a good idea of his or her attitude before he or she starts to speak. And inside language, attitude is conveyed by the choice of words. Words which mean or refer to more or less the same thing can differ markedly in the attitude they convey. For instance, *television set* and *goggle box* both refer to the same machine and have the same cognitive meaning: but the latter displays a marked negative attitude towards it. Similarly, *man, chap* and *bloke* all refer to adult male human beings, but a *chap* is 'up-market' compared to a *bloke*. Some apparently 'meaningless' words add attitudinal colouring, e.g. *She wants a horse* is attitudinally neutral, but the addition of *bloody* in *She wants a bloody horse* gives it a negative colouring.

In view of these other effective ways of conveying attitude, it is not clear what is left for intonation – that is, the 'spoken punctuation' aspect of intonation that we have described in earlier chapters and as opposed to paralinguistic features – to convey. It is extremely unlikely that there are any attitudes which are conveyed uniquely by intonation: it is rather the case that intonation offers an alternative or additional channel to convey attitude.

It is possible that intonation patterns that are regarded as attitudinally marked use the intonation system in an unexpected way, and possibly in conjunction with other linguistic patterns. To return to our da Vinci example, the expected reply to the question *Who painted the Mona Lisa?* would have the nucleus on the new information, and in addition the given information would be ellipted:

da ＼ VINci.

Now suppose the questioner has already asked the question half a dozen times: the addressee would be justified in feeling annoyed or impatient. A marked attitude would be conveyed by switching to the – unexpected – citation intonation:

da VINci painted the mona ＼ LIsa.

The correct interpretation depends on all parties knowing the relevant information, i.e. that the question has already been asked. The attitude is conveyed by mismatching the answer to the question, and leaving the addressee to find an interpretation that reconciles the conflicting signals. The intonation does not itself contain any clue as to what attitude is involved.

As a general rule, a peripheral feature mismatches a more central feature, and indicates that it is not to be taken at face value. We have already seen in Chapter 9 how the interpretation of social rituals depends on the nuclear tone. Paralinguistic features in the same way affect the interpretation of intonation. We shall say that a pattern is used 'strategically' if it mismatches more central aspects of the message, or if the type which occurs is markedly different from the one that might be expected.

Mismatching may seem an odd way to go about communicating. Why, it might be asked, do we not say exactly what we mean? One reason is that people are subject to social conventions which restrain the display of certain emotions and attitudes, such as anger or sexual attraction, and the most direct and efficient signals may be blocked. Actors on stage are allowed to shout and rant and rage to convey their anger, but in real life this kind of behaviour is socially unacceptable, and an auxiliary means has to be found if the anger is to be conveyed.

Although the attitudinal approach to intonation is a long-established one, very little is actually known in this area. Until the direct meanings of intonational phenomena are properly understood, it is difficult to analyse their strategic uses, and this is an area in which further research is needed.

10.2 Tone of voice

According to the old maxim 'it's not what you say that's important, but the way you say it'. The phrase TONE OF VOICE is a rather vague cover term for a range of paralinguistic features which make up 'the way something is said' as opposed to 'what is said'. Among the constituent parts of tone of voice that we shall consider are pitch range, tempo, and loudness. We have already considered the kind of local variations in these that contribute to the rhythm and intonation of speech. We now come to the more general levels of pitch, tempo and loudness in speech.

To explain the difference here, a comparison with music may be helpful. When you play a melody, you move between high and low notes, you make some longer than others, and some stronger and louder than others. In other words, the melody has lots of local changes in pitch, tempo and loudness. You can change the pitch in a general fashion by retuning the instrument or by changing key; you can vary the general tempo on the scale from lento to allegro; and general loudness can vary on the scale from forte to piano. The value of an isolated note cannot be ascertained without reference to these general scales. You cannot plot it on the sol-fa scale without knowing the key; you cannot class it as a crotchet or a minim without knowing the tempo; and you cannot class it as loud or soft without knowing the general loudness level. Corresponding to the melody we have in speech the intonation pattern with its rhythm and accentuation: this intonation pattern involves local variations in more general paralinguistic settings of pitch, tempo and loudness.

The setting on these general scales may depend on external circumstances. The guitarist who plays loudly in the living room may be scarcely audible in the concert hall. The settings may be related to norms; for instance if someone can be said to play a minuet fast, this implies that there is a recognized tempo for a minuet. Norms of this kind do of course vary in time and from one social group to another.

Pitch

The general location of the speaker's pitch on an objective scale from low to high depends on anatomy, and in particular on the size of the larynx: women generally use higher pitches than men, and young children use higher pitches than adults of the same sex. The 'same' intonation pattern spoken by a man, a woman and a child is rather like the 'same' melody played on a cello, a viola, and a violin. It is possible, however, for human beings to modify the top and bottom of their range. Sex differences are exaggerated in certain social circles, men having lower voices and women higher voices than is anatomically determined. When adults talk to babies and children under about six they tend to raise the pitch range by several semi-tones; this is rather like retuning an instrument to change its key. If the child is otherwise more of a spectator than a participant in the conversation, this change of pitch is a clear signal 'this one is for you'.

The speaker's PITCH RANGE is the difference between the highest and lowest pitches. For instance, if a man's vocal folds vibrate 180 times per second for his highest pitch, and 90 times per second for his lowest pitch, he is using a range of 90 cycles per second $(90 = 180 - 90)$. The range can also be measured on a musical scale of octaves or semitones; in this last case, where the highest note has twice the frequency of the lowest note, the range is one octave. In our discussion of pitch levels and pitch movements, we have assumed a top and bottom for the range of pitch used. Intonation is concerned with what is going on inside this pitch range: the question we come to now is how to describe that range as a whole.

Speakers of British English – and particularly RP – seem habitually to use a wider range of pitch than speakers of some other languages. A range of an octave is not unusual, whereas in Dutch for example, a range of a whole octave would appear to be significantly widened. The range used by a Dutch speaker – which to him or her may be neither widened nor narrowed – is likely to correspond to what is English is a narrowed range. In this way, it may mistakenly seem to the native speaker of English that the Dutch person is uninterested, bored or even being deliberately rude. The width of range expected in English, on the other hand, may be the foreigner seem artificially effusive. Pitch range is an area where misunderstanding is likely to occur between native speakers of English and others who superficially know the language very well.

Tempo

The tempo or rate of speaking is governed in some measure by the time available. In broadcasts, for instance, the speaker may have to speed up in order to finish in the time allotted, e.g. in reading the headlines at the end of a news programme, making announcements between programmes, or giving the weather forecast. Speech rate can slow down when plenty of time is available, such as when the speaker has the floor to give a speech, a sermon or a lecture.

Tempo has an obvious strategic use: when there are no external constraints, it can reflect the importance attached to given chunks by the speaker. Less important items – such as items in parenthesis – are skipped over quickly. Increased tempo may indicate impatience, 'I'm not spending much time on this'.

Loudness

The general loudness or 'volume' of speaking is determined in part both by personality, and by ambient noise. Some people habitually speak more loudy than others; in fact it is possible that the generally accepted loudness level varies from one dialect to another, and even across languages. In any case one has to speak loudly enough to be heard above the surrounding noise. This last point explains the 'inflation' of loudness in a classroom or at a party. At first, in an almost silent room, people talk quietly, but they progress-ively raise their voices in response to the noise of other conversations (and perhaps also a record player), and end up shouting.

Loudness greater than required to be heard, or which

is greater than normal for the speaker, may be communicatively significant. It is used in a rather obvious way to underline the fact that the speaker is in control. A sergeant-major gives his commands more loudly than is necessary for them just to be heard. The chairperson of a meeting is entitled to speak more loudly than other members; he or she may, for instance, override discussion by a loud intervention. The tutor of a seminar tends to speak more loudly than the students. Of course, if the speaker manages to command authority in some other way, the loudness may be rendered superfluous.

'Raising' and 'Lowering' the voice

Pitch, tempo and loudness work together to 'raise' and 'lower' the voice. In order to reach the higher pitches, one has to push more air out of the lungs, and this action automatically makes the voice louder as well as higher. A raised voice is also likely to have increased tempo. Conversely a lowered voice has a lowered pitch range, a decrease in loudness, and probably a reduction in tempo.

Raising or lowering the voice controls the gradient of pitch movements. If a narrow rise or fall is spread over slowly delivered, drawn-out syllables, then there will be a gentle change of pitch; but if the range is increased and the time interval curtailed, the pitch jumps suddenly from one level to another.

The stereotype emotional impression of raised voice and steep gradients is negative, while a lowered voice is positive: one thinks of a voice raised in anger and lowered in humility. In reality there is no such simple correlation. One is expected to raise the voice to express genuine gratitude, and lower it for a genuine apology: *thank you* with a lowered voice sounds grudging, while *I'm sorry* with a raised voice sounds over-cheerful. Raising the voice probably has more to do with projecting one's personality, and forcing oneself on the attention of the addressee: raised voice can convey confidence, enthusiasm and interest as well as anger and domination, while lowered voice can communicate boredom, lack of confidence and reluctance as well as humility.

In reading from a script, the appropriate height of the

voice depends on whether the reader is concerned merely to put the words across, or whether he is trying to give the impression that he has just composed them fresh. In dictating a letter, or even reciting some kinds of poetry, the interest is in the text itself rather than in its transmission, and a lowered voice is in order. A lecture or political speech which has been written out as prose beforehand has all the characteristics of written language, and therefore the intonation is actually required only to put the words across; but if it is delivered with a lowered voice it quickly gets boring and unlistenable to. A raised voice, on the other hand, gives the impression that the speaker is highly involved and interested, and making up the words as he or she goes along. Parents reading stories to young children are likely to use very wide ranges, with exaggerated sweeps of pitch on rises and falls, to keep the child's attention and interest.

Tone of voice has to be taken into account when judging the alleged attitudinal value of intonation patterns. The conventional mismatch of intonation and tone of voice in the case of some phrases like *all right* and *not bad* has produced what almost amounts to intonational idioms. On their own these phrases are non-committal, and fairly neutral on the scale from good to bad. With a raised voice and a falling nucleus, they mean 'very good', e.g.

A: How did you like the film?
B: It wasn't ＼ BAD (it was all ＼ RIGHT).

On the other hand, with a lowered voice and rising nucleus to suggest 'don't take this at its face value' they can amount to a polite and face-saving way of saying something like 'pretty awful':

A: How did you like the film?
B: It wasn't ／ BAD (it was all ／ RIGHT).

10.3 Voice quality

The role of the vocal folds in producing voice was discussed above in Chapter 2. Except for short intervals corresponding to voiceless sounds, the vocal folds vibrate throughout speech. But we simplified the position somewhat by assuming that there was just one mode of vibration. In fact an individual can put on a wide range of 'voices', and these involve different modes of glottal vibration or settings of the musculature of the larynx or of the vocal tract. These different 'voices' are technically known as VOICE QUALITIES.

Voice quality is an important factor in recognizing a particular individual's voice, or in recognizing a regional accent. It also conveys attitude involuntarily. Tension or emotional arousal which is communicated to the larynx has an effect on the mode of vibration of the vocal folds, and this can be heard in the resulting voice quality. Some variations in quality are used to accompany the kinds of feature we have covered under the heading of tone of voice. The norm of voice quality is known as MODAL VOICE, and is produced when the larynx is neither raised nor lowered, neither tensed nor laxed, and the vocal folds vibrate efficiently.

Modal voice makes efficient use of the air passing through the glottis, and it can be heard easily. In 'breathy' voice, the vocal folds are held further apart than for modal voice, with the result that more air passes through. When people speak in 'hushed tones' they possibly combine breathy voice with lowered voice. Perhaps on account of its 'soft', 'soothing' effect, a breathy voice accords more with the sexual stereotype of a woman than of a man. In the case of a man who is effeminate in other respects, a breathy voice is a mannerism which is likely to be picked on as evidence of his effeminacy. Together with lisping – substituting /θ/ or a dental [ṣ] for the normal alveolar [s] – and a defective /r/ and so on, breathy voice is an essential ingredient of the stereotype 'homosexual' voice.

High pitches may be produced by means of FALSETTO, and low pitches by CREAK. To produce falsetto, the mass of the vocal folds is held stiff, so that they vibrate only along their thin inner margins: these margins vibrate naturally at a higher pitch than the whole mass of the vocal folds. Falsetto is useful for reaching high pitches which would be difficult or impossible with modal voice. Men also use it, of course, to imitate the voices of women and children. Creak is produced by vocal folds thickened by muscular action which only allows them to vibrate slowly along a short section at the front end. Whereas in modal voice the individual vibrations of the vocal folds merge in a continuous stream of sound, the individual clicks of creak are separated by very brief but audible moments of silence. In this way creak may be compared to the click-click-click of a pawl on a ratchet, or the sound of an old clock being wound up. Creak is used to accompany or replace modal voice during low pitched stretches of speech.

The pitch of the voice can be apparently raised or lowered by vertical movements of the larynx. A woman whose voice sounds low and like a man's may not in fact be using low pitches at all: she may have lowered the larynx and thus changed the voice quality. Similarly, men who seem to have high-pitched voices may in fact use a normal male range, but with a raised larynx.

Voice quality is affected by the general degree of tension in and above the larynx. A high degree of tension has the effect of concentrating the energy in the sound wave in the part of the spectrum to which the ear is most sensitive. In this way a tense voice is perceived as louder and more penetrating than a lax one, even though it may not be objectively louder as measured by laboratory instruments.

A tense voice may sound emotionally negative, but this is not necessarily so. If you speak clearly for the benefit of a deaf person, you will probably tense the voice to make it carry better. You are also likely to raise the pitch and the loudness for the same reason, but this does not quite produce raised voice as we have described it, as the tempo will be reduced rather than increased.

We mentioned above that the volume level is normally set to make the voice audible above the ambient noise level. Whisper, on the other hand, makes the voice blend in with the ambient noise. The obvious uses of whisper are for conspiratorial or confidential utterances which the speaker wishes to keep from a third party; but it is also used in church, or by children talking in class, where the speaker does not wish to break the silence. To produce whisper, a V-shaped gap is left open at the rear end of the vocal folds, the folds being held together forward of the gap: air passing through the gap generates turbulence which is recognized as the whisper.

A variant of whisper is used on stage. In this special

case, the speaker has to project his voice to the audience, while apparently keeping it from a third party on the stage. Stage whisper is produced by vibrating the front portion of the vocal folds as for modal voice, while simultaneously leaving the V-shaped gap at the back as for whisper.

Calling

If we have occasion to speak to somebody at a distance, we can make the voice louder, or shout. In view of the way loudness is likely to be interpreted, this may not be a good strategy. An alternative is to adjust the voice quality to make it carry more effectively: instead of speaking, we CALL to the addressee.

Called nuclear tones take on some of the characteristics of musical tones. In music, (leaving aside ornaments), a pitch is set and maintained for the duration of the note; a note sung in this way is said to be 'intoned'. In speech, on the other hand, the rises and falls are constantly moving, and even so-called 'level' tones actually fluctuate considerably. In calling, these pitch fluctuations are levelled out, and even intoned. Rising tones may be levelled completely, or split into two level parts, the first level marking the initial pitch, and the second the final pitch.

We have already discussed examples such as

COME \//IN.
\//Dinner's ready.

These are likely to be called, to someone on the other side of the door, or from the kitchen to someone in another part of the house. The called fall-rise begins with a high-pitched level tone, followed by a second tone a few semi-tones lower. We shall indicate this with the symbol (−_):

COME −_IN.
−_DInner's ready.

This pattern is used for calls for attention, e.g.

−_heLLO

The phrase *thank you* can be used in this way – 'come and serve me' – to call an assistant in a large store. (It is interpreted differently in different regions, in some places being taken as polite, but elsewhere as rather rude.) Since the phrase has nothing to do with gratitude here, a rising nucleus is appropriate, and since it is called rather than spoken, it takes the form

–_THANK you!

In the case of farewells, there is a convention whereby people taking leave of each other act as though they were already distant. Instead of saying goodbye, it is common to call it, thus

good –_BYE

or simply

–_BYE

This may be accompanied by a farewell wave, even though speaker and addressee are less than a metre apart. In extreme cases, farewells can be rather comic to observe.

Calling over apparent distance rather than real distance is found in examples like

wakey –_WAkey!

or attempts to rouse the addressee

–_JOHN, you're not paying –_aT-TENtion!

The small child, who when told to apologize to Auntie Jane calls

–_SOrry!

is not really apologizing at all: he goes through the motions of apologizing, although perhaps absent in spirit.

The simple rise is also called and split into two level tones: in this case the second is higher in pitch than the first, and will be written (_–), e.g.

_–MORning.

As a general rule, we would expect the accented syllable to be louder than a trailing syllable. In the case of the called rise, either syllable can carry the peak of loudness: a loud accented syllable represents the normal use of loudness for audibility, but a loud trailing syllable probably indicates an exaggerated use of loudness to convey that the utterance is a ritual, and so not really sincere. Examples of this kind,

marked with the crescendo mark above the trailing syllable,
are close to commands. If a man knocks a little old lady
down in the street and responds with

_–SOrry!

he is probably saying 'get out of my way', albeit disguised
as an apology. A called vocative, such as

_–MAry!

may convey 'I'm looking for you' if the loudness peaks on
the first syllable, but 'come here!' if it peaks on the second.

Called nuclear tones are common in everyday language
use, but they are also found in some special styles of public
speaking. Before the invention of the loudspeaker, it was
necessary to find some means of projecting the voice to
make it audible to a large audience. This declamatory style
may now be considered old-fashioned, but it survives in
liturgical usage and in verse recital.

The priest may still need to project his voice to the
back of the church, particularly when speaking from the
altar in an acoustically ill-designed building. Nuclei which
would be rises in ordinary speech, become very narrow
rises or level tones, and they may be almost sung, e.g. in

Almighty Father, we have erred and strayed like lost
sheep, . . .

Father, strayed and *sheep* are likely to be 'intoned' in this
way. On the other hand, a trendy vicar having an informal
chat with the Almighty may use conversational rises on
these words. Of course, with a microphone, or even in a
pulpit with an effective canopy, the voice may carry
anyway, and there is no need for calling. Calling is likely
to survive as an ingredient of the 'vicar voice' long after the
practical need for it has disappeared. Some politicians and
trade unionists delivering their speeches sound like fun-
damentalist preachers: and this may be partly due to intoned
nuclei similar to those in liturgical use.

In the case of verse recital, it must be extremely rare
nowadays for the speaker to have practical difficulty
reaching his audience. It may have been very different in
former times, e.g. for the Anglo-Saxon bard reciting
Beowulf or *The Battle of Maldon* to an assembled multitude.

At any rate, there survives a style of verse recitation in which rises and falls are narrowed in a way which is strongly reminiscent of the liturgical style. This is typically how children's rhymes are recited, for instance:

ONE potato, TWO potato   THREE potato, FOUR
FIVE potato, SIX potato   SEVEN potato, MORE.

In each half line except the last, the first accent is high pitched for the onset, and the second has a low level pitch representing a levelled rise. This pattern of high onset and low levelled nucleus, possibly intoned, is also found in the self-conscious recitation style of literary verse. If you listen to different people reciting verse, you can expect them to vary from this self-conscious verse style to the style used for reading prose aloud, just as you can expect vicars to vary from the liturgical style to an everyday conversational style of delivery.

10.4 Turns and paragraphs

Vocal and non-vocal features combine to divide a long spoken text into 'paragraphs'. If you listen to a lecture or a sermon you will probably hear such spoken paragraphs marked off by raising and lowering the voice. The speaker raises the voice at the beginning of a paragraph, and lowers it at the end. The lowering of the voice will normally coincide with the end of a syntactic sentence. The change of paragraph may also be accompanied by a shift of posture, by a change in the standing or sitting position. The voice may be raised at the beginning of sentences inside the paragraph, but not to the same extent as at the beginning; the accompanying gestures are likely to be minor ones, such as a shift of the arm or leg rather than the body as a whole. You can expect to find some clear 'initial' signals and some clear 'ending' signals, but this is unlikely to be consistently or systematically done. Except perhaps in a well-rehearsed performance, you cannot expect a close correlation between the size of the chunk delimited and the clarity of the signal.

In conversation, the speaker takes a 'turn', and then hands over the right to speak to someone else. The handover signals are essentially similar to the end of paragraph signals, but the speaker can indicate 'this is the end of the paragraph but I haven't finished' by means of a loud 'pause filler' such as *er* or *um*, or by an appropriate gesture. Handing over is generally performed remarkably smoothly, even though the participants are quite unaware of how it is done. If a person interprets a handover signal where none is intended, or abandons politeness and just interrupts, then two people speak simultaneously. In such a situation one person is likely to yield the floor to the other. But in an argument, or when the speakers are otherwise competing with each other, they are likely to engage in a paralinguistic battle for the floor. Both speakers may use raised voice to take over or keep the floor.

Alongside the main turntaking, there may be a 'back channel' of communication giving a running commentary on how successfully the speaker is conveying his meaning. The speaker signals 'are you receiving me?' in the expectation of 'loud and clear' in response. The speaker's signals may be facial gestures, or a phrase such as *you know*. In recent years the word *right* has come to be used in this way; some varieties of English have highly ornate expressions, e.g. *You know what I mean, like?* The addressee's response may be a pseudo-word, the sort of thing written *mmm, mhm, uh-uh* etc., the word *yes*, or a head nod or facial gesture. On the telephone, where the physical gestures cannot be seen, *yes* may be used so frequently that casual observers comment upon it. The back-channel feedback is important to the speaker, and if it stops, the addressee may be taken to have not understood, or even be accused of not paying attention.

The speaker's feedback requests are dual purpose, as they also act as pause fillers. The addressee's response is also dual purpose, but in a different way. If it is given a rising pitch, similar to that for non-final items in a sentence, it is a signal for the speaker to carry on. But falling pitch, as at the end of a sentence, acts as a 'final' signal, here suggesting that it is time to hand over. Although this feedback is simultaneous with the speaker's turn, it is essentially co-operative rather than competitive. With lowered voice, it is not intrusive, and even if the addressee echoes the speaker's words, or supplies them during a hesitation pause, it does not count as an interruption.

10.5 Reporting conversation

The kinds of paralinguistic features we have discussed in this chapter play an auxiliary role in conversation, and have no exact counterpart in the written language. They do not feature in prose or verse, and they are difficult to identify and describe. For this reason there have been no exercises in this chapter: the only possible exercise would be to study a video recording and observe what is going on.

The time that it is necessary to describe paralinguistic features is when we are reporting a conversation. Reports of this kind may occur in conversation, but more commonly they are included in reported speech in novels, e.g.

"No!", cried Elizabeth angrily.

Paralinguistic hints are also given occasionally in plays, e.g.

Elizabeth (angrily): No!

In order to interpret these examples you have to reconstruct the kind of paralinguistic features which might have been used. However, the characters whose words are reported belong to a literary world where our normal expectations about social behaviour may not be fulfilled. In this literary world, for instance, people quite often cry things angrily, free of the convention which limits the show of anger in the real world. Reports of paralanguage do not necessarily reflect normal paralinguistic behaviour.

There are a large number of verbs which are used in literary style to reflect the paralinguistic context in which something is said. Some of these have to do with raising or lowering of the voice. The emphasis may be on loudness, e.g.

"Quick march!" shouted/bellowed/thundered/roared the sergeant-major.

"I hope you do" he murmured/muttered.

or on pitch:

"Go away!" she cried/screamed/shrieked/screeched.

Note the frequency of 'high pitched' vowels here to reflect

the rise in pitch (refer back to section 5 of Chapter 2 for the connection between high pitch and close front vowels like /iː/ and /i̯/.)

Or the emphasis may be on tempo:

> "Tomorrow morning," he drawled/snapped.

Voice quality is also indicated:

> "They've gone," she whispered/croaked/gasped/breathed/murmured/purred.

or even vocal gestures can be included:

> "Of course you won't," she laughed/sobbed/giggled.
> "That was absolutely delicious," belched the stranger.

Where there is no verb readily available, paralinguistically neutral verbs such as *say*, *tell* or *reply* can be combined with adverbs or adverbial phrases:

> "You are probably right" he replied gloomily/timidly/scornfully/sternly.

When you read the direct speech aloud, you have the choice of just saying the words, or attempting to reproduce the speech as indicated. The latter requires the skill of an actor, not just the normal literacy skills of reading aloud:

> "It's a wee bit expensive, so it is," replied the Irish girl, with an air of disappointment.

Unless you can speak with an Irish accent, complete with the appropriate intonation pattern, and combine it with a means of communicating disappointment, then you have little choice here but to say the words.

As you read novels and plays, you probably take reports of conversations for granted, without really thinking about them. As a final exercise, go through a chapter of a favourite novel, picking out examples. Identify the kind of paralinguistic feature they are intended to suggest.

A List of English Phonemes

Each phoneme is identified by its symbol and a key word: the key word is given in ordinary spelling and in phonemic transcription. The set of characters adopted is the one used by Daniel Jones for the 'broad' transcription of RP in *The Principles of the IPA*. As far as possible, the key words have been chosen for their relative stability from one variety of English to another.

Vowels

1.	i:	reed	/ri:d/
2.	i	rid	/rid/
3.	e	red	/red/
4.	a	bad	/bad/
5.	a:	shah	/ʃa:/
6.	o	cod	/kod/
7.	o:	law	/lo:/
8.	u	could	/kud/
9.	u:	mood	/mu:d/
10.	ʌ	bud	/bʌd/
11.	ə:	bird	/bə:d/
12.	ə	the	/ðə/
		about	/əbaut/
		sofa	/soufə/
13.	ei	raise	/reiz/
14.	ou	rose	/rouz/
15.	ai	rise	/raiz/
16.	au	rouse	/rauz/
17.	oi	toy	/toi/
18.	iə	beer	/biə/
19.	eə	there	/ðeə/
20.	uə	lure	/luə/

Consonants

p	pop	/pop/
b	Bob	/bob/
t	tight	/tait/
d	dead	/ded/
k	cake	/keik/
g	gag	/gag/
tʃ	church	/tʃə:tʃ/
dʒ	judge	/dʒʌdʒ/
f	fife	/faif/
v	van	/van/
θ	thirtieth	/θə:tiəθ/
ð	then	/ðen/
s	sauce	/so:s/
z	zoos	/zu:z/
ʃ	sheep	/ʃi:p/
ʒ	leisure	/leʒə/
h	hat	/hat/
m	mime	/maim/
n	noon	/nu:n/
ŋ	singing	/siŋiŋ/
l	lull	/lʌl/

Consonants

r	rain	/rein/
j	yacht	/jɒt/
w	will	/wil/

The numbering of the vowels is conventional, and follows the order originally used by Jones in 1918 in his *Outline of English Phonetics* (Cambridge: Heffer), and since adopted by a number of phonetics textbooks.

Phoneme Frequency

A knowledge of phoneme frequency is occasionally useful, for instance in the study of literary texts. The writer may appear to have used a lot of /s/s or /r/s, or more than the usual number of open vowels or nasal consonants. The first thing you need to know is what kind of frequency you can expect anyway, arising purely by chance. If you have a text in which one phoneme in ten is a shwa, that is not very interesting if you can expect 10 per cent shwa in any text chosen at random.

Published frequency distributions are available, but you cannot use them unless you know what phonological assumptions are built into them. Digraph symbols – e.g. for /tʃ, dʒ/ and the diphthongs – can be counted once, or the two parts can be counted separately, and this obviously leads to different frequencies. The variety of English is also relevant: Northern English may have 0 per cent /ʌ/, and a correspondingly higher figure for /u/. Further, the frequency of phonemes is different in British and American English on account of the different development of the vowel system before /r/.

The following table is for RP transcribed according to assumptions made in this book. Ten different types of text, five written and five spoken, ranging from a seed catalogue to a passage from *Pygmalion* to recorded interviews, were transcribed. The first 1000 phonemes of each text were counted, making a total of 10 000 phonemes. The frequency of each phoneme was divided by 100, to give an average frequency per 100 phonemes of text. The phonemes are ordered according to frequency.

| ə | 10.49 | ou | 1.59 |
| i | 8.26 | ei | 1.54 |

n	7.65	u:	1.46
t	7.48	ʌ	1.41
s	4.77	o:	1.36
d	4.12	j	1.26
l	3.91	h	1.00
r	3.62	ŋ	0.94
ð	3.37	g	0.93
z	3.05	ʃ	0.82
k	2.89	au	0.65
e	2.57	dʒ	0.63
w	2.53	ə:	0.62
m	2.29	θ	0.57
ai	2.22	a:	0.56
b	2.17	tʃ	0.53
p	2.05	u	0.38
f	1.66	iə	0.36
v	1.94	eə	0.31
a	1.80	oi	0.26
i:	1.80	ʒ	0.04
o	1.73	uə	0.04

In any text, we can expect an inflated frequency of the phonemes of the key words. For instance, in a text about Lloyd George we can expect an unusually high frequency of /oi/ and /dʒ/. Severe distortions can be expected in very short texts, e.g. the exclamation *Ah!* is made up 100 per cent of /a:/, which normally occurs only one per 180-odd phonemes. The sample on which the above figures are based is probably too small to prevent some distortion of this kind.

You have to be aware of the possibility of distortion, especially if the extract you are dealing with is very short, and perhaps just one or two lines of verse. Unless a phoneme or group of phonemes occurs with a frequency several percentage points away from the figure given above, it is unlikely to be significant. If about 8 per cent of the phonemes in a poem about a snake are sibilants, this is no more to be wondered at than the fact that one Christian in seven is born on a Sunday, while one Muslim in seven is born on a Friday.

Phoneme frequency on its own does not explain very much about a poem or any other text: you have to explain how the frequency of phonemes contributes to your response to the text. If you feel that the writer is manipulating the sound of the text, you should first check the key words to rule out the possibility that your feeling about the 'sound' is actually a response to the meaning of the key words. Next check for onomatopoeia, and phonaesthemes: in these cases your response is to the sounds themselves, and not strictly to their frequency. In cases of sound parallelism, the parallel structure itself boosts the frequency of the sounds which are repeated.

The interesting cases are the ones which are not so easily explained. You may find an unusually high or low frequency of stops or of close front vowels which is not tied down to particular words or syllables. In such cases the aesthetic properties of the sounds – of the kind which we discussed in section 5 of Chapter 2 – relate to whole phrases, lines or longer stretches of text.

The Organs of Speech

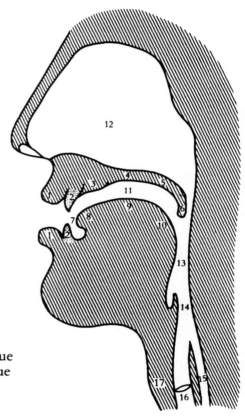

1. lips
2. teeth
3. alveolar ridge
4. (hard) palate
5. velum
6. uvula
7. tongue tip
8. tongue blade
9. front of the tongue
10. back of the tongue
11. mouth cavity
12. nose cavity
13. pharynx
14. epiglottis
15. oesophagus
16. glottis
17. larynx

Vowel and Consonant Charts

The consonants do not vary much from one variety of English to another. The vowels plotted on the Cardinal Vowel charts are the vowels of RP.

(a) Consonants

	Labial	Dental	Alveolar	Palatal	Velar	Glottal
Stop	p b		t d	tʃ dʒ	k g	
Fricative	f v	θ ð	s z	ʃ ʒ		h
Nasal	m		n		ŋ	
Lateral			l			
Approximant	w		r	j	(w)	

(b) Short vowels

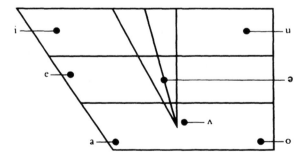

(c) Long Monophthongs

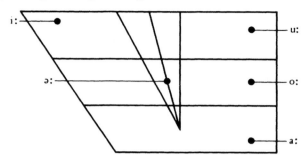

(d) Closing Diphthongs

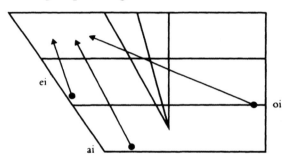

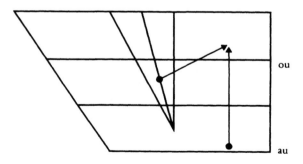

(e) Centring Diphthongs

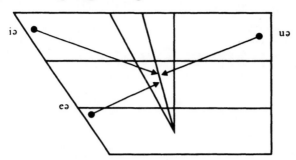

Phonemic Symbols for RP

The symbols used in RP textbooks are the result of a compromise between two often conflicting principles: the need for a legible script with familiar characters, and the need to represent phonemes according to the IPA value of symbols. Several of the vowel symbols in the 'broad' transcription are replaced by more exotic symbols. It is debatable whether this really serves a useful purpose, even for the foreign learner of English: most people who have a sufficiently detailed knowledge of the Cardinal Vowel system to benefit from the exotic symbols already know what the RP vowels sound like anyway. And for anyone with a knowledge of the RP vowels, the exotic symbols give no more information than the broad ones. Nevertheless, certain systems of transcription are well established, and you will find it useful to know about them and the differences between them.

Daniel Jones introduced some exotic characters in the system used for his *Everyman's English Pronouncing Dictionary* (London: Dent) first published in 1917. This system is still generally known as the 'EPD' system. In the Cardinal Vowel system the Roman letter **o** is reserved for vowels in the region of Cardinal 7, and so in the EPD system the Cardinal 6 character is adopted in the symbols for the vowels of *cod, law, toy* e.g. /kɔd, lɔː, tɔi/. Since the vowel of *there* in RP starts nearer Cardinal 3 than Cardinal 2, it is written /ɛə/, e.g. *there* /ðɛə/. The vowel of *shah* is written with the Cardinal 5 symbol, thus /ʃɑː/. Also the letter æ is used to replace /a/: this has nothing to do with Cardinal Vowel theory, for æ happens to be a letter of the Anglo-Saxon alphabet conventionally used by nineteenth century philologists to represent the English **short-a**.

The EPD notation is perfectly clear for native speakers of English, but for foreign learners the use of the colon for 'long' vowels can be confusing. The system now most widely used for RP is the one used by A. C. Gimson in *An Introduction to the Pronunciation of English* (Edward Arnold), the third edition of which was published in 1980. This system – referred to in the chart below as the 'A.C.G.' system – introduces new characters to highlight the fact that 'long' and 'short' vowels differ significantly in quality. These are /ɪ/ for short /i/, /ʊ/ for short /u/, /ɒ/ for short /ɔ/ (this is the symbol for a rounded Cardinal 5, and can be used on the grounds that the RP vowel is actually more open than Cardinal 6) and /ɜː/ for the long shwa /əː/. The symbols /ɪ, ʊ/ are also used for diphthongs, e.g. /eɪ, ɔɪ, ʊə/. Gimson also reflects the new central starting point of **long-o** in the symbol /əʊ/, and distinguishes the starting points of /aɪ/ and /aʊ/.

If 'long' and 'short' vowels have different characters, the colon is redundant. Colons are omitted in the transcriptions used by J. C. Wells and G. Colson in their *Practical Phonetics* (1971, London: Pitman), which is referred to below as the 'W & C' system. They also adopt the symbol /ɒɪ/ in place of Gimson's /ɔɪ/. J. Windsor Lewis, in *A Concise Pronouncing Dictionary of British and American English* (the 'J.W.L.' system) also omits colons, retains /ɔɪ/, but changes /aɪ/ to /ɑɪ/, restores the Roman **e** in /eə/, and reintroduces the letter **o** for the vowel of *hot*.

The table summarizes these differences in vowel symbols

Key word	'Broad'	EPD	A.C.G.	W & C	J.W.L.
reed	iː	iː	iː	i	i
rid	i	i	ɪ	ɪ	ɪ
red	e	e	e	ɛ	e
bad	a	æ	æ	æ	æ
shah	aː	ɑː	ɑː	ɑ	ɑ
cod	o	ɔ	ɒ	ɒ	ɒ
law	oː	ɔː	ɔː	ɔ	ɔ
could	u	u	ʊ	ʊ	ʊ
mood	uː	uː	uː	u	u
bud	ʌ	ʌ	ʌ	ʌ	ʌ
bird	əː	əː	ɜː	ɜ	ɜ

Key word	'Broad'	EPD	A.C.G.	W & C	J.W.L.
the	ə	ə	ə	ə	ə
raise	ei	ei	eɪ	eɪ	eɪ
rose	ou	ou	əʊ	əʊ	əʊ
rise	ai	ai	aɪ	aɪ	ɑɪ
rouse	au	au	ɑʊ	ɑʊ	ɑʊ
toy	oi	ɔɪ	ɔɪ	ɒɪ	ɔɪ
beer	iə	iə	ɪə	ɪə	ɪə
there	eə	ɛə	ɛə	ɛə	eə
lure	uə	uə	ʊə	ʊə	ʊə

Note that some characters, including /i, u, ɔ/ represent different phonemes according to which system is being used. You cannot interpret /rid/ or /ful/ without first identifying the system: they could represent *rid, full* or *read, fool.* Some linguists and phoneticians, especially those connected with the University of Edinburgh, use the characters /ɪ/ and /ᴕ/ in place of /ɪ, ʊ/ respectively.

There are signs that the conventions of transcription – like spelling in the middle ages – are beginning to fossilize, and to show a reluctance to reflect changes in pronunciation since the early years of the century. For example, most young RP speakers have an [o]-like vowel in *law* and *short,* but all the above systems still indicate the older pronunciation. Moreover, the impression is sometimes given that existing practice is to be regarded not as just a matter of convention, or as one solution of the problem, but as objectively correct, much as, say, *tough* is regarded as the only correct spelling for /tʌf/. There are people who have objected to the use of /o/ for the vowel of *hot* on the grounds that its normal pronunciation is too far removed from Cardinal 7, the IPA value of the character **o**. However, a similar objection might be made to the use of ʌ for the vowel of *shut* on the grounds that it is too far removed from its IPA value, unrounded Cardinal 6. In any case, there is no general principle to account for the use of a letter borrowed from the Anglo-Saxon alphabet to represent the pre-war RP vowel of *hat*.

Transcription practice is likely to be influenced in the next few years by the computer, and in particular by the need to store transcriptions in machine-readable form. Since all the different systems for RP derive historically from

Daniel Jones's 'broad' system, a very simple computer program will convert 'broad' symbols into any of the others. A text can be stored as a sequence of characters which match the 'broad' transcription one-to-one, and this can be printed out or displayed on the screen in any desired system. Although the conversion is a very simple process, it is strictly unnecessary: the 'broad' system does exactly the same job as the others and more simply.

Suggestions for Further Reading

The titles suggested here for further reading are either standard works or books which are reasonably accessible to the non-specialist. They should also be readily available, at least in the United Kingdom.

Chapter 1

On the history of English, see D. Leith (1982) *A Social History of English* (London: Routledge), or A. C. Baugh (1951) *A History of the English Language* (London: Routledge) revised and co-authored in 1978 by T. Cable.

On English spelling, see G. H. Vallins (1954) *Spelling* (London: André Deutsch) revised 1965 by D. G. Scragg, or D. G. Scragg (1974) *A History of English Spelling* (Manchester University Press).

Chapter 2

J. C. Wells and G. Colson (1971) *Practical Phonetics*, (London: Pitman), and P. J. Roach (1983) *English Phonetics and Phonology: a Practical Course* (London: Cambridge University Press) give a good introduction to the production of sounds.

The anatomy and physiology of speech is dealt with in some detail by W. Hardcastle (1976) *Physiology of Speech Production*, (London: Academic Press).

Chapters 3, 4, 5

For a detailed account of different varieties of English see J. C. Wells (1982) *Accents of English* (London: Cambridge University Press). An older account of the development of the standard pronunciation is given in H. C. Wyld (1920) *A History of Modern Colloquial English* (Oxford: Blackwell). The standard work on contemporary R.P. is A. C. Gimson (1980, 3rd edn) *An Introduction to the Pronunciation of English* (London: Edward Arnold).

The Principles of the International Phonetic Association is obtainable from the secretary of the I.P.A. at the Department of Linguistics and Phonetics, The University of Leeds, LS2 9JT. A recording of the Cardinal Vowels made by Daniel Jones is available on two 45 rpm records from Linguaphone (ENG. 252, 253, 254A, 255).

On the aesthetic properties of sounds, see G. N. Leech (1969) *A Linguistic Guide to English Poetry* (London: Longman), ch. 6.

Chapter 6

A useful account of English verse is given by D. Attridge (1982) *The Rhythms of English Poetry* (London: Longman); this is particularly good on 'binary' verse.

Chapter 7

Accentuation is discussed in R. Quirk, S. Greenbaum, G. Leech and J. Svartvik (1972) *A Grammar of Contemporary English* (London: Longman) – henceforth *GCE* – ch. 14, 'Focus, Theme and Emphasis', and Appendix II, 'Stress, rhythm and intonation'. The corresponding sections of a new work by the same authors and publisher (1985) *A Comprehensive Grammar of the English Language* – henceforth *CGEL* – are ch. 18, 'Theme, focus and information processing', and Appendix II, 'Stress, rhythm and intonation'.

The accentuation of words is dealt with by R. Kingdon (1958) *The Groundwork of English Stress* (London: Longman), and by E. C. Fudge (1984) *English Word-Stress* (London: Allen & Unwin). If you are familiar with generative phonology, try N. Chomsky and M. Halle (1968) *The Sound Pattern of English* (New York: Harper & Row).

Chapter 8

The 'two tunes' approach to intonation has a long history, and was popularized in the present century by L. E. Armstrong and I. C. Ward (1926) *A Handbook of English Intonation* (Cambridge: Heffer). For an interpretation of rises and falls as 'referring' and 'proclaiming' tones, see D. Brazil, M. Coulthard & C. Johns (1980) *Discourse Intonation and Language Teaching*, (London: Longman).

For a useful discussion of the relationship of spoken to written language from the point of view of writing, see G. Kress (1982) *Learning to Write* (London: Routledge), and F. Smith (1982) *Writing and the Writer* (London: Heinemann).

Punctuation is discussed in *GCE* Appendix III, 'Punctuation', and in *CGEL* Appendix III, also entitled 'Punctuation'.

Chapter 9

The connection between intonation and force is discussed in R. Kingdon (1958) *The Groundwork of English Intonation* (London: Longman).

Chapter 10

On the 'attitudinal' approach to intonation, see J. D. O'Connor and G. F. Arnold (1973, 2nd edn) *Intonation of Colloquial English* (London: Arnold). On voice quality see J. D. Laver (1980) *The Phonetic Description of Voice Quality*, (London: Cambridge University Press), and on non-verbal communication see M. Argyle (1975) *Bodily Communication* (London: Methuen); on tone of voice in general see D.

Crystal (1975) *The English Tone of Voice* (London: Edward Arnold). The section on turn-taking is partly based on S. Duncan (1972) 'Some signals and rules for taking speaking turns in conversations.' in *J. Pers. & Soc. Psych.* **23**. The idea for the final section is taken from G. Brown (1977) *Listening to Spoken English* (London: Longman).

Answers to Exercises

For several of these exercises, it is not possible to give a single definitive answer in view of the many different varieties of English. I have provided phonetic transcriptions for RP, and indicated other possibilities either in round brackets, or in a separate note.

Chapter 1: Spoken and Written English

p 5:

See page 186 for a short extract from a conversation.

p 15:

cat, quick, was, shall, theft, bring, this, Jack, yak, fix

/wig, baŋ, nat, jel, siks, kwik, tʃop, puʃ, ðis, dʒak/

p 16:

/lam, pin, pet, top, pul, kof, tʌf, riðm, swop, flʌd/

Northern English people may have /flud/ for *flood*.

p 17:

/milkmən, kotidʒ, skotlənd, wimin, wumən, gudnəs, kiŋdəm, witnəs, pidʒən, beriəl, medsən/

An older pronunciation for *witness* is /witnis/; older forms for *medicine* include /medsin, medisin/ etc.

Chapter 2: The Formation of Sounds

p 26:

/f, p, θ, k/ are in the 'noise' category, and /u:, l, o, ə/ in the 'resonance' category.

In the following transcriptions, I have put "n" below a symbol to represent 'noise' and "r" for 'resonance':

/ka:m, piktʃə, me:məriŋ, eləfnt/
nr r nrnnnr rr rrrrr rrrnrn

Very careful speakers may say /piktjə/ for *picture*, and in some dialects the word ends in /r/, e.g. pɪktʃər/. Acceptable alternatives for *elephant* include /elifnt, eləfənt/ etc.

p 30:

k–g; ʃ–ʒ; p–b; θ–ð; f–v; s–z; t–d.

In the following transcriptions, "0" below a symbol represents a voiceless sound, and "1" a voiced sound:

pan, krak, bend, tofi, ʃo:ts
011 0110 1111 0101 01 00

These values are for the phonemes in isolation. Some sounds may lose some or all of their voicing in context. After /k/, /r/ will be devoiced in *crack*, and after /p, t/ the vowel will begin voiceless in *pan* and *toffee*.

p 42:

These are just my personal impressions:

gloom: /u/ suggests something indistinct and ill-focused; /gl/ suggests light (see PHONAESTHEMES in section 5 of chapter 5).

screetch: /i/ suggests a high-pitched noise. This is reinforced by a concentration of high frequency energy in the voiceless fricatives /s, ʃ/.

plop: the initial and final stops /p, p/ suggest a sound that begins and ends suddenly, while the open vowel /o/ perhaps indicates loudness.

thwack: the fricative /θ/ and devoiced /w/ suggest the sound of a cane passing through the air; the sound stops suddenly with /k/. The vowel /a/ suggests a loud sound.

clunk-click: two sounds, the first /ʌ/ louder than the other /i/; both sounds end abruptly with /k/.

whoosh: /u:/ suggests a distant, ill-defined sound, and /ʃ/ indicates that it ends gradually. In older pronunciations, the voiceless fricative spelt *wh* represents this sound in a more direct way.

glimmer: /gl/ suggests light (see PHONAESTHEMES in section 5 of chapter 5), and /i/ suggests a small light.

In examples (1) – (3) the same or similar words are used for both visual and auditory sensations:

(1) if *loud* music overloads the ear, *loud* clothes overload the eye.

(2) a *chink* is a tiny light; a *clink* is a tiny sound

(3) a *peep* is either a little look or a little noise.

Chapter 3: The English Sound System

p 44:

/l, θ, b, ŋ, d, h, ʒ, i, s, tʃ/

In the following descriptions, the term *voiced* is placed in square brackets wherever it is predictable.

g:	voiced velar stop
dʒ:	voiced palato-alveolar affricate
r:	[voiced] (post-)alveolar approximant
m:	[voiced] bilabial nasal
s:	voiceless alveolar fricative
θ:	voiceless dental fricative
v:	voiced labio-dental fricative
w:	[voiced] labial and velar approximant
k:	voiceless velar stop
b:	voiced bilabial stop

In this next series, the main difference between successive sounds is given in italics. In some cases there are additional minor differences.

k: voiceless velar stop
t: voiceless *alveolar* stop
s: voiceless alveolar *fricative*
ʃ: voiceless *palato-alveolar* fricative
tʃ: voiceless palato–alveolar *affricate*
dʒ: *voiced* palato–alveolar affricate
ʒ: voiced palato–alveolar *fricative*
ð: voiced *dental* fricative
θ: *voiceless* dental fricative
f: voiceless *labio*–dental fricative
v: *voiced* labio–dental fricative
b: voiced bilabial *stop*
m: voiced bilabial *nasal*
ŋ: voiced *velar* nasal
g: voiced velar *stop*
d: voiced *alveolar* stop
l: voiced alveolar *lateral*
r: voiced (post-)alveolar *approximant*
j: voiced *palatal* approximant
w: voiced *labial and velar* approximant
g voiced velar *stop*
k· *voiceless* velar stop

p 51:

/mʌd, pudiŋ, bʌt, buʃ, sʌtʃ, brʌʃ, gʌm, puʃ, put, bʌtə, bul, tʌmi, ʃʌn, gʌn, hʌm, kʌt/

People from the North of England can expect to have /ʊ/ wherever /ʌ/ is given here. Those who use a compromise vowel, intermediate between /ʊ/ and /ʌ/, can transcribe this with /ə/, thus /məd, pudiŋ, bət, buʃ, sətʃ/, etc.

p 63:

There is an obvious link here between the noise of the train wheels passing over joins in the railway lines, and the syllables of the verse (in particular, the peaks of loudness on the vowels). There is much more of course to the sound of a train, as there is to the sound of syllables, but these other things play no role in the onomatopoeia. Since the onomatopoeic link is so simple in nature, it continues through the poem.

When the train builds up speed, the 'clackety-clack' becomes regular, and this is imitated in the first line of section III: I "hear" the train at full speed in this section. The repeated rhythm is reinforced by the repetition of *letters*. When it slows down and crosses the points, the rhythm of the noise from the wheels becomes irregular: this is imitated in section IV, where I can "hear" the train coming into a main station.

My imagination having been excited, I can now go back to sections I and II, and "hear" a lot more: the train going up hill and down dale, and even the shaking of the bedroom jug. I can even "hear" the hiss of steam in *shovelling*! But if you can also "hear" these things, you should note that we are responding to the meaning of the text, and not just to the sound of the phonemes and the rhythm of the lines.

Chapter 4: The Syllable

p 67:

/l<i>n<ə>n, l<a>ŋ>g<w<i>dʒ, d<r<i>ŋ>k<i>ŋ,
 s b s   s   b   s   s   b s

b<j<u>t<i>f<ə>l, k<r<i>s<m<ə>s,
 s b s b s   s b   s

p<e>l<ə>g<o>u>n<j<ə>m,
 s b s b s   b   s

t<e>l<ə>v<i>ʒ<ə>n,   h<a>tʃ<ə>t,
 s b s b s b s   s b s

r<o>u>d<ə>d<e>n>d<r<ə>n/
 s   b s b s   b   s

If your phonemes are different from mine, you can expect slight differences in your syllabification, e.g. you might have an extra syllable in *pelargonium*: -n<i> <ə>m. There is no consonant here between the last two syllables, and this is marked by the blank space between ">" and "<"

p 69:

/wet, (h)wet, weðə(r), (h)weðə(r), wain, (h)wain, wɜ:(r), (h)weə(r)/

Note that *were* is also pronounced /weə(r)/.

p 71:

/siŋ, siŋə(r), loŋ, loŋgə(r), fiŋgə(r), baŋiŋ, baŋə(r), baŋgə(r), eniθiŋ, aŋgə(r)/

In the 'North-Western' type, /ŋ/ is followed by /g/ in all of these words.

p 73:

In this answer, I use semi-colons to separate words, and commas to separate common alternative pronunciations. Since this cannot be an exhaustive answer, your pronunciation may not be included.

/bruːz; priz(j)uːm, priʒuːm; vjuː; bjuːti; s(j)uːə(r); luːk; s(j)uːpəː(r)b; mjuːzik; n(j)uːsəns; s(j)uːit; t(j)uːzdi, tʃuːzdi; dʒuːəl; d(j)uːəl, dʒuːəl; t(j)uːb, tʃuːb; zjuːgmə; n(j)uːkliə(r); ruːl; luːt; l(j)uə(r)/

p 78:

[boiɫ, gleid, madli, miljən, dʌɫ, dʌlə(r)d, teɫ, teliŋ, kɭuː, liliən, lili, liɫ, pɭei]

p 88:

This answer will only list the parallelisms in each example. The general effect of parallelism is to highlight the structure of the verse, and to give unity to the stanza within the whole poem, and to the line within the stanza.

(1) *Khan* rhymes with *ran* and *man*, and *decree* with *sea*. Each line ends with an alliteration: *Kubla Khan, dome decree, river, ran, measureless to man, sunless sea*. The /an/ rhyme is reinforced by internal rhyme *Xan-, Khan*, and by assonance in *Alph* and *caverns*. In mid-line, *pleasure* rhymes with *measure-*, and there is a near-reverse-rhyme in *stately* and *sacred*. This initial /s/ reinforces the alliteration of *sunless sea*, and the /d/ of *Down* reinforces the alliteration of *dome decree*. In this way, every accented word in this stanza is linked by parallelism to at least one other word.

I have assumed that Coleridge intended *Khan* to be pronounced /kan/: in contemporary RP it is /kaːn/.

(2) There is much alliteration here: *coign . . . cliff, round . . . rocks, inland . . . island, ghost . . . garden . . . girdle, brushwood . . . blossomless bed, steep square slope, grew green . . . graves.* There is also a regular rhyme pattern: *highland . . . island, lea . . . sea, encloses . . . roses,* and *bed . . . dead.* In addition there is the repeated unaccented syllable in *lowland . . . highland . . . island.*

(3) This stanza takes parallelism to the extreme. Here are just some examples:

> RHYME: Oh . . . sloe . . . go; lash . . . flash; worst . . . burst . . . first; lush . . . plush . . . gush . . . flush; sweet . . . feet;

> ALLITERATION: sour . . . sweet; flash . . . full; Calvary, Christ's;

> REVERSE RHYME: lash . . . last; worst Word;

> CONSONANCE: best . . . worst . . . last . . . first;

> PARARHYME: lash . . . lush; flesh . . . flush . . . flash; kept . . . capped

There is a further kind of parallelism in *meaning it, wanting it, warned of it,* which does not really come into any of the above categories.

Chapter 5: Rhythm

p 94:

These are transcribed for RP:

> /gra:s, gas, pasindʒə, ba:θ, kras, na:sti, va:st, ofn, broθ, hot dog, froθ, froθi, kros, krosiŋ/

You may have the short vowel where RP has the long one, or vice versa.

p 95:

I cannot answer this for you! But note that *spook* generally retains the old vowel: /spu:k/. Some older dictionaries give /snuk/ for *snook,* but I have only ever heard /snu:k/; the game *snooker* can only be /snu:kə(r)/.

p 97:

BUcket, aLOUD, BLACKboard, WINdow, deFY, PICture, aLARming, beLOW, BIllow, SUddenly, specTROgraphy puncTIliously.

p 105:

HAmmer (/ha/ is light, shorter than /mə/, and its duration is unaffected by /m/)

BINgo (/biŋ/ is heavy, about the same in duration as /gou/, and longer before /g/ than before /k/)

GRUMble (/grʌm/ is heavy, about the same in duration as /bl̩/, and longer before /b/ than before /p/)

BOttle (/bo/ is light, shorter than /tl̩/ and its duration is unaffected by /t/)

HOUses (/hau/ is heavy, about the same in duration as /iz/, and longer before /z/ than before /s/)

PAper (/pei/ is heavy, about equal in duration to /pə/, and shorter before /p/ than before /b/)

p 114:

(i) This final /l/ comes from many sources, one of which indicated repeated movement or action: the *Oxford English Dictionary* gives several examples including *crumple, dazzle, hobble, sparkle, wriggle,* and suggests that several words are based on onomatopoeic roots, e.g. *babble, cackle, giggle.* I think /l/ also often suggests aimless or uncontrolled activity. But this interpretation does not apply to *little, ladle* or *puddle.*

(ii) in most of these words, /st/ suggests something like 'standing firm and erect'. In the case of words with several meanings, you have to choose the right one, e.g. you have to take *staff* to mean 'stick, stave' not 'group of employees'. In other cases you have to choose the right image: you think of the stork in its upright posture, not with a new-born baby in its beak! Where no such image can be found, /st/ is not expressive at all, e.g. *stew, stone, statistics.*

(iii) /sw/ suggests rapid movement in *sweep* and *swoop* (and also in *swift* and *swipe*); but these words are etymologically related. Perhaps there is a rapid movement too in *swirl* (and also *swerve*). But I do not think /sw/ is expressive in the other words.

(iv) /dr/ is a common initial cluster in English, and it does not suggest meaning in any consistent way. The first three examples – *drip, drop, droop* – are historically different forms of the same word: if you concentrate too much on these, you may be misled into thinking that /dr/ is a phonaestheme.

p 115:

/dʒabəwoki   brilig   slaiði   touvz   gaiə   gimbl   weib
mimzi   borəgouvz   moum   raːθs   autgreib   dʒabəwok
dʒʌbdʒʌb   fruːmiəs   bandəsnatʃ   voːpl   maŋksm   tʌmtʌm
ʌfiʃ   wifliŋ   tʌldʒi   bəːbld   snikəsnak   gəlʌmfiŋ   biːmiʃ
frabdʒəs   kəluː   kəlei   tʃoːtld/

All these nonsense words do in fact conform to the normal rules for legal syllables and words. The two words *gyre* and *gimble* are presumably intended to alliterate, and so I have given them both the same value for the *g*, and transcribed with /g/ rather than /dʒ/, but the evidence offered by Humpty Dumpty in chapter 6 of *Through the Looking Glass* is inconclusive. He defines *gimble* as 'to make holes like a gimlet' (/gimlət/), and *gyre* as 'to go round and round like a gyroscope'. This last word seems to have been pronounced with initial /dʒ/ in Carroll's time. So if you transcribed them with /dʒ/, that must also be accepted as correct.

Gimble, whiffling, burbled and *chortle* contain the phonaestheme /l/. But in general I think the nonsense words are expressive at a higher level, suggesting real English words rather than general areas of meaning: *slithy* (?lithe, slimy), *gyre and gimble* (?gyrate and gambol), *manxome* (?fearsome), *whiffling* (?whiff, whistling), *galumphing* (?galloping, triumph), *frabjous* (?rapturous), and *chortled* (?chuckled, snort). A word like *slithy, galumphing* or *chortled*, which combines the sounds and meanings of two words is known as a *portmanteau*.

Note also the pararhyme in *snicker-snack; Callooh! Callay!* is a kind of alliteration which includes the whole of the first syllable.

Chapter 6: Words and Phrases

p 118:

Unless otherwise stated, the addition of the suffix has no effect on the accentuation.

\laik, \laiknəs; \leit, \leitli; \nesəsri, \nesəsrili; \voləntri, \voləntrili; ni\gousieit, ni\gousieitiŋ; \dʒu:k, \dʒu:kdəm; \buʃ, \buʃiz; \praiməri, \praimərili; \edʒu:keit, \edʒu:keitid; \reit, \reits/

Words ending *-ary* can be pronounced -/eri/, in which case there is an optional shift of accent in the adverb, e.g. / \nesəseri, nesə\serili; \volənteri, volən\terili; \praimeri, prai\merili/. In the North of England, the verb ending *-ate* is sometimes accented before *-ing* or *-ed*, e.g. /ni\gousieit, nigousi\eitiŋ; \edʒu:keit, edʒu:\keitid/.

p 119:

> viBRAto: the ending is *o*, and the preceding syllable *bra* is heavy and accented.
>
> canTAta: the ending is *a*, and the preceding syllable *ta* is heavy and accented.
>
> aMErica: the ending is *a*, and the preceding syllable *ri* is light, so the accent passes back to the second syllable *me*.
>
> coNUNdrum: the ending is *um*, and the preceding syllable *nun* is heavy and accented.
>
> EMphasis: the ending is *is*, and the preceding syllable *pha* is light, so the accent passes back to the first syllable *em*.
>
> maLAria: the ending is *a*, and the preceding syllable *ri* is light, so the accent passes back to the second syllable *la*.
>
> BROccoli: the ending is *i*, and the preceding syllable *cco* is light, and so the accent passes back to the first syllable *bro*.
>
> THEsis: the ending is *is*, and the preceding syllable *the* is heavy and accented.

p 121:

Endings that lose the accent are marked with square brackets.

COMpuTAtion[al],   SESquipeDAli[an],   PROtoZOa,
LYMpho[blast],   HElio[trope],   TEtraHEdron,   DIa[lect],
CONtraPUNt[al],   PHOnoLOgic[al],   TEleGRAph[ic],
POlyANthus, MARseiLLAISE, LEUco[cyte], EpiDERmis,
HOmin[oid],   anHYdrous,   VInaiGRETTE,
VErisiMIlit[ude].

p 122:

In each phrase, the last accented syllable is the nucleus, and
out of context probably has a fall in pitch. If there are two
accented syllables, the first one is the onset, and at this point
the pitch rises to a high level.

BAcon and EGGS; for the TIME BEing; at PREsent; Every
DAY; JOHN SMITH; LONdon ROAD.

p 125:

Syllables   which   lose   their   accent   according   to   the
intermediate accent rule are marked in square brackets.

NINE TEEN EIGHty FOUR → NINE[teen eigh]ty FOUR
the M P for NORwich → the M [p] for NORwich
a TALE of TWO CIties → a TALE of [two] CIties
the FErry aCROSS the MERsey → the FErry a[cross] the
MERsey.

p 128:

/wot wəz i duːiŋ
ə dʌzn l duː
dʒon əd biːn bifoː
ʃi brouk ə(ː) leg
(h)i had eg on iz feis
(h)əv ðei staːtid
wen (w)əd ju gou
luk ət mi (luk ət miː, luk at mi)
wi wont tə si ðəm
juː kən duː ði ʌðəz fə mi (. . . fə miː, foː mi)/

Outside RP, *you* may be reduced to /jə/.

p 130:

/stʌft təmaːtouz/   →   /stʌf təmaːtouz/
/tʃeind təgeðə/   →   /tʃein təgeðə/
/rould gould/   →   /roul gould/

/kaind tə handz/ → /kain tə hanz/
/ə tʃaildz vois/ → /ə tʃailz vois/

p 132:

/klouðz ʃop/ →/klouðʒ ʃop/
/fan klʌb/ →/faŋ klʌb/
/graund flo:/ →/graun flo:/ → /graum flo:/
/a:nt meəri/ →/a:np meəri/ → /a:mp meəri/
/laind peipə/ →/lain peipə/ → /laim peipə/
/dount gou/ →/dounk gou/ → /douŋk gou/
/lost ʃi:p/ →/los ʃi:p/ → /loʃ ʃi:p/

In /graum flo:/, /m/ represents a labio–dental nasal.

p 134:

/krakt kʌps/ → /krak kʌps/
/hai ʌp/ →haiʲʌp/
/vəronikə edwədz/ → /vəronikər edwədz/
/ro: egz/ → /ro:r egz/
/ə ka: endʒən/ → /ə ka:r endʒən/
/pit klouʒəz/ → /pik klouʒəz/
/wet peint/ → /wep peint/
/nou ʌðəz/ → /nouʷʌðəz/
/blaind mais/ → /blain mais/ → /blaim mais/

p 139:

(1) This is indeed 'binary' verse, but subtly different from the popular type. The predominant line movement goes

DUM de DUM   de DUM de DUM

with a break after the second beat. But in several lines that second beat falls in the middle of a word: YOUTHful, WRINkled, HOLding. In other cases the words on either side of this break position are closely connected, and are naturally run together in the rhythm of speech: *trip it*, *light fantastick*, *right hand*. This means that you cannot actually recite this as binary verse without doing violence to the natural rhythm of the text.

(2) This is also 'binary' verse, with two beats per half line, as long as you delete intermediate accents where necessary, e.g. 1879 (EIGHteen seventy NINE). And as in Milton's verse, the connections between words stops the reader from pausing in mid-line, e.g. *very sorry* in the second line.

I think that MacGonagall is derided for the wrong reasons. (Even effects very similar to those which are admired in the 'sprung rhythm' of Hopkins are derided for having too many syllables.) The problem of MacGonagall's verse lies in his use of grammar, vocabulary, phraseology, and the banality of his poetic message: but I do not see anything wrong at the level of the sound patterning.

Chapter 7: Accentuation

p 147:

    (i) /juː kəŋ gou wen juːv finiʃt/ (*you've*)
    (ii) /tuː impres ə(ː)r id duː eniθiŋ/ (*he'd*)
    (iii) /((w)ə)d ʒuː laik ə glaːs ə milk/ (*D'you*)
    (iv) /ai wondər uːl bi peiiŋ fər oːl ðis/ (*who'll*)
    (v) /ðeiv disaidid ðət ðeə betər of ðən ʌs/ (*they've, they're*)

In (v), *they're* can be weakened further to /ðə/ in some varieties of English.

p 149:

    (i) /wudnt ʃuː laik tə nou/ (*Wouldn't*)
    (ii) /it s mai təːn nau izn(t) it/ (*isn't*)
    (iii) woznt ðə doːr oupn̩/ (*Wasn't*)
    (iv) /havnt ʃuː biːn driŋkiŋ//juːb betə lep miː draiv hadnt ʃuː/ (*Haven't, hadn't*)
    (v) /wount ʃuː kʌm bak əgen/ (*Won't*)

p 150:

Items deaccented by the compound rule are marked with square brackets.

    a FOUNtain [pen] (compound)
    ICE CREAM (non-compound) *or* ICE [cream] (compound)
    a COULdn't-care-LESS [attitude] (compound)
    FARM[house] CHEESE (non-compound, but it contains the compound word FARM[house])
    a BOX of MAtches (non–compound)
    a MATCH[box] (compound)

Note that in the phrase *COULdn't-care-LESS*, *care* is deaccented by the intermediate accent rule.

p 152:

the GREAter [Lon]don COUNCIL (the intermediate accent rule)

the RANK [Organization] (the compound rule)

ALL'S [Well] that ENDS [Well] (the parallelism rule)

there's a FLY [in my soup] (the dynamic predicate rule)

the OXford [Eng]lish DICtionary (the intermediate accent rule)

a DISK [operating [system]] (the compounding rule applying twice)

the CRIME [prevention] [officer] (the compounding rule applying twice)

the uNIted [States] of aMErica (the intermediate accent rule)

the BRItish [High] coMMIssion (the intermediate accent rule)

the camPAIGN for [Nu]clear diSARmament (the intermediate accent rule)

a MAN for [All] SEAsons (the intermediate accent rule)

GEORGE [Ber]nard SHAW (the intermediate accent rule)

the CANterbury TALES

NEW [York] City (the intermediate accent rule)

the FIRE [brigade] (the compound rule)

WHAT the BUtler [saw] (the dynamic predicate rule)

the SIdney Opera [House] (the compound rule)

DOUble [ye]llow LINES (the intermediate accent rule)

the LAtest oPInion [poll] (the compound rule)

p 153:

   (i) Did da Vinci own the Mona Lisa?
   (ii) Who painted the Mona Lisa?
  (iii) What did da Vinci paint?
  (iv) What did da Vinci do?
   (v) What did he paint?
  (vi) Did da Vinci paint the Mona Lisa?
 (vii) What is the connection between da Vinci and the Mona Lisa?
(viii) Did da Vinci paint a Mona Lisa?
  (ix) Did Giotto paint the Mona Lisa?
   (x) Who painted the Mona Lisa?

p 156:

Both parts of *FOUR-TEEN* and *TWEnty-FOUR* are accented in isolation, but if the number of tens or the number of units is constant, the corresponding part of the numeral is deaccented.

The higher overall pitch usually indicates the winner. In the case of a draw, the score is a constant and therefore deaccented, e.g. if someone starts

> LIverpool [one] . . .

you can tell – just because the score *one* is unaccented – that the other team has also scored one, i.e. it is a draw.

p 158:

> (i) /(h)əz eniwʌn got ə boks ə matʃiz/ /jes ai hav/ (*have* cannot be reduced as 'got a box of matches' has been ellipted)
> (ii) /ju: dount haf tə dʒoin bət ai fi:l ju: o:t tu: in fakt/ (the second *to* cannot be reduced as 'join' has been ellipted)
> (iii) /wot wəz ðat ju: sed it woz andʒələ/ (the second *was* cannot be reduced as it comes after *what*)
> (iv) /(h)i(:)z lukiŋ fər ə boks tə ki:p iz to:təs in fə ðə wintə/ (*in* could not be reduced here as it is placed after the relative *which* 'in which to keep his tortoise', and *which* has been omitted anyway)
> (v) /wot dʒu: wont tə nou weər ik kʌmz from fo:/ (*from* and *for* cannot be reduced as they come after *where* and *what* respectively)

A reduced *was* is followed by the complement *two*, i.e. *Mary was two*. An unreduced *was* indicates that the complement has been omitted, in which case /tu:/ must be interpreted as *too*, i.e. *Mary was three, too.*

p 164:

Both were right in their own ways! Monboddo described the de-DUM de-DUM of the metre, while Steele described the rhythm of a recitation with 'the proper expression'.

Chapter 8: Intonation Structures

p 172:

When I have asked people to read this, they have generally

taken it a pair of clauses at a time, highlighting the parallelisms, e.g.

> it was the ╱ BEST of times, it was the ╲ WORST of times
> it was the age of ╱ WISdom, it was the age of
> ╲ FOOlishness

No attempt is generally made to group these paired clauses as
a list.

p 176:

First identify the paired items, and treat these as lists as in the
Dickens passage on p 171. This overrides the distinction between 'stopping points' and 'continuation points':

> on GRAVE subjects not ╱FORmal, on LIGHT occasions
> not ╲GROvelling
> GLOWing ╱WORDS or POINted ╲SENtences
> neither STUdied ╱AMplitude, nor afFECted ╲BREvity
> ╱faMIliar but NOT ╲COARSE
> etc.

The remainder of the text follows the normal rules. The first
sentence begins with a non-final chunk *His prose* to which I
would give a rise, and the first stopping point comes after
style, which I would mark with a fall. The second sentence is
made up entirely of paired items. The third sentence has only
two unpaired chunks, *his Sentences* and *his periods*, both of
which are non-final, and to both of which I would give a rise.
In the last sentence, the first comma marks a continuation
point: the sentence cannot end after *Whoever wishes to attain an
English style,* , and so I would put a rise on *style*. The second
and third commas mark off paired items. In the final part of
the sentence, you might treat *days and nights* as a pair, and put
a fall on *nights*; or if you regard it as too trivial to count, you
may treat the whole of *must give his days and nights* as a non-
final chunk with a rise on *nights*. All readers will surely agree
on putting a final fall on *Addison*.

p 177:

To convey the intended meaning, you change several of the
boundaries. My version is based on the re-punctuated text of
scene v. I have kept the initial capital letters, but otherwise

disregarded the original line divisions. I have presented the text in sequences of chunks ending at a stopping point. Any preceding boundaries are at continuation points. I have inserted commas enclosed in round brackets to mark possible boundaries which are not marked by the punctuation.

> Sweet mistress, whereas I love you, nothing at all Regarding your richesse and substance: chief of all For your personage, demeanour, and wit(,) I commend me unto you:
>
> never a whit Sorry(,) to hear report of your good welfare.
>
> For (as I hear say) such your conditions are, That ye be worthy of favour:
>
> of no living man(,) To be abhorred:
>
> of every honest man(,) To be taken for a woman inclined to vice(,) Nothing at all:
>
> to virtue(,) giving her due price.
>
> Wherefore concerning marriage, ye are thought Such a fine paragon, as ne'er honest man bought.
>
> And now by these presents(,) I do you advertise, That I am minded to marry you:
>
> in no wise . . .

p 183:

Sonnet 7 divides naturally into octave and sestet, and all the lines are end-stopped. The rhythm of recitation matches the metre closely, with the exception of some words – *my, am, and* – which are in ictus position, but unlikely to be accented.

Sonnet 19 is superficially similar, with the rhyme scheme ABBAABBA CDECDE dividing it into octave and sestet, but this has no connection with the meaning. The opening section is six lines long, the middle section five lines and a bit, ending after *Kingly,* and the concluding section just under three lines. The middle section sub-divides after *ask* in the middle of line 8. The first two lines, line 6 and the last three lines are end-stopped, but the others run on:

> And that one Talent which is death to hide, Lodg'd with me
>   useless,
> though my Soul more bent To serve therewith my Maker,
> and present My true account, least he returning chide,
> Doth God exact day-labour, light deny'd, I fondly ask;
> But patience to prevent That murmur, soon replies,

> God doth not need Either man's work or his own gifts,
> who best Bear his milde yoak, they serve him best,
> his State is Kingly.

The match between rhythm and metre is similar to that in Sonnet 7, but the salience of the metrical pattern is much reduced by the lack of fit between the chunks of text and lines of verse.

Chapter 9: Colloquial Intonation

p 187:

Here is my version for you to improve upon:

> When I was first called up, I went to Margate, and we marched up and down the prom. It was February, and so cold that I had to have tablets for my neuralgia.

p 199:

Baron Hardy surrounded by commas looks like a vocative, but in fact it is the subject. If you read it

> you see BAron HARdy your majesty. . .

this will correctly indicate that the baron is the subject and *your majesty* the vocative.

If you interpret *character* to mean 'moral backbone, good reputation' you may accent it. But if you treat it as a predictable property of a man, you are more likely to deaccent it:

> a MAN of STRONG character.

If you take for granted that the person the baron married was a lady, you may deaccent the word *lady* in the phrase

> to the KINdest GENtlest of ladies.

There are several parallelisms in the text (see pp 152–6). If you spot them, you may choose to bring out the parallelism in your reading:

> (i) *she had TWO daughters* . . . indicates that at least one more daughter is to be mentioned;
> (ii) *by her FIRST marriage* follows the mention of her second marriage;

(iii) *by HER first marriage* would anticipate the information that the baron had also had a second marriage;

(iv) *the BAron had ALso been married before* follows the mention of the lady having been married before;

(v) *the BIRTH of THEIR daughter* follows the mention of the daughters of the other marriage;

(vi) *became exACtly like HER mother* follows the mention of other children exactly like their mother

p 200:

Superficially, this is conventional blank verse. The lines are unrhymed, but they are iambic pentameters in which the de-DUM de-DUM of the metre matches quite well the accentuation of a recitation. In this respect, the text is unremarkable.

On the other hand, interpreting the text is a bit like making sense of a conversation. Who is the speaker talking to? Is it the reader or a third person? What is going on? Have they just finished dinner? What are they talking about? Are they talking about wine-drinking? Or is that just a side-issue before they get down to the conversation proper?

The opening question is grammatically incomplete, as we might expect in conversation: it is very difficult to read this as verse. Other conversational features include the informal tag *eh?*, and the exclamations *cool, i' faith!* and *bless his heart!* In line 7, the subject *those chalk rosettes* is replaced by the pronoun *they* and delayed to the end of the line: this structure is characteristic of spoken rather than written language. In line 9, "it" is like breathing in a lime-kiln: but what does "it" refer to? In written language we normally expect such references to be clear.

In other circumstances the conversational features might be judged inappropriate in blank verse, and the result humorous or ridiculous. If called upon to read this text aloud, I would take it seriously, and produce a hybrid intonation, with the rhythm of blank verse and the pitch patterns of conversation. Actually, I prefer to read it silently, and try to avoid the issue altogether!

p 202:

If you start this

you KNOW the old bailey ╱ WELL, no doubt

the rise in pitch continues over *said one of the oldest of clerks to Jerry the messenger*. If you pitch this rise too steep, you will quickly get into difficulties at the top of your pitch-range!

If you put a fall-rise on

MUCH ╲╱ BEtter

the pitch falls on the nucleus BE-, and the rise is delayed to the end. Since this direct speech is followed by the long reporting phrase *said Jerry, not unlike a reluctant witness at the establishment in question*, the rise is delayed until *question*. This feels at best extremely awkward.

Immediately after this there follows a case of apposition

╲╱ I, as an HOnest ╲╱ TRADESman

in which *I* and *TRADESman* have the same type of nucleus. If this is a fall-rise, then counting the fall-rise on *better*, this makes three fall-rises in a row.

This is immediately followed by a parallelism in which *to know the Bailey* is the constant:

╲WISH to know the bailey.

You are indeed a highly skilled reader if you can read these last three lines aloud without preparation, without stumbling, and without making any mistakes!

Index

In the case of common phonetic terms, references are only given to the definition or other substantial discussion.